A BAG OF BOILED SWEETS

Julian Critchley, who once described Lady Thatcher as the label on a can of worms, has been a Conservative MP for nearly thirty years. His memoirs, which he has called *A Bag of Boiled Sweets* – sweets being the only safe pleasure for a politician – are a different kind of political autobiography.

Put simply, Julian Critchley has done nothing to boast about. Elected MP for Rochester in 1959, his long career in Parliament was to see out five Tory Prime Ministers. Over the years, he has become an acute and disarmingly frank observer of political life, particularly of the changing nature of the Conservative Party. Julian Critchley was knighted in the Queen's Birthday Honours List, 1995.

Julian Critchley, whose wry humour and irreverence have made him one of our most liked and entertaining politicians, has written a charming account of his life and loves, his many failures and few successes.

'Critchley could have been a serious politician – but he wasn't quite. Liberal sympathies marked him out as "not one of us". More fatal, though, two nice qualities were his downfall: complete loyalty to his friends; and a certain *insouciance* – the Whips would call it indifference. These qualities have been the downfall of Critchley the serious politician, but they are the making of Critchley the light columnist. You may judge for yourself which, in these self-important times, we have needed most.' Matthew Parris, *The Times*.

by the same author

non-fiction

THE CONSERVATIVE OPPORTUNITY
(contributor; Batsford)

COLLECTIVE SECURITY
(with Otto Pick; Macmillan)

THE NORTH ATLANTIC ALLIANCE AND THE SOVIET UNION IN THE 1980s
(Macmillan)

WARNING AND RESPONSE:
A HISTORY OF SURPRISE IN THE TWENTIETH CENTURY
(Leo Cooper)

WESTMINSTER BLUES
(Elm Tree Books)

THE UNAUTHORISED BIOGRAPHY OF MICHAEL HESELTINE
(André Deutsch)

PALACE OF VARIETIES
(John Murray)

SOME OF US
(John Murray)

BORDERLANDS: SHROPSHIRE AND THE WELSH MARSHES
(with David Paterson; Alan Sutton)

fiction

HUNG PARLIAMENT
(Hutchinson)

FLOATING VOTER
(Hutchinson)

A Bag of Boiled Sweets

An Autobiography

JULIAN CRITCHLEY

faber and faber

LONDON · BOSTON

First published in 1994
by Faber and Faber Limited
3 Queen Square London WC1N 3AU

This paperback edition first published in 1995

Phototypeset by Intype, London
Printed in England by Clays Ltd, St Ives plc

© Julian Critchley, 1995

Julian Critchley is hereby identified as the author of this
work in accordance with Section 77 of the Copyright,
Designs and Patents Act 1988

A CIP record for this book
is available from the British Library

ISBN 0–571–17496–5

4 6 8 10 9 7 5

Contents

List of Illustrations

To Prue who came and went, and came back again.

George Orwell contended that autobiography can only be trusted when it is about failure. 'A man who gives a good account of himself is probably lying, since any life when viewed from the inside is simply a series of defeats.'

The reader has been warned.

Rectory Cottage, Wistanstow, by Susannah Critchley

The only safe pleasure for a politician is a bag of boiled sweets.

Westminster Blues

Introduction

When I was at Oxford in the early fifties, a callow youth wearing a brown velvet jacket and a spotted bow-tie, I was a close friend of Michael Heseltine. We dined together frequently with Ian Josephs, a mutual friend who drove a red MG. Michael, when asked what he wanted from life, said 'power'. Josephs said 'wealth', I, who secretly felt that neither power nor riches were ever likely to come my way, said 'fame'. A few votes more and Michael Heseltine might have become Prime Minister, Ian Josephs lives in Monaco and has made serious money from setting up language schools across Europe. I am occasionally described in the newspapers as 'a senior back-bencher', or, by the old-fashioned as 'an anti-Thatcher Tory'. I have some fame but no power and no money to speak of. Which is why I am writing the brief story of my life.

I was born on 8 December 1930 in the Royal Northern Hospital in London, the first child of Edna and Macdonald Critchley. My mother was a nurse and midwife; my father, who was thirty, a consulting neurologist at King's College Hospital, Denmark Hill and the National Hospital. He was tall, dark and cerebral; she was pert, witty and not unmalicious. My father, 'Mac' to his friends; 'Donald' to my mother, was a Bristolian; later to become the first British president of the World Federation of Neurology; my mother was one of six children of a Shropshire railway worker; she married the brightest young doctor on the ward. My parents lived in a rented flat in Chelsea at a time when that borough was not particularly fashionable. Today they would be classified as upwardly mobile young professionals, drawn from the thin line that divides the lower middle from the 'respectable' working class.

In later life I have been called a snob by Teresa Gorman. This could be due to a plummy voice and the portliness of late middle age; Tory MPs tend to be double-breasted. It might also relate to my invention of Essex Man (an assertion that will be challenged by the writer, Simon Heffer), a character much trumpeted in the national press as representative of the 'new' working-class Conservative. It could also be due to my comment on the ideal number of buttons on an MP's cuff, the party having lost one during the thirty years I have sat in the House of Commons. This phenomenon had been pointed out to me one day at lunch by an elderly Knight of the Shire. It appears that a decent suit has four buttons on the cuff; the ready-made having three and sometimes as few as two. As I wanted to tease the more zealous Thatcherites whose role model was Norman Tebbit, I made much of the missing buttons in a newspaper article. Nicholas Soames, Churchill's grandson, was not to be outdone; he promptly instructed his tailor to make him a suit with five buttons. No doubt Alan Clark has six.

John Major's desire to achieve a classless society seems a harmless enough aspiration, although given the tendency of the English to judge people by their vowels, it is unlikely ever to come about. Class is fun, or it should be; it is also fascinating with its infinite nuances and gradations. It is every Englishman's parlour game. A snob, in the derogatory sense, is someone who takes the whole ridiculous business seriously. This, I hope, I have never done. Of my grandfathers, my paternal was a clerk in the Bristol Gas Works whose trouser pockets were especially strengthened to take the amount of copper coins he was obliged to collect going from door to door. My maternal grandfather worked as a bridge builder on the London and North Western Railway. He was killed by a rogue engine at Leominster in 1902. His moustache, according to family legend, was found a mile down the line. My father's success as a doctor catapulted him and his family into the professional middle class. In consequence, Shrewsbury, the Sorbonne and Pembroke College, Oxford, permitted me to pass for white in the Tory party. I do not think, however, I would have fooled 'Chips' Channon (an American adventurer with an ear for English nuance) or Lord Margadale, once chairman of the 1922 Committee.

1 Put in the Girls' Half for Protection

My first memory is of having my head thrust through the sun-roof of my father's Lanchester at the age of four in order to admire the flame-coloured sky above south London. Crystal Palace burned down in 1935, a harbinger of the Bristol blitzes of 1940–41, of which I was a spectator. We lived in a rented house, 4 Harben Road, Swiss Cottage, Hampstead. The house, which consisted of a basement and three storeys, was of a South Hampstead stucco, built I imagine in the 1850s; tall, thin and a touch shabby. A flight of stone steps ran down to the front garden and a gate flanked by two smut-covered acacia trees. Two hundred or more feet below the house ran the London Midland and Scottish Railway's main line from Euston; trains and their smoke could be glimpsed from the maid's bedroom at the top of the house. Like most families of the pre-war professional class, we had a maid (Laura?), and a nanny, my Shropshire cousin Daisy. Mother did the cooking. She could manage a decent Sunday lunch – a joint and two veg – but nothing 'fancy'.

Between the wall of the road opposite and the main line to Scotland below (I can remember seeing the blue, streamlined *Coronation Scot* emerging from the tunnel's mouth and steaming through south Hampstead station in 1937) ran the Great Central line from Marylebone to Manchester. The trains emerged from the mouth of one tunnel only to disappear almost immediately into another. This surfeit of trains made 4 Harben Road a little (but only a little) like the house behind St Pancras station in which the respectable widow, played by Katie Johnson, lived with her parrot in the Ealing comedy, *The Ladykillers*.

Number 4 Harben Road (replaced by Hampstead council flats *circa* 1954) was to be found at the junction of three postal districts: NW8 which covered St John's Wood with its pretty early-Victorian villas; NW3 that included most of Hampstead proper, including the village, and NW6 which embraces the much less salubrious Kilburn and West Hampstead. Sadly, our house was just in NW6, a fact which went unrecognized by my mother, an oversight that meant many of our letters were delivered a day late. It was the same with my paternal grandmother: she lived in Bristol just on the wrong side of the line that divides Clifton from Redland.

My mother was born in 1898 in Rectory Cottage, Leamore Common, Wistanstow, a stone-built village in south Shropshire. The cottage had two rooms and a kitchen downstairs, with a staircase hidden by a door leading to three interconnecting bedrooms upstairs. There was a wash-house, a well and a two-seater lavatory at the bottom of a long garden over which hung an enormous pear tree; beyond the barn was a small field, the 'Patch'. There was a pig and many 'fowl', the Shropshire word for chickens. When I was evacuated to the cottage in August 1939 it was much as my grandmother (who died of cancer in 1924) would have remembered: oil lamps, black-leaded kitchen range with cast-iron pans to match, and a Monday washday from which Auntie May (the wife of Campbell Morris, my mother's eldest brother) would emerge like a locomotive swathed in steam. My aunt had been in service in Wales. She wore her hair in an enormous bun in the style of an Edwardian beauty with ankle-length skirts to match, a uniform she never changed until her sudden death of a heart attack in the sixties.

My Uncle Campbell, whom for some forgotten reason I called Jack, had started work as a boy of fourteen upon his father's death in 1902, and had subsequently worked as head gardener at The Grove, the big house near Craven Arms owned by Mrs Harriet Greene, until his retirement. He had joined up in 1914 at Kitchener's call and had survived four years in France and Flanders as a sergeant in the Royal Artillery. Like his two brothers, Sidney and Oscar, he stammered badly, an affliction which at second hand much intrigued my neurologist father. Did all three brothers stammer when the trio were alone? The three sisters (my mother, Edna; Daisy, the eldest, who emigrated to New Zealand in 1925; Beth the youngest) did not, but their brothers were seriously handicapped throughout their lives.

A stammer is a nervous, not a physical, condition, and it is one from which I have suffered, although only very moderately when compared with my uncles. I did not 'catch' it from them, I developed it later at prep school as a result of being thrown into the deep end of the swimming-pool by my headmaster. It was a handicap at Shrewsbury (I used to dread being required to read out loud in form), and I could never have become an actor. To this day I avoid scripts, wishing to be left free to exercise that skill in verbal substitution which a stutterer develops as a means of self-defence. I might not have relished making ministerial statements from the dispatch box. The civil service is not geared to deal with word-substitution. It is also a matter of self-confidence. As I grew older my self-esteem, which had taken a battering from schoolmasters, waxed, and the affliction slowly waned. None of my children has ever stammered.

Life in a cottage, far from the *Luftwaffe* and the rumours of war, was idyllic. It had been built by a long-forgotten parson (hence Rectory Cottage), sold by him to Mrs Harriet Greene and much later, when The Grove estate was wound up, sold for next to nothing to my uncle. In the late eighties, when Jack died in Bishop's Castle hospital aged ninety-six, it passed out of the family, selling for £30,000. 'A lot needs doing to it,' I was told by Jack's son John, who lives at Berry Mill nearby. Sadly, it did. I wondered whether to buy it, but I hadn't the money. When last I saw it, it looked tatty and ill-kempt.

The cottage faced south-east, looking towards Wenlock Edge and The Monument, a hundred-foot tower planted by a Ludlow merchant called Flounder on the summit of Callow Hill. The Edge ran in two forested steps, in a north-easterly direction as far as the eye could see, ending, so I was told, at Much Wenlock. It cut the cottage off from the rest of the world. To the south the view towards Ludlow was blocked by Norton's camp, while behind the cottage the land rose steadily. When climbed, the views encompassed the Long Mynd, the Stretton Hills and, to the east, the peaks of the two Clee Hills that rose above Wenlock Edge. The Brown Clee, said my uncle, was the highest land in a straight line between here and the Urals. I was most impressed although I later realized that as much could be said for the Gog and Magog hills outside Cambridge. Nevertheless, Shropshire was silent, green and very beautiful. I felt about it as did the young Marcel Pagnol in the film *La Gloire de mon père* when, as a small boy, he was taken for the first time from Marseilles into the limestone hills of Provence. London I never loved; Shropshire was a magical land. It was the start of a lifelong love affair.

Summers were hot in the years before Hitler's war. The August journey from Paddington to Shropshire took all of five hours; we would leave our house in Swiss Cottage by taxi-cab, swoop down the ramp which led into the station and scramble for the Shrewsbury train. We invariably travelled third class (I only acquired the first-class habit years later when sustained by an MP's pass). Luggage safely on the rack, seat facing the engine (would it be hauled as far as Wolverhampton by a King or a Castle?), encompassed by the reek of buttoned carriage-cloth, waiting nervously for the arrival of the ticket collector and my mother's frantic search in her bag displacing keys, lipsticks and packets of Players cork-tipped in search of one and a half monthly returns to Wistanstow Halt. 'Change at Shrewsbury for the Hereford line,' said the collector, his accent more Ladbroke Grove than Ludlow. Three and a half hours later we steamed into the great vault of Shrewsbury station where the trains of two companies met, the green-and-gold engines of the Great Western, and the maroon of the LMS. We had five minutes to spare. Across in the bay stood the Hereford train. The line was jointly owned, and it was a toss-up whether the train would consist of the Great Western's chocolate-and-cream carriages or the duller red of the London, Midland and Scottish. My favourite was the GWR with its engines of Brunswick green and gleaming brasswork. As soon as the train left the platform my mother would begin her recitation: 'Condover, Dorrington, Leebotwood, All Stretton, Church Stretton and Little Stretton, Marshbrook and (pause for effect) Wistanstow Halt.' It was a litany of delights.

The halt was just that, two small, windy platforms, a hut and stern notices in cast-iron imploring us to look and listen before crossing the line. We did as we were told and, luggage to hand, walked the mile or more through the village, past Auntie Lizzie's house, the shop, the school and 'up the Common'. The welcome was warm, the cake made using dripping and with a sugared top, and then came the joy of running wild over the three surrounding fields: Church Field, the Pottocks and the Poorsland, which fifty years ago was undrained and marshy. Across the Pottocks was an oak wood, long-felled and now replaced with dull pines. A stream ran through the garden feeding the well. At one side of the Patch it was overhung by an oak tree and there the shallow stream could be dammed by stones, old tomato-tins and much mud. There was a large yew tree by the gate. At the bottom of the garden were the pigsty, an old, dilapidated barn and a Shropshire two-seater, the sides of which were made of corrugated iron. The lavatory paper consisted of squares of last Sunday's *News of the World*, my introduction to the wonders of British journalism. It was my pleasure to wait until my cousin Edna had gone to the lavatory after dark (a torch stood by the cottage door), creep after her and run a stick along the iron side of the privy. This gave rise to some squealing and, after a decent interval, hot pursuit. There is much to be said for being eight years old.

The living-room contained a cottage picture of a small girl winningly presenting a bouquet of flowers within a maple frame which I have since acquired, and a grandfather clock which, by being kept twenty minutes fast, aped the clocks of King George V at Sandringham. There was a small parlour with a country-oak corner cupboard 'in which your grandmother kept her treasures'. I paid £250 for it in my uncle's sale. The mattresses were of feathers and the upstairs windows small. I can remember reading *What Katy Did* by the light of a candle, safe against the rumble of distant thunder. In those hot summer days the front door was kept open and the window-sills smelt of geraniums, a scent I have long associated with dead wasps. Indeed, a jar smeared with jam and half-filled with water would hang outside the front door, next to the Victoria plum. It seethed with drowning wasps, like so many desperate sailors.

On the morning of Sunday 3 September 1939, the wireless was taken into the garden and we sat and listened to Neville Chamberlain's broadcast. He seemed strangely peevish, as if Herr Hitler had behaved badly to spite him. My uncle and aunt were silent; their only son, John, was of military age. My cousin Edna, in her teens, was more cheerful. She told us that the initials KSLI stood not for The King's Shropshire Light Infantry (A. E. Housman's 'the 53rd') but, when reversed, 'I Love Soldiers' Kisses'. I laughed politely along with the rest.

Thanks to the war I was sent to the village school, a nervous child with a piping west London accent. The headmaster kindly put me in the girls' half for my protection. He was wise. I had been placed in the care of Rosemary Price, a red-haired, pale-complexioned daughter of a neighbour, and once the final afternoon bell had rung, she and I ran for our lives up the lane towards Leamore Common and safety, pursued by Shropshire Lads crying 'rotten taters'. It was my first taste of the mob. It was not so much my ordeal but my accent, which had swiftly acquired a Shropshire burr, that compelled my mother to pay a flying visit. Had she not spent twenty years ridding herself of hers? I was promptly sent to Brockhurst preparatory school at Church Stretton where the English was standard and the conditions Spartan. There I was thumped for talking Shropshire.

2 Palma non sine Pulvere

I had been happy at my various kindergartens. My parents were progressive enough to send me to Froebel (we were then living in Barnes) and for years I retained two half-forgotten memories of that institution: a large, brightly coloured form-room picture of a small boy sitting on the edge of a steep hillside (it may still be there) and a dim recollection of caves, a grotto. To my delight I was told fifty years later after making a speech at a dinner at the school in favour of Britain in Europe, that there are indeed artificial caves to be found in the garden. Merrion House was a pre-preparatory school across the road from our house in Hampstead. I was taken there every day by Daisy, my cousin/nanny. She opened a garden door set in a length of wall, and shoved me gently in. I have no memories so I must have been happy there; childish recollections are more usually of trauma. Certainly I cannot remember being taught to read and write. Sometime in 1939 I was sent to Peterbrough Lodge near John Barnes's store on the Finchley Road. I wore a cap of black and white roundels, and once again was delivered and fetched by the devoted and much loved Daisy. Of the school I remember nothing. After this, a month in the girl's half at Wistanstow Village School could not be other than something of a shock to the system.

My daily flight up the lane back to Rectory Cottage (the mob was finally routed by my broom-wielding aunt) prompted my uncle to teach me to box. He found some gloves, got on his knees and insisted I square up to him. He asked which was my stronger arm, and I told him my right. As a natural left-hander, he made me stand right-foot foremost in the southpaw style and told me to hit him as hard as I could. The lessons continued for several weeks, and were to stand me in good stead. Greatly daring I squared up to Geoffrey Brick, a toughie of about my age, but he did not accept the challenge. Uncle Jack told me all about the great fighters of the past: Jimmy Wilde, Jem Driscoll, and the great Tommy Farr who in 1937 had taken Joe Louis the distance in New York for the heavyweight title, only to be robbed by some American referee. (In fact, Louis won easily.) He lit a lifetime's interest in the sport and, more importantly perhaps, gave me this bit of advice: 'If you're being mobbed, pick out the smallest and hit him as hard as you can on the nose.' His advice was to come in very handy.

The preparatory school is a peculiarly English invention which has not had a good press. If the accounts of the more sensitive are to be believed, many of these institutions were little better than penitentiaries governed by sadistic old men who bullied the 'screws' (poorly paid and poorly qualified staff) every bit as badly as they did their fee-paying pupils. From Charles Dickens's Dotheboys Hall, via Waugh's Lanabba Castle to the stories of Jeffrey Bernard's travail as told to Graham Lord, the record is a grim one. My experience at prep school took me from the depths to a kind of liberation later accompanied by farce. But we should start with Brockhurst under R. P. Marshall, known invariably as 'RP'.

I was a naturally timid child much given to secret fears. When I was about four or five I was terrified of thunder. August in Shropshire saw the culmination of those hot, pre-war summers, a climax expressed with mighty claps of thunder accompanied by two kinds of lightning: forked that could kill (especially if you were sheltering under a tree in the middle of a field) and sheet which was harmless, all accompanied by torrential rain. My Onibury cousins, Campbell and Clive, children of my mother's sister Beth and five years or more older than I, would point to the south at the first rumble of thunder and exclaim with relish 'there's a black cloud over Wart Hill', news that would set me running tearfully to take refuge inside the cottage. I was also afraid of hornets, the sting of two of which, or so said my Uncle Oscar, a gamekeeper, 'could kill an 'orse', and the berries of the deadly nightshade, a sinister plant that featured so vividly in L. P. Hartley's novel *The Go-Between*: 'There's nowt the doctor can do'. I was also scared of gypsies; my Aunt would warn me of their presence, telling me they were fond of kidnapping children. And there was always 'Big Jim'. Big Jim's job was cleaning out the lavatories of half the county: he was a huge, smelly and sinister figure, clearly to be avoided. I was a neurotic child, and by the early autumn of 1940 I had to face a fresh set of fears. Although I had spent time away from home, I had always been to day schools. Now I was to be caught up in that curious British custom of educating their children at arm's length. Three times a year the main London railway termini were the scene of distraught mothers pushing pale eight-year-olds into third-class compartments to the accompaniment of the thump of trunks and tuck-boxes. Perhaps they still are. My weekly departures from Rectory Cottage were not such public affairs.

Perhaps as a concession to my frailty I was made a weekly boarder, leaving in dark and frost-bound Monday dawns and walking 'well wrapped up' a mile or more down the lanes that led to the main road. I stood by the Traveller's Rest at

Bushmoor Corner waiting for the Midland Red bus to appear, squat, noisy and with a silver roof, its lights ablaze. Fifteen minutes later it would drop me at the World's End outside Church Stretton and I would then trudge with a heavy heart up the hill to Brockhurst School, motto *Palma non sine Pulvere*: No reward without effort. (I wonder if there were agencies that supplied novice headmasters with trite mottoes, just as there were similar bodies that sent inarticulate or idle parsons a weekly sermon?) I did not always travel by Midland Red; occasionally Peter Robson's father's Rolls would swoop to a stop and I would sink into its blue leather upholstery. Robson *père* had made money opening cinemas and owned, among others, the Regal at Craven Arms. His son Peter was the only other weekly boarder; his daughter Rosemary sold tickets from behind the guichet. I think I fancied her. She might, for a time, have taken the place of Jessie Matthews, the thirties singing star with whom I had fallen gently in love in pre-war London.

If I have been slow to come to the point, it is because my subconscious has taken over. My early weeks at the school have been covered by layers of protective paint. Let me first describe the school, its situation and its cast. It was situated on a small hill in the Stretton valley with the ruins of a castle at its southern end. It was overlooked to the west by the great wall of the Long Mynd, and to the east by Ragleth Hill; consequently the sun arrived late and left early. The school was a gloomy red palatial Edwardian building set in a garden large enough for a cricket pitch. It smelt of sweat, stew, embrocation, fear and excrement. As a sign of the times one of the changing-rooms had been fitted with a set of curved steel bars to serve as an air-raid shelter. This was trumpeted along with 'a healthy upland position' and 'a fully qualified matron' in the school's prospectus. Church Stretton was only bombed once: a Heinkel III on its way back to Normandy from Merseyside dropped its load on the Little Caradoc on the night of Tuesday 22 October 1940, leaving three 'enormous craters' in the volcanic rock. We slept through it, but at breakfast RP took the opportunity to break the news. 'The Hun', he said, 'will never get the better of us.' They were certainly never likely to get the better of him. Had he not served in the Royal Navy during the Great War? We stood to sing the National Anthem, and sat to bangers and fried bread. Those of us with experiences of the blitz – I had spent most of 1940 living with my parents at Barrow Gurney, seven miles outside Bristol – could adopt a tone of having seen it all before. As indeed I had: I can remember reading a newspaper by the light of Bristol burning.

R. P. Marshall seemed as old as the hills. He was, at sixty-two, a little younger than I am today. He was tall, stooped, clean-shaven and hook-nosed with thin strands of fairish hair drawn tightly across his pink-domed skull. He wore shapeless tweed suits. He had been an instructor at the Royal Naval College, Osborne, where he had taught the Prince of Wales and the Duke of York, and had bought Brockhurst in the early twenties. In his prime he won a reputation for running 'a tight ship'; by the early forties he had deteriorated physically and his temper, never sanguine, had become alarming in the extreme. Perhaps he was suffering from some disease we could not imagine, and was continually in pain? The young take their bodies for granted, it is only in old age that one is imprisoned by them. At nine or ten I was either 'fit for games' or 'seedy' which meant a short stay in the San.

RP was a ferocious teacher of Latin in particular, inspiring so much fear that I never failed in my daily task of learning the conjugations of verbs and the gender of nouns. We were also obliged to learn each Sunday's collect. God help those who were not word perfect. Even away from the form-room, RP was a man to avoid. His quarter-deck manner made him brusque and appear alarmingly unfriendly. At his entry the room fell silent. He was an evangelical Christian of the muscular type. I would never have dared to essay a joke, not even a comment on the state of play. I still have somewhere a form prize, a red-leathered copy of '*Black Beauty*' in which, under the school motto, can be found his neatly written initials. I won it at the end of my first term.

For the greater part of my time with him, we had little to do with each other. Like every new boy I was ritually mobbed, an unpleasant playground ceremony in which the newcomer is jostled by a circle of jeering boys. Luckily, I remembered Jack's advice and punched one of the smaller of my tormentors twice on the nose. He bawled and ran off, blood everywhere; his mates fell silent and then they turned away, going quietly about their business. I was never attacked again. RP, however, became fiercer and more unpredictable. He was a great 'swisher', summoning boys to attend outside his study after breakfast to await punishment, a delay which meant a night of apprehension. On one occasion, he thrashed three boys publicly (I do not recall their offence), an appalling ceremony in which I shared the agonies of their humiliations if not the pain. Thankfully, he never beat me.

RP's daughter, Mrs Lazenby, taught maths and was a restraining influence on her irritable father. In the dorm we would lie awake waiting for the lights of her car signifying her return from the nameless pleasures of wartime Shropshire. (I wonder where she got the petrol. Did prep schools have a special allocation of coupons?) I never did discover what had befallen Mr Lazenby. Her daughter called Yvonne or 'Duch' was of my age, and belonged unofficially to the school. We became friends (indeed fifty years later she told me she had fallen in love with me), a relationship that was marked on her part by a curious ceremony: as proof of her favours she would remove her glass eye and let you hold it in the palm of your hand. I was intrigued but more interested in Dinky toys.

It was soon decided that my status as a weekly boarder was unsettling, and I became a full boarder from the start of the spring term. I also returned to live at Barrow Gurney which was far enough out of Bristol to be safe from the *Luftwaffe*. This meant a train journey from Bristol Temple Meads, through the Severn Tunnel to Pontypool Road, Hereford and Church Stretton. Shropshire winters are bleak. On many days the clouds and mist would cover the Long Mynd and the Stretton Hills in a grey shroud; in January and February snow lay on the ground, and chains were fixed to the wheels of Mrs Lazenby's car (I think it was a Riley Nine). Yet there were winter days of blinding sunshine and brittle cold when the younger boys would climb to the top of the Caradoc, a puffing elderly assistant master brought out of retirement by the war bringing up the rear. Caradoc, an elegant hill of ancient lava fifteen hundred feet high, was believed by some to have been the site of Caractacus's last stand against the legions of Rome. We cheerfully refought the battle with clods of earth.

The school was divided into four competing 'houses': the Trojans who were given yellow badges; the Greeks who were allocated green, the Spartans, red, and the Corinthians, to whom I belonged, sported blue; once a Corinthian always a Corinthian. Had there been a choice I would have been a Trojan, as Hector had long been a hero of mine. Boys were awarded stars and stripes, too many of the latter leading inevitably to their physical equivalent. The food was rather good, although the weekly menu never varied and the day could be told by a glance at one's lunchtime plate. There was also a supply of very filling cake. The summer term should have been the best. The school owned the hill upon which it stood, and there were free afternoons in which hordes of small boys, sporting their rival house colours, ranged freely among the bracken-clad slopes and the oak woods that fringed the western flank of Brockhurst Hill, fighting mock battles. I would have been happy enough had it not been for the compulsory swimming.

Why I should have been afraid of water I cannot tell. Probably just another neurosis. I was truly terrifed of getting out of my depth. The open-air swimming-pool was at the top of a slight rise, beyond the masters' cottage, in full if distant view of the windows of the Long Mynd Hotel, an enormous riviera-type establishment across the valley which is open for business to this day. RP had believed in nude bathing but the weight of complaint from the peculiarly longsighted residents of the hotel had obliged him to kit us out with thongs.

Several of the staff had tried in vain to lure me into the deep end. I would cavort in the shallows, hoping against hope that it would not be my turn to wriggle into a harness from which one was suspended like a fish from the rod of the instructor. We would begin at the side of the shallow end, and progress, puffing and blowing, into deeper water. The moment I could not feel land under my foot I would make a grab for the rail and no amount of threats, or cajoling by Nora Lazenby, could make me budge. I hung there snivelling miserably.

After several unsuccessful public attempts to make me seaworthy, I was told by a master that RP himself would put a stop to my nonsense. I was ordered to attend upon him at five o'clock the next day. I can recall the date: Friday 11 July 1941. I sat alone in the main classroom for most of that afternoon watching the unforgiving clock. At fifteen minutes to the hour I climbed the hill in order to report to the headmaster. He hung me from his line and, scarlet-faced, exhorted me to play the man. I was frightened of him, but more terrified of drowning. As soon as I felt insecure I grabbed the rail and clung to it for dear life. After much upbraiding and talk of 'funk' (all of which attracted an ever-growing and eager audience of boys), he plucked me from the water and carried me kicking and yelling to the deep end into which I was unceremoniously tossed. I sank like a stone, surfaced, and sank again. It was at that stage that someone plucked me out of the pool minus my modest thong which somehow had worked loose in the fracas. RP promptly set about smacking my bottom only to be thwarted by the arrival of Mrs Lazenby who had been summoned, so I was told later, by an anxious assistant master. They had 'words'. I was bundled into a towel and put to bed. I was ten years old.

I suppose that from the perspective of fifty or more years one can find excuses for him. He was old and he was sick. He was in the midst of negotiating the sale of his beloved school which, I suspect, was losing money despite its remoteness from the *Luftwaffe*. He might have feared lest I write home complaining of my ordeal, but he was an experienced enough headmaster to know that whatever the traumas suffered, and at whomsoever's hand, small boys were loyal to the code. We did not sneak, not even to our parents. Many years later a friend in Ludlow, the Reverend Richard Hill, a fellow Old Brock, told me how much he had admired the Old Man. Hill showed me a chapter written about his life at Brockhurst in the twenties. Marshall was then in his prime and the portrait, although recognizable, bore little resemblance to the tyrant I remembered. Perhaps I was just unfortunate in my timing.

3 Under New Management

A year later, in the early summer of 1942, it was announced that the school had been sold and we were to have a new headmaster, a Mr John Park. Not only did he have three daughters, Rosemary, Priscilla and Muriel, all of whom were of prep-school age, he was also bringing three ponies with him. Boys who wished would be taught to ride. Brockhurst, the house that is, was sold to St Dunstan's, while the school was to reassemble for the Michaelmas term at Broughton Hall near Eccleshall in Staffordshire where, we were further informed, a prep school of the same name was already in occupation. We were to share a large Elizabethan manor house with our peers. (Just how large can be determined by its sale by the nuns to a local businessman for £750,000 in 1993.) This was good news indeed, an act of liberation, a mercy from heaven. By some miracle, I was to see the last of RP, who like all good schoolmasters retired to south Devon.

John Park was a widower in his late forties. Large, pipe-smoking and tweedy (smelly, heather-coloured tweeds seem on reflection to have been the prep-school master's uniform), he had spent much of his time in Spain and the Argentine, doing quite what I was never able to discover. Despite an ulcer, he was affable, approachable and friendly. So too were his daughters, while the ponies (to whom I was introduced in the summer holidays, the Parks having rented Prior's Holt, a house on the flanks of the Long Mynd), were either large and placid (Wiseman), highly spirited (an arab called Robin which only Rosemary Park could manage), or docile like Black Bess upon whose back I was destined to learn to ride. The journey from Bristol Temple Meads back to school at the end of the summer holidays was more exciting than usual. The wartime express, dirty and packed with servicemen, the Great Western's cream-and-chocolate carriages a dull mud colour, did not stop at Church Stretton. I waved the school goodbye and changed at Shrewsbury for an LMS train to Stafford where the boys congregated beneath the station clock in order to 'embus' for Eccleshall and Broughton Hall. Great was our excitement; the pangs of homesickness long assuaged.

As I grew older the size of the houses in which I lodged increased exponentially. Our house in Harben Road had six bedrooms, our cottage at the Royal Naval Hospital, Barrow Gurney, only three (my mother called it 'the council house', which it had been, although it was enhanced by the sight of my father's Daimler ELT 34 parked outside), Brockhurst ran to dormitories named after admirals with a world of unknown rooms beyond the green-baize door. But Broughton Hall was vast, a black and white warren of twisted oak, spiral staircases and a minstrels' gallery, the bedrooms too many to count. The bus paused at the top of the drive and Park commended to us the view. It was very splendid. Over the multi-chimneyed Tudor roof flew a strange green flag, the standard of the rival school, or so we were informed. 'I have brought ours to fly beside it,' declaimed our new headmaster, unwrapping a dull red banner on which was a badger's head. 'The Brocks for ever'. Tired from our journey, we could still raise a ragged cheer. Park's gesture was to be the harbinger of a clash of loyalties that was to drive the progress of the war from the front pages of the tabloid press.

Broughton Hall was in 1942 the home of eighty or so boys, half Green, half Red in their allegiances, two matrons, a bevy of ageing assistant masters brought back to life by the war, sundry cooks and bottle-washers, an Aga (or was it an Esse?), a kitchen garden, a Wolseley motor car and two prima donnas: Captain G. K. Thompson who led Broughton from the front, and 'JFP' who had brought what was left of Brockhurst through the Red Sea. Would remote Staffordshire turn out to be the promised land? At least there was no R. P. Marshall.

A new and smaller wing had been added to the Elizabethan original some-time in the twenties; it was built mainly of sandstone and was in harmony with the whole. Pevsner writes well of it. There were extensive grounds and gardens, including a walled kitchen-garden from which we stole nectarines and peaches, and a large stable block which, if today's *Country Life* is to be believed, has been converted into several flats. In 1942, there were two rooms over the stables into which John Park moved, a slight unnoticed by his boys but not by the Great Man himself. He must have slept uneasily, discomfited by the sound of his ponies breaking wind.

I never knew the legal arrangements into which Park and Thompson had entered, and over which there were to be a series of court cases. We Brocks were not much concerned with the niceties: Red was good; Green bad. It did not take long for evidence of headmasterly disharmony to become apparent. Yet for a time the schools co-existed happily enough. We were taught and slept separ-ately, but took our meals communally. We played daily ball games, the Reds versus the Greens. In what spare time we were allowed, we formed rival gangs and spent happy afternoons skirmishing in the woods that surrounded the Great House. The Brocks were perhaps the more formidable physically, such long-forgotten names of toughs like Anthony de Crespigny (whose father was an air marshal, thus bestowing much prestige on his son and the school), 'Roo' Enderby, Peter MacVicar and myself comprising a praetorian guard of sorts. Prominent among the Broughton boys was an eleven-year-old blond as a Viking, who was called Heseltine. He was not very strong, but he seemed to possess leadership qualities. He was later to make a name for himself in the witness box.

All schools suffer from crazes of one kind or another. At Stretton it had been Dinky toys, especially guns, planes and army lorries. I would have sold my soul for a squadron of Vickers Mk I tanks. A replica of a Fairy Battle was worth a block of Cadbury's wartime chocolate. At Broughton, it was model warships made of wood. I made a replica of a landing-raft ship which I sold at a profit to Michael Heseltine, an untypical lapse on his part. And when it came to mock warfare, the Brocks had the light cavalry. Every afternoon, Park's daughters would take a selected few out riding, first on a leading rein and then, greatly daring, releasing us to thunder solo across the fields. John Park fancied himself as Wellington, seated upon his Copenhagen; Robin, who was liable to bite, was Rosemary's pride and joy, Black Bess who was inclined to kick, showed a surprising turn of speed, given that she had little legs. I think there was also a grey pony, but its name escapes me. We were taught to ride like gauchos, long in the saddle, rarely if ever rising to the trot, a foreign style that later was to bring the school's hunting contingent into disrepute.

Our daily rides out into the fields revealed to us the wartime countryside. Hedges and their borders were no longer trimmed and in June the cow parsley was magnificent. Lanes became sun-dappled tunnels. The fields were all under the plough. The roads were devoid of traffic; a rare motor bus on the main roads, the vicar's Austin Seven on some parish errand, the district nurse on her bike, a soldier riding a motor cycle and sidecar. There was nothing else apart from some occasional military traffic, a convoy of lorries. It was a silent world, except for the distant drone of a Blenheim bomber. Behind the hedges were Nissen huts covered in camouflage netting inside which were stored dark-green metal boxes of ammunition. We left them well alone. Land Girls in khaki with green leggings and unflattering hats (designed by Vita Sackville-West) tossed hay on to carts and swopped unintelligible obscenities with Italian prisoners of war. We forget how popular were the 'Eyeties', handsome, hard-working and friendly, forever bursting into song. Cowards they might have been, if British propaganda was to be believed, but no one thought the worse of them for that. By contrast the German POWs were sullen and hostile. All the signposts had been stored away for the duration but that did not seem to matter much. Give Black Bess her head and she would find her way home. The nearby village was Wetwood with its shop owned by a burly ex-petty officer; the main road led either to Eccleshall in the east or to Loggerheads in the west, with a series of lanes running down from the ridge on which Broughton sat south-westwards towards Shropshire. On a fine day I could make out the faint profiles of the Stretton Hills, the Lawley and the Caradoc on the distant horizon.

We did our bit for Mrs Churchill. So as to raise money for her Aid to Russia Fund, Brockhurst would spend cold, wet mornings lifting potatoes in a field next to Broughton church, a building that seemed to serve none save for the residents of the Great House, and us who attended matins on Sunday. Potato picking is a back-breaking, dirty job. The monotony was relieved by throwing potatoes at the master in charge who was a dear old boy called Lewis, as blind as he was deaf, whose services had been recruited by John Park via a postcard displayed in the local shop. I once went to tea with him on a Sunday afternoon in his cottage where he lived with his genteel, elderly, unmarried sister; seed cake, but no ale. We gobbled up his grub and mocked him behind his back. Little boys are beastly.

I was not particularly homesick at Broughton, although I had been initially at Church Stretton. Routine coupled with high spirits narrowed one's focus: pleasures included riding, football and the cheerful exchange of abuse with any Green; pain was the remorselessness of each day's 'prep' and frequent sickness: both schools seemed always to be suffering from epidemics of one sort or another. Matron was forever thrusting thermometers into our mouths. Thompson beat his boys, Park did not – an indulgence that we were reluctant to exploit. I liked John Park and was given the daily task of mixing his powdery-white stomach medicine which he took each morning before the first lesson. 'You, too, Critchley, should become a doctor like your distinguished father.' This reference was pleasing, for the rank of one's father (along with the make of the family's motor car) constituted a pecking order in which I became second only to de Crespigny. Father seldom wrote, but I received a weekly letter from my mother. Sometimes there would be enclosed along with all the Barrow Gurney gossip a brown ten-shilling note, or even a blue pound. Once or twice a term a parcel would be delivered containing cake and sweets.

The Greens' headmaster, Kenneth Thompson, was a dapper little man, dark-haired, wearing a 1915 moustache. He looked young enough to be serving in the Western Desert, but prep-school headmasters enjoyed the status of a reserved occupation. I thought him a nasty piece of work, a disciplinarian in the Marshall mould. He was a donkey (*vide* Alan Clark), but he did not lead lions. The Greens were generally the first to give ground. His pleasure was to oblige his boys (not ours) to squat head down on his study sofa so that he could conveniently beat their bums. The Reds steered well clear of him. John Park, on the other hand, did not believe in beating boys, and kept order by the force of his personality, a task which became increasingly difficult. His natural buoyancy was deflated by his ulcer about which, and despite my ministrations, he would loudly complain. Events were to serve to irritate it still further. There was in fact a tribe of Parks besides his three mounted daughters: Miss Park, an unmarried sister, taught the younger boys while Mrs Turner, his mother-in-law, was a dear old body ever ready with a tin of sweets. We had come under new and congenial management, and some of us were quick to take advantage of it.

It would be hard to describe the passion with which in the forties we sought chocolate and sweets. The joint-school rule was an inflexible one. At the beginning of term we were told to hand over our sweet rations to Matron, every block of chocolate and bag of sweets marked carefully with its owner's name. Our coupons were also confiscated in order to prevent what would have become a flourishing black market. Cigarettes were the currency of occupied Europe; sweets and chocs were ours. The school's sweets, the rations for two months for more than eighty boys, were locked away in a cupboard in Matron's ante-room; every Saturday morning before lunch we queued to receive our week's ration. Miss Hardman, a plain spinster with a cavalryman's moustache, was in charge of the key, which, when she had completed her dispensation, was tucked away in the folds of her ample person. But could the lock be forced?

The senior Brockhurst dormitory was two flights of oak stairs beneath Matron's surgery. We would keep awake until midnight by telling each other stories, then creep like mice up the stairs and into the ante-room. The sweet cupboard's lock was swiftly pushed back by the blade of a penknife, and an Aladdin's cave revealed. We had taken care to make two rules: to steal small amounts only and to make victims of the Broughton Hall boys. I expect I must have lived off Michael Heseltine's gobstoppers, but so skilled did we become that no one ever noticed. We expunged any feelings of guilt by pretending to ourselves that we were British prisoners of war, imprisoned in Colditz.

The hostility between Park and Thompson, their staff, and by extension the rival schools, slowly became more evident. The headmasters contradicted one another at morning assembly and Park, perhaps unwisely, took his senior boys into his confidence. Thompson was, in some way we did not properly understand, going back on his undertakings. We became committed partisans, probably to the detriment of discipline and good order. When we could get away with it we cheeked the Broughton masters, although not Captain Thompson. We set up ambushes in the woods where we lay in wait for unsuspecting Greens whose butterfly nets we snapped in two before driving them back into the Hall for safety. The Brock's head flew proudly over the stables. Our private 'war' was matched by the intense interest most of us took in the progress of the real one overseas. The form-rooms were lined with maps taken from the *Daily Telegraph* showing the arrows of the 8th Army's advances and retreats. General Auchinleck's portrait was replaced by that of General Bernard Montgomery, and posters of Spitfires and Hurricanes fuelled our morale. Because my father was in the Royal Navy I followed the war at sea with a peculiar interest, my prize possession being a copy of the 1941 edition of *Jane's Fighting Ships*. The contents of this handsome volume I soon knew by heart; my favourite ships being the battle-cruiser *Renown*, the cruiser *Cleopatra* and the destroyer *Zulu*. Force H based on Gibraltar commanded by Admiral Jimmy Somerville seemed to embody the Nelsonian traditions of the navy, and I can still remember the gloom with which both Reds and Greens greeted the news of the sinking of the aircraft carrier *Ark Royal*. In peace, the outside world would have passed most prep schools by; in war, we were subjected to an intensive course in what later came to be called 'current affairs', something that doubtless stimulated my interest in politics. There was not an aircraft, friendly or no, that we could not spot, no Allied or enemy commander we did not recognize.

The Park versus Thompson quarrel soon came to a dramatic head. At the beginning of the autumn term of 1943 the returning Brocks reassembled under the clock at Stafford station. John Park, tweedy in the September sunshine, pipe grasped between his teeth, shook our hands warmly, promising us all an 'exciting term'. Little did he know. Thirty-five or so boys embussed (rumblings had caused the withdrawal from the school of one or two of the more faint-hearted, a loss which was more than made up for by the arrival of 'Johore', a dusky prince of whose presence the Parks made much). We rattled off in the direction of Eccleshall, tuck-boxes bumping on the roof to the accompaniment of much merriment and the exchange of playful punches. Park being in a particularly benign mood, we went unrebuked. We passed Wetwood with its retired chief petty officer waving to us from beneath his shop's façade ('Capstan, Navy Cut') and then turned right into the short drive which led down to the gravel frontage of Broughton Hall.

The gravel, usually immaculate, was littered with what appeared at first sight to be the detritus of a retreating army. Desks were piled on desks, blackboards sat on easels, books were scattered everywhere, saucepans, pots, pans and brushes lay on the ground in no good order, beds and bed-linen were strewn over the grass verges, and the stuffed badger that had been brought reverently from Marshall's Brockhurst lay feet up on the gravel, minus its glass case. We got out of the bus to find the windows of the Hall lined with Greens, their thumbs to their noses. The young Heseltine, his eyes pink with triumph, opened a bedroom window and yelled some imprecation. We were out on the street, lock, stock and barrel.

But not for long. John Park, finding the huge oak door of the old building barred against him (it had, after all, withstood a Roundhead siege), exercised his leadership qualities. He ordered us to stay put and to do nothing until he returned from the village 'with reinforcements'. The bus drove him off while we swopped insults eagerly with the occupiers and shied a few stones in the direction of the mullioned windows. There was no sign of Thompson. When it returned some fifteen minutes later, the bus contained the chief petty officer and several of his mates, large men armed with house-breaking equipment. A side door was quickly forced and at Park's command we charged into the Hall giving voice to the rebel yell. (John Park, besides having Falangist sympathies, was a strong supporter of the South. 'Slavery had nothing whatever to do with it' was his view.) After much scuffling the Greens retreated in bad order to the new wing. Thompson made a sudden appearance at the top of a flight of stairs. We made way for Park who climbed past us, his dander up. Thompson spreadeagled himself across a doorway, crying in a high-pitched voice 'touch me and it's assault', a point of view to which the press was later to give currency. Park ran past him up a further flight, followed by his exultant boys, 'Take over your old rooms,' he ordered. We did so with pleasure. That evening the Parks, that is the three girls, Miss Park and old Mrs Turner, gave us a celebratory supper, bangers, bacon and tins of Heinz beans. We were all very overexcited. It had been a famous victory.

Sadly, the tide turned. John Park (who had, I believe, qualified as a barrister) represented himself in the first of three court cases held in London. In spite of the old adage about having a fool for a client, he won, and great was the rejoicing. We Brocks were staying put, the stuffed badger was back in the common-room and the Greens scarcely dared to put their faces out of doors. The second round, however, was won by Kenneth Thompson. The newspapers, tired of the Second World War, made much of the 'battle' of Broughton Hall, and the young Heseltine, then eleven years old, was reported to have given evidence to some effect on behalf of his headmaster. His piping tones were said to have won the day. It was his first public appearance. The final round was fought out after the end of term, and Thompson was once again the winner. My parents who had listened to my account of so many brave deeds and remarkable goings-on with growing anxiety, made half-hearted arrangements to find me another school only to receive a handwritten letter from John Park. Our headmaster was a man of winning ways. He announced with some pride that Brockhurst, despite the vagaries of His Majesty's judges, was back in business. We would be housed from the beginning of next term in Maer Hall, Maer, Staffordshire, the palatial home of the Misses Harrisons of the Harrison shipping line. A photograph of an early-Victorian mansion (Pevsner is perhaps lukewarm) the length of several cricket pitches was enclosed. It contained bedrooms without number. In January 1944 the bulk of the Brocks (there had been casualties) assembled at Whitmore station whence we embussed for pastures new.

Three terms at Maer could not help but be something of an anti-climax. The house, in which Darwin had once lived, had a lake in the grounds across which was stretched a steel hawser, its purpose being to discourage the Germans from landing a seaplane on it (an act that given our battle-hardiness, would have been foolish in the extreme). The elder Miss Harrison was in her sixties, frail and elegant; her sister was a stout party who was also the master of the North Staffordshire Hunt. A small party of Brocks would ride regularly to hounds, not least when the meet was at Maer itself. The sight, however, of small boys 'riding like cowhands', tall in the saddle, did not endear us to the MFH who made her disapproval plain to the headmaster. Like King Charles II, Park had no wish to go on his travels yet again and we were promptly urged by him to rise in the trot like English gentlemen. Park's ulcer, which showed no signs of improvement, prompted not only an eccentric belief in the properties of the 'black box', which given a strand of hair could diagnose a sufferer's complaint, but also an obsession with our bowel movements. We had to 'take our line' and sign a book after doing so each morning. In the summer I took the common entrance examination and passed into Shrewsbury, although I had to wait until January 1945 until a place became vacant. I was just fourteen by the time I left Brockhurst, head of school and cock of the walk. Academically I might have suffered (I was placed in the top form of the lower school), but post-RP Brockhurst had been enormous fun. The Battle of Broughton Hall has passed into prep-school legend, a cautionary tale for all headmasters tempted by exigency to share premises with another; it also prompted the film *The Happiest Days of Your Life* in which a girls' school led by Margaret Rutherford is billeted on a boys' school, the headmaster of which was Alastair Sim. I liked the Parks who were good to me; at Shrewsbury I was to come down to earth with a bump.

4 Floreat Salopia

Corporal punishment, fines, the imposition of lines and the unreasonable deprivation of liberty are all inadmissible at Shrewsbury.

Shrewsbury Handbook, 1993

Graham Greene has asserted that fear is the dominant emotion of childhood, a sentiment which can be explained by his equivocal position as a pupil in his father's public school. Happiness, in his case, was to be found if at all on the other side of the green-baize door. My father who was a remote, if somewhat splendid figure (he was consulting neurologist to the Royal Navy by the age of 39), accompanied me on my first journey to Shrewsbury in January 1945. We trundled northwards by train from Bristol, passing all my familar Shropshire landmarks, the Clee Hill at Ludlow, my Uncle Arnold and Auntie Beth's village shop at Onibury, a deserted Wistanstow Halt, and more sinister, R. P. Marshall's Brockhurst at Church Stretton, now given over to blind servicemen in the care of St Dunstan's. My journeys towards Shrewsbury have always been more doleful than my departures from that pretty town. My dutiful father was largely silent (we had little to say to one another until his old age); his anxious son fearful of what a new chapter would bring. The gulf that separates a prep-school head-boy, biggest fish in the pond from that of a 'new scum' thrust into the lowest ranks of a traditional public school is one of life's widest, a trauma reserved for the children of the fee-paying classes.

Shrewsbury school stands proudly on a high bluff overlooking the town, its principal building an eighteenth-century workhouse converted into classrooms. It was a 'Clarendon' school, one of the top five public schools in the country, its once-high reputation restored during the last century by several formidably bearded headmasters whose bad portraits lined the walls of the Alington Hall. We had to learn their names by heart: Butler, Kennedy (of the Latin primer) and Moss. There might well have been others. I found myself in S. S. Sopwith's house, called officially Oldham's Hall, a large building regarded somewhat unjustly by boys in other houses as being unduly luxurious. The western end was barrack-like, its sole form of heating a hot-water pipe, its windows always open to the wet Welsh wind.

My father took a cab from the station and we drove over the Kingsland toll bridge into the 'site', as the large grounds of the school are called, past chapel, tuck-shop, fives courts, indoor swimming-pool and library to Oldham's Hall. Sopwith gave us both his limp hand, and put us in the charge of the head of the house, a large and relatively good-natured eighteen-year-old called Downie. He gave us a perfunctory tour of grim cream-and-green studies, large cold bedrooms (never 'dorms') and Lysol-smelling changing-rooms which led to the communal lavatories. There was a dining-room, its walls covered with names and dates painted in gold, about which hung the smell of last term's Irish stews, also a room full of swills (bathtubs) and a small paved yard with high, imprisoning walls. We passed small old Mr Rushbrook, who swung along the corridor on permanently bent knees like one of the lesser apes. He, we were told, was the odd-job man who rang the bells that were to govern my life, and whose wife did the cooking. I was later to point him out to a prospective parent as our housemaster. My father said a hurried goodbye (we would never have dreamed of kissing each other) and departed happily no doubt, for the railway station, Bristol and what was left of the Second World War. I was left to my own devices, but not for long.

Horror stories of life in the old-style public school, written by the sensitive and misunderstood, are two-a-penny and I have no wish to add to the genre. Life at Shrewsbury in the late forties had its moments, scattered as they were between fear and discomfort on one hand, and high excitement on the other. The headmaster, who had the term before succeeded H. H. Hardy, was J. F. Wolfenden, later to take up sex in a big way. He seemed curiously young to be a headmaster (he was in his thirties); a pompous, bespectacled figure, remote, if not particularly god-like, whose principal aim in life besides promotion outside and beyond the school was to stop boys coughing in chapel. As we all suffered almost permanently from colds this was not easily accomplished. He also was accustomed to take prayers on a Monday morning, not in chapel but in the Alington Hall (the 'Ali-barn') where he would take the opportunity to upbraid the whole school for some nameless, and thus intriguing, vice. I learnt much later from a disaffected master that JFW was in the habit of quitting Shrewsbury by the milk train for London, returning from the metropolis on the last train of the day. Clearly, he had bigger fish to fry. I was at Shrewsbury for eleven terms in all; Wolfenden for fourteen. He went on to become the vice-chancellor of Reading University and the author of the Wolfenden Report on homosexuality. But he was by no means gay: the site was littered by his many children. I ran into him years later when I was MP for Rochester and he claimed to remember me, but I did not believe him. At Shrewsbury, we had never exchanged a word.

The fashionable wave of liberalism that was to swamp the Arnoldian traditions of the British public school didn't reach Shrewsbury until the mid-sixties. In 1945, nothing had changed since the turn of the century. The routine was remorseless; every minute of every day of the week was accounted for. There was one exception; unlike Brockhurst one could crap at will, if and when one could find the time. The many houses were run not so much by the housemasters (Sopwith was barely visible) as by the monitors who set up a not always benign tyranny of their own. They ran the fagging (in Shrewsbury, so as to emphasize its classical tradition, fags were called 'douls' after the Greek word for slave), and had the power to administer corporal punishment after lights-out with a slipper. The school prefects, called praepostors (this time Latin), had the authority to beat the especially wicked with a cane. The first I suffered from, although not very often; the second I happily escaped completely. In Sopwith's the studies, like the bedrooms, were put in the charge of a monitor and filled by boys from each of the school years. We were all graded like so many eggs; one-year-olds, two-year-olds and so on, the great divide coming at the end of the second year when one no longer lived with an ear cocked for the raucous cry of 'doul' which meant dropping whatever you were doing and running as fast as possible so as not to be the last person to arrive at the monitors' room door. The unfortunate, or just slow, were then sent on some errand to another house or obliged to clean shoes or make toast. To be a three-year-old was to taste freedom for the first time since I left Maer. Left very much to their devices, three-year-olds were almost free of the threat of punishment.

I suppose the first two years at Shrewsbury were the longest two years of my life. They were certainly the most uncomfortable. The food was dreadful although the tuck-shop carried a stock of wads, sticky buns that unrolled to reveal a sugary centre, and glasses of milkshake. You could also spend your coupons there on an assortment of sweets. The house was bitterly cold, we slept in our overcoats (it was thought unmanly to shut the windows), and I suffered along with everyone else from chilblains on my fingers and the tips of my ears. The winter of 1946/47 was intensely cold, so cold in fact as to almost bring down the Labour government. I survived part of 'Shinwell's winter' by a ruse. The boy in the next bed got the measles and I was put in the San under observation having assured the house matron that I had not previously suffered from the disease. This was not strictly true as I had groaned through an attack of something very much like it while at Broughton Hall. It could have been the

German sort. The San was warm, the food was good, the matron was kind. Happy in the knowledge that I was very unlikely indeed to come down with the disease I spent a luxurious fortnight reading the novels of Mary Webb and watching ten-foot drifts of snow pile up against my window. In the meantime, as old newsreels bear witness, the nation ground to a halt, but not the school. From the warmth of my bed I could watch the boys blown along before breakfast to 'first lesson' at 7.45 a.m. When I was returned finally to Sopwith's the boys resembled the *Grande Armée* on its retreat from Moscow. We sat huddled together on the hot-water pipe, stamping our feet in unison, smearing unguents on our swollen fingers. Despite the arctic weather, the house was still obliged to take a cold bath every morning, thus breaking the ice. The idea was to stop us thinking about sex. It did not succeed in doing so.

I was remarkably fit. We were forced to do a 'change' a day, that is some sort of athletic activity. We were a soccer school, rugger being kept for the Lent term only. In the summer we played cricket or rowed. Some of us boxed, others played Eton fives, everyone ran like mad. Running or 'towing' as it was called, was a Salopian speciality. In the winter the whole school was obliged to do the 'tucks', a five-mile run across country, and there were many other such, the names of which I have long forgotten, on which we were encouraged to go. Once a week we were compelled to do a 'benjers', a run of a mile and a half around the red-bricked Edwardian villas of Shrewsbury. The fleet of foot were made 'huntsmen', and proudly sported a whip sewn upon their sweaty shirts. My chief memory of three and a half undistinguished years at Shrewsbury school is running for my life through the mud and filth of some Shropshire farmyard pursued by savage dogs.

Memory may hold the door, but happily the uglier recollections of my life at Shrewsbury have been buried deep, accessible only under hypnosis. The happier events remain, coloured by the passage of time. Could all the masters have been tweedy eccentrics, stout to the point of parody? Surely not; rationing and the size of the site itself must have kept them neat and trim. Was it really as bitterly cold as I have suggested? I can remember sleeping in the long summer grass, a flannelled fool listening to the crack of bat on ball. Was I always hungry? I can recall one triumphant term when I so arranged the seating in hall that I was squeezed between Jew and Muslim, the grateful recipient of rashers of dry-cured bacon, and gifts of fat, porky sausages. Was I always bored? I was most certainly bored in chapel to which we were obliged to go twice on Sundays and five other mornings a week. It was all good low-church, middle-stump, muscular Christianity with robust, cheerful hymns and sermons by either the chaplain or the headmaster. Sometimes Sunday evensong would be enlivened by a sermon delivered by a dotty and aged country parson, taking a busman's holiday from some damp but beautiful Marches church.

At least chapel provided the commodity in shortest supply at school: privacy. The hour-long services, through which one bobbed and knelt unthinkingly, allowed me to sink into reveries which became increasingly sexual as I grew older. 'Sexual' is probably not the correct word; 'romantic' would be better. Although it was not considered to be quite manly, I used to boast about my girlfriends acquired on holiday, totally innocent affairs consummated by the exchange of infrequent letters. I also was the first (as a three-year-old) to stick up a picture of Ingrid Bergman in my study, a welcome addition to coloured pictures of Generals Alexander and Montgomery and Winston Leonard Spencer Churchill.

At sixteen I knew nothing about girls, but lusted after them a great deal, so much so that I broke out in an unlovely rash of spots. The Park girls at Brockhurst, pink-faced and pigtailed, passed as boys (save on one shameful occasion when several of us fumbled them half-heartedly in the hay; the girls were discreet and mercifully did not tell their father). At Barrow Gurney I had two close 'girlfriends', Clare Allison and Alison Brown, but they were chums in the sense of *Boy's Own*, handsome tomboys whose long, brown legs were forever disappearing up trees. Clare, the daughter of Sydney Allison, a Belfast neurologist, was my particular favourite; she had the engaging habit of pinching a handful of her mother's Craven 'A', and sticking them up the leg of her drawers. She is still a heavy smoker.

When I was about eleven we had a stunningly handsome Wren cook who took her clothes off and paraded in the road outside the officers' cottages. This was a dodge, fashionable at the time, that invariably led to discharge from the service. I rushed outside in order to see the fun only to have my mother clap her hands over my eyes. At Shrewsbury there were no women worthy of the name. S. S. Sopwith, a bachelor every bit as limp as his handshake, interviewed maids, cooks and matrons with an eye to their non-existent charms, there were no women on the teaching staff and JFW's many daughters were far too young. My friends and I would discuss film stars in a desultory fashion. Was Pat Roc 'sexier' than Phyllis Calvert? Without a doubt. But not as sexy as Gloria Grahame. Did your mother cry during *Brief Encounter*? Wasn't Jennifer Jones terrific as Hazel Woodus in *Gone to Earth*? In truth we were pig-ignorant, virgin soldiers, spotty youths, for whom 'relief' was possible only during the holidays. There was no homosexual activity in Sopwith's during my time. I am not sure why this should have been so. We were either too God-fearing or clean-living, or perhaps too closely supervised.

I later discovered a pleasure attainable only in the summer term. We were allowed into town on Saturday afternoons having first sought permission from the housemaster. A watch that needed mending, a book to be collected from W. H. Smith or a visit to the dentist. But there was a catch. At four o'clock there was always a roll-call in the house yard (we stood in ranks like so many POWs), the afternoon being divided into two halves in order to discourage an illicit visit to the pictures, or too long spent in the fleshpots of the town. Two hours, however, was long enough to watch the girls of the Shrewsbury high school playing tennis which they did most energetically, my friend Taff Jenkins and I solemnly changing ends in harmony with a neat blonde girl with a disturbing figure. I think she was called Denise. After several Saturdays spent in rapturous if silent contemplation, we were driven away by a schoolmistress with threats to report us to the headmaster. Dressed as we were in shiny black jackets, grubby white shirts, black ties and grey flannel bags, our provenance was only too obvious. We quickly withdrew.

I think it was a Shrewsbury housemaster who once boasted to a parent that he knew at any hour of the night and day precisely what it was that any of his boys was doing. He was very nearly right. Summer Sundays were the exception. We rose an hour later, enjoyed a breakfast of sausage and egg, went to Matins (where I day-dreamed of partnering Denise in doubles), ate a lunch of vilely overcooked beef and Bisto, and, after the stewed apple and Bird's custard, leapt upon our bikes and rode off to freedom.

In the late forties the Sunday roads were empty of traffic and we had four and half hours on our own before returning to the house at six o'clock. Three or four of us would ride together, tyres hissing on the hot tarmac, heads down, bottoms up, pumping the pedals, eating up the twelve uphill miles to Church Stretton where we would buy bottles of Tizer and spend an hour climbing the steep slopes of the Long Mynd before turning north up an empty A49 to Shrewsbury. We rode east to Uriconium and climbed The Wrekin, south-east to Much Wenlock and its Edge, south-west to Pontesbury Hill and Stiperstones, west to the Breiddens, calling in on the way back at a pub in Nesscliffe where we stoked up on bacon and eggs. I do not remember ever going north across the flatter lands to dull, red Cheshire.

Coming downhill fast on my bike was as near as I could get to the hard-riding randy Shropshire squires about whom I read so avidly in the novels of Mary Webb. Her heroes were forever in pursuit of fleet-footed virgins called Hazel or Prue, but with little success. They went to earth. Salopians were encouraged to model themselves on Sir Philip Sidney who at the battle of Zutphen gave the last of his water to a dying soldier, although gravely wounded himself. Sidney was, of course, a famous Old Salopian (so was Darwin, but less fuss was made of him). I was happier to take as my model Squire Jack Reddin of Undern who although very much a Shropshire man was certainly not an Old Salopian.

I was also a train-spotter, a word which is now used by my children as a term of abuse. I had long nursed a passion for railways, especially the Great Western, and Shrewsbury station in the late forties was a paradise for locomotive buffs. It was a junction for six lines, and until nationalization in 1947 jointly owned by the LMS and Great Western. There was even a through train, Birkenhead to Southampton, with green Southern Railway stock. I spent much of my little spare time in my first two years noting down the numbers of Halls, Castles, Manors and Granges in a shiny black-backed notebook. Sopwith encouraged me in this harmless pursuit as long as I was in the company of a large, unspectacular, hairy older boy called Platts whose hobby was photographing engines and who was regarded as a trusty. But there was, as the curate said of Cardinal Wiseman, if not a lobster-salad side to the Cardinal, a more dashing side to Humphrey Platts. He was not content with light and shade but, greatly daring, led me on Sunday afternoons to the engine sheds where he mounted the footplates of unattended locomotives, still in steam, and drove them up to the points on to the main line and back. It was highly dangerous but great fun. He also discovered a box of thunder-flashes, explosive caps which when attached to the railway line warned the passing driver of the danger of fog. These we fixed to the through line at Shrewsbury station on the following Sunday afternoon when the place was almost deserted. We then sat giggling in the refreshment room waiting for the passage of the next through train, a heavy freight, hauled by a class 47, which steamed slowly through the station to a fusillade that drove a thousand starlings into the sky, and sent sleepy railwaymen running in all directions. We made our excuses and left, but thought it wise to stay away for some weeks from Shrewsbury station.

When I did return in the following term, some of the excitement I had felt previously had gone. One locomotive looked much like another. I hung around the station bookstall until I finally plucked up courage to buy a copy of *Health and Efficiency* wherein were pages filled with naked women, their private parts suitably air-brushed for the sake of decency. My copy surreptitiously did the rounds of Sopwith's until it fell to pieces. Somehow the *Railway Gazette* was never quite the same again.

Once again, as it had done at Brockhurst, boxing came to my rescue. It was very much a minor school sport, competitions being organized only twice a year. But it was prestigious. Over four years I had about twelve fights, winning all but one. My most famous victory was a first-round knockout of Abel of Moser's Hall; I was then boxing at middleweight in my final year. Abel, an all-round athlete rather like 'Caesar' Desmond in *The Hill*, had a fearsome reputation. I hit him with a jab, he hit me with a right-hand punch that I can still feel, and then as he charged towards me I caught him with a sweeping right hook which had him staggering drunkenly around the ring. Sergeant Joyce, gym instructor and referee, sixty-something and as trim as a girl, ever mindful of the risk of injury and the resultant scandal, promptly stopped the fight. My reward for so brief and brutal a contest was to be invited to box an exhibition against Jimmy Wilde.

The great Jimmy Wilde, a Welshman who had been flyweight champion of the world, was a hero of my Uncle Jack's. He had seen him fight in Merthyr during the Kaiser's war. Known to the fancy as 'The Ghost with a Hammer in his Hand', Wilde has been rated by *Ring* magazine as the best boxer ever known. In the late forties he had been reduced to a life of gentle exhibitions for which the school no doubt paid him a fee and his expenses. He climbed into the ring, an elderly man quite as wide as he was tall, white haired and ruddy complexioned. He wore a pair of silk drawers down to his knees. In his prime, he weighed no more than six stones, knocking out opponents two stones heavier than himself. Mindful of both his great age and greater reputation I moved round him with extreme care, jabbing gingerly in his direction, keeping out of distance. He made fierce Welsh grunting noises and clipped me round the ear in a matey manner. After a minute or two of ballet, he raised my arm in mock victory and told the crowd I was a lovely feller. It was the apogee of my school career.

As a new boy I had been against the system, although I believed discretion to be the better part. The rules and regulations were trivial and often silly, the year-distinctions being marked by prohibitions and privileges all of which have long since disappeared. But such is their longevity I would never, even today, put pens and pencils in my jacket's top pocket. As a three-year-old I became more openly nonconformist to the extent of joining an older boy called Heath in support of the Labour party. This was done in order to shock, the rest of the house being as unthinkingly Tory as the 1922 Committee. My nonconformity extended to criticizing the house monitors for the power they sometimes unreasonably exercised, and I poured scorn upon the simpler verities of school and house life, the 'house spirit' and the 'voluntary' attendance at boring house matches of one kind or another. In part, it was all a pose; in truth, I rather hankered after promotion, and had thought quite carefully about the ways I would change and soften the system. I played the poacher, but deep down

I wanted to be a gamekeeper. This pattern, first established at Shrewsbury, was to be repeated when I became a Tory MP. I have been dogged by housemasters all my life.

I had a final brush with Sopwith before he retired to be succeeded as housemaster by a W. E. Matthews. I did not want to be confirmed, fearing, wrongly as it turned out, that my newly acquired status would lead to more compulsory religious observations. Sopwith, turning nasty, would have none of it and I was obliged to kneel before the Bishop of Lichfield, my hair free of any kind of dressing. (In fact it was regarded in the house as a bad thing to oil one's hair, an act done only by 'good men', a subtle term of abuse applied to the more worldly wise.) Putting religion to one side, Matthews took as little trouble with me as had Sopwith, although to be fair Sopwith was at least a very good teacher of English. By and large the masters all ran to type. Leather-patched and shabby with tobacco they taught whatever it was they had to teach with vigour and a numbing conventionality. Those with character tended towards dottiness; a boy once asked his form master, famous for his fecundity, how many children he had. 'I don't know,' was the reply, 'I haven't been home since breakfast.'

The master I liked best was the crime-writer Edmund Crispin whose real name was Bruce Montgomery. Red-haired, lame and flamboyant, he introduced me to the ghost stories of Montague James which he would read aloud to us in form. 'Oh Whistle and I'll Come to You' remains to this day my favourite short story. Although I had no means of knowing, Montgomery was a drinking companion of Philip Larkin's – Larkin was then a librarian at Wellington. We could have done with a poet on the staff.

In the middle of the summer term of 1948, towards the end of my third year, Matthews told me that however long I stayed on in the house he would never make me a house monitor. I believe he felt me to be a bad influence. He must have thought that I combined a threatening physical presence with a dangerous cynicism. I told him I would quit Shrewsbury at the end of term and take my higher school certificate elsewhere. Many years later I lunched with David Wright who had been headmaster of Shrewsbury in the middle sixties. I asked him whether he had to strive to bring about reform. He told me that he had done little. The Arnoldian system had collapsed 'under the weight of its own contradictions', the house monitors had freely abandoned their privileges and the housemasters were, at long last, prepared to pull their weight. Matthews was mentioned, although not by me. 'Quite the worst housemaster I ever knew' was Wright's opinion. I was pleased to hear it. He certainly robbed me of two years in the History Sixth, which was what being at the school for the three previous years was supposed to be all about. It put me at a severe disadvantage. It was many years before I learnt to work properly on my own.

As a postscript, I was invited to speak to the sixth form in 1983 and spent a day on the 'site', including taking tea with the housemaster of Oldham's Hall, his wife and the head boy. They gave me a tour of the boys' half which had been much improved, the studies being covered with the kind of girlie photos that would have given Sopwith a seizure. The housemaster also showed me a copy of my confidential report which read 'Curious mixture. Would work hard and do well at anything he was keen on. Pleasant fellow on the whole.'

5 Life among the Hampstead Young Conservatives

I celebrated my eighteenth birthday on 8 December 1948, at 4 Harben Road, the house which my parents had reoccupied, not without difficulty, in 1946. My birthday was a downbeat affair as I had few friends. My brother Nicholas, five years younger than I, would have been at school at Bryanston. The house had survived the blitz and a legion of non-statutory subtenants and was no more shabby than every other house in north-west London. It was not until the sixties that London sparkled with new paint and the acres of bomb damage with their crop of purple-flowering weeds and buddleias, finally disappeared. 'Swiss Cottage,' said my mother, who had a countrywoman's prejudices, 'is full of German Jews.' It was. Hardly anyone seemed to speak English. Sad survivors of the Holocaust would sit sipping coffee and eating strudels in mock Austrian cafés along the Finchley Road. I was a student at Eaton and Wallis, a crammer in Maida Vale, where I took my higher school certificate in history, English and divinity. It occupied another large, peeling and dilapidated west London family house. It was co-educational (the writer Gillian Freeman was a pupil) and, after Shrewsbury, rather jolly. Not only did I study, I also taught, being paid a salary of £4 10s. a week to teach the smaller children the rudiments of English and French. Today, it would be the equivalent of a sixth-form college.

I had two immediate problems and one overriding anxiety. My first problem was loneliness, I knew nobody. My Shrewsbury friends were all still at school, or from the North (the school was largely patronized by the sons of Liverpudlian merchant princes). I also suffered from acne, a problem which an ointment called Eskamel did little to overcome. The pains of old age are as nothing when compared with the pangs caused by the appearance while shaving of yet another unsightly red spot. Just as colds are three days coming, three days here and three days going, so too were my blemishes. Girls seemed never to have spots, and found boys with 'blips' most unattractive. Or so I had been told. I was near despair.

My chief anxiety was the prospect of National Service. Conscription for a period of two years into the armed service of one's choice was obligatory. It was clearly wiser to get it over with before going up to Oxford; after the rigours of Shrewsbury and its Junior Training Corps (where I had won my Certificate A, the first step for some, at least, towards the acquisition of a field marshal's baton), the privations of army life, at that point even active service in Korea, would be little when compared with the shock of joining the army after three years at Oxford spent revisiting Brideshead. I was due to sign up once I had taken my higher school certificate examination, my call-up date expected towards the end of 1949.

In the late summer of that year I was summoned to attend a medical which was held in a vast hall in the vicinity of Neasden. Having reported at the gate I was obliged to strip naked and stand in a long line of my fellows to whom I had not been introduced. A doctor and two senior officers moved slowly down the line casting six beady eyes over the sacrificial lambs. When they came to me the party stopped dead, and one of the officers barked 'I can see you're a public-school boy. What regiment are ye joinin'?' I mumbled something to the effect that I didn't quite know and, still naked, was marched into a small hut contained under the roof, where I was told to join the Greenjackets. I signed my name. 'Damn good regiment,' said my patron. The Rifle Brigade, of which the Greenjackets became a part, is known throughout the army as the 'Black Mafia'. Light infantrymen, they are not quite as smart as the footguards, but a lot more clever. However, I now know what it is they all have in common, or rather what it is they have all lost, such was the medical fashion among the aspiring middle classes in the early thirties.

It was not long before my mother despaired of my hanging around Swiss Cottage 'eating her out of house and home'. I was tall, thin and very greedy. I spent much of my time going to the pictures; sometimes I would go not once but twice a day, ending up with a splitting headache. The Swiss Cottage Odeon was three minutes away, a huge picture-palace opened just before the outbreak of war by Alexander Korda and his wife Merle Oberon. Even in 1948 it was the last word in vulgar luxury with ankle-deep carpets and Wardour Street chic. I would sit in the one-and-nines seeing for the first time films destined eventually for Channel 4. Its rival cinema was even larger, the Gaumont State in the Kilburn High Road, a number 31 bus ride away where the local Irish waited patiently for the world's largest cinema organ to come through the floor to the music of some Celtic ballad. There was always a long, a short, a trailer (mercifully brief) and the Gaumont British News in which Ernest Bevin and Clement Attlee boarded aircraft, raised their hats and waved farewell, all in time to loud patriotic music. In the intervals cheap chocolate and ice-cream made from groundnut oil were sold by girls called Maureen. I think there was an ABC cinema on the Maida Vale side of Kilburn LMS station where I saw *The Third Man*, surely the best British film of all time. London rang to the music of Anton Karas and his zither.

The rich of Hampstead Village were protected from the rest of the borough by the long climb up Fitzjohn's Avenue. There was no direct bus route except up Haverstock Hill, which meant a pull up the avenue past the site of the Eve Curie Institute beneath the ruins of which, so said my mother, lay chunks of unrecovered radium, a discouragement for those who wanted to see French films at the Everyman cinema. Had it not been for my mother's inspiration I might have spent a year sitting alone in darkened cinemas, consumed with lust for Deborah Kerr (an English rose) or Gloria Grahame (who was plainly nothing of the sort). My mother, aware of a slight interest in politics on my part, made it her business to pay visits to the Hampstead Young Liberals, the local Young Socialists and the Young Conservatives. She thought the YCs to contain 'much the nicest class of girl', and after much pushing and shoving made me go one Tuesday evening to the Conservatives' HQ in College Crescent. As an event it was hardly comparable to St Paul's trip to Damascus, but it was a conversion of a kind. My first sight of the Tories in action was of the young Geoffrey Finsberg telling thirty or so pretty girls of Captain Macmillan's intention to build 300,000 houses a year. The room was large and furnished with wooden chairs. The walls were decorated by large coloured posters of 'The Tory Team' which included, besides Captain Macmillan, Harry Crookshank, Oliver Stanley and Lord Woolton. After the oratory, such as it was, came cups of milky Nescafé.

Thanks to Fred Woolton, the chairman of the party, the Young Conservatives had become the marriage bureau of the middle classes; 200,000 nubile girls in search of 10,000 politically ambitious young men. Forty years ago mothers kept anxious eyes upon their daughters who did not enjoy the freedom they do today. The only 'pill' was an aspirin. There was much titillation, little consummation. And throughout Hampstead bells tolled the ten-thirty curfew. The YCs paid a price of gentle political indoctrination and in return were permitted to fall in and out of love, play tennis during long summer evenings, badminton in the winter, and on Saturday nights to penetrate the West End in order to see the latest big films in and around Piccadilly (seats at 12s. 6d and 15s) and to eat Chinese at the Hong Kong restaurant in Shaftesbury Avenue. It was then the only chop-suey house in central London, famous for its crispy meatballs.

The friendships of youth are the most intense. I was enraptured by the Pats, Marions and Sues, hairdressers, shop girls and secretaries; sweet, trim but very respectable. I was even persuaded to march through the streets of Hammersmith in support of Anthony Fell's candidature in a by-election ('Get Fell in'). Two thousand YCs, mainly men, dressed in tweed jackets and grey flannel trousers paraded before Winston Churchill who was perched, a little precariously we thought, on the balcony of the Hammersmith Conservative Club. People in the crowd shouted 'fascist' but we didn't care; it would have been hard to imagine a less threatening procession. Most if not all of those taking part had done so in order to attend a Gala Evening to be held at the Hammersmith Palais which Conservative Central Office had taken over for the evening. We danced the night away to the music of big bands, saving the tango for the girl of our choice, foxtrotting with branch secretaries from the smarter suburbs, quickstepping our way in noisy groups to catch the last tube home. Winston Churchill was, no doubt, dining at the Savoy, but Anthony Eden 'said a few words', an elegant figure with a languid voice later to be imitated so cruelly on record by Peter Sellers.

We spent most Saturday evenings playing tennis at the Hampstead tennis club, supping on cold pork pie, pickles and potato salad. If we drank at all, it was sweet cider. Then the long walk home across a silent Hampstead to NW6 and fumbling doorstep goodnights. It was all brief and unsatisfactory, for 'Mother' was clearly up and waiting, and my own mother's stern injunction, delivered stentoriously whenever the front door of Number 4 shut behind me, 'Don't get that girl in the family way', rang inside my head. That would indeed have been the day. Even in the gladdest of their glad rags, the Sues and Pats were armoured against all assault, such was the wiring of their bras; while their knickers were *terra incognita*. In the meantime, we dillied and dallied, hoping that there was more to life than necking on sofas, counting our 'conquests', such as they were and lusting in the watches of the night over the remote possibility of going one step further. Small wonder I suffered from spots.

We did our bit politically. We conspired successfully to replace Charles Challen with Henry Brooke as MP for the borough of Hampstead. I attended a noisy meeting at the Embassy Theatre, Swiss Cottage, and cast my vote as instructed against Challen. It seemed that he had neglected the constituency. On Tuesday evenings we sat in our large, dingy room at College Crescent decorated with posters of Walter Elliot and Oliver Lyttelton, listening politely to the speaker and holding hands with Marion, Pat or Sue. It was all very painless. We were not encouraged to think, still less to write. It was not our pens that were wanted but our feet. At elections we went canvassing, climbing the front steps of tall, grubbily stuccoed houses in Belsize Park, pressing the battery of bells, marking up the doubtfuls by the light of street lamps.

Sometimes expeditions were mounted into enemy territory, such as Kilburn or Kentish Town. In the 1950 election we were continuously engaged, the foot-soldiers of the counter-revolution, canvassing with the girl of the moment, deployed around the marginal seats of London, ready to do or die. We had the time of our lives.

6 Doctor in the House

In 1945 my father was demobilized and returned to London to practise medicine. He was a consultant neurologist working partly for the Health Service, attached to the National Hospital for Nervous Diseases, Queen Square (where he later became dean to the Institute of Neurology), and partly for King's College Hospital in south London. He had abandoned Harley Street for a set of consulting rooms at the National. The pre-war Daimler ELT 34 had been exchanged for an older Rolls-Royce with the registration number EGO 125, the letters affording my somewhat waspish mother a good deal of pleasure. Richard Gordon's fictional Sir Lancelot Spratt also drove an old Rolls, a type of motor car that after the war became the hallmark of the successful medical consultant. Father for some mysterious reason never received a knighthood, much to my mother's chagrin, stopping on the ladder of recognition in 1962 when he was awarded the CBE. He certainly deserved one. He was later to become the first president of the World Federation of Neurology. But knighthoods for doctors are comparatively rare; unlike in politics when they are frequently a reward for long, silent service.

My mother's health had begun to deteriorate during the war, when she suffered terribly from attacks of renal colic. By the time I was due to join up she had recovered somewhat, a chain-smoker and gin-drinker who was, when on form, an immensely amusing companion with a wickedly malicious wit. I may have inherited this trait from her: there were to be times enough when, in later life, I should have bitten my tongue. She was fiercely loyal of Father's reputation. 'Your father,' she would say, somewhat dauntingly 'is a very clever man indeed.' Having been told more than once by masters at Shrewsbury that I would amount to nothing, I found this depressing. But I was happy living in Harben Road. I would, on occasion, slip into my father's bedroom and count the number of his hand-made suits (never fewer than a dozen), and run covetous hands over his battery of heavy silk French ties. Not until I reviewed the television series *The Life and Times of Lord Mount-*

batten for *The Times* in the late sixties did I glimpse so extensive a wardrobe.

Mother ran Number 4 with the help of Mary Teevendale, an Irishwoman married to a man from Onibury, Auntie Beth's village in Shropshire. Mary was the cook. My brother Nicholas and I had outgrown Daisy, our pre-war cousin/ nanny, and there was no longer a second living-in maid. We dined at seven o'clock sharp, assembling in a large dining-room through the floor of which sprang a lift, preceded by subterranean rumblings, driven by a handle in the kitchen below. As small boys, we would elevate the cat in this way. On a good day the lift would contain a generous dish of rissoles made of twice-cooked meat and fried onion, which must have been an Irish speciality. They were delicious. But this was a middle-class household before Elizabeth David taught the English how to cook. The food was aggressively plain, scrambled eggs smothered in HP sauce being a favourite dish of mine, the sauce bottle itself with its label part written in French ('*Cette sauce de haute qualité . . .*') took up a prominent position on sideboard or table; part of a Trinity of red, yellow and brown. Not until the days of Harold Wilson's premiership did the satirists succeed in banishing HP from the tables of the bourgeoisie. Garlic was unknown and an avocado a gleam in Elaine Dunday's eye. We had salads (hard-boiled eggs, tomato, spring onion and lettuce) with Heinz Salad Cream for dressing, and much of what we ate was fried. Sunday night's supper was inevitably cold lamb and bubble and squeak. There were echoes of my mother's rural poverty. The Sunday roast – beef, lamb or pork – was resurrected in different form on Mondays, Tuesdays and Wednesdays. As Friday was a fish day, Thursdays presented something of a problem; but I never went hungry.

As Mother's health deteriorated so we entertained infrequently; hospitality being reserved for Mother's sister Beth, Father's brother Michael and his wife Doris (never a favourite of my mother's) and my Shropshire cousins, Clive and Campbell Jones. My mother was inordinately proud of a remark she had overheard in the local Cullens, 'The Critchleys,' said someone darkly 'are the sort of people who drink wine with their meals.' This was an exaggeration. We only drank wine when Father was at home, and then from what I can remember it was a dull white Bordeaux, like Entre Deux Mers. I drank sweet cider. Besides the rissoles, there were chops and stews, and lots of puddings, bread-and-butter pud and queenie pudding being the two favourites. Mother, who claimed to be a bad cook, was not much interested in food, although she would become lyrical when recalling the special treat of her cottage childhood; 'peas, beans and bacon', peas and little broad beans, fresh out of the garden, with home-cured bacon. This is to be highly recommended, although I cannot say as much for my paternal grandmother's Bristolian salad-dressing that consisted of milk mixed with sweetened malt vinegar.

Number 4 Harben Road was not a temple to gastronomy, but it was a house full to overflowing with books. My father bought books by the score, especially anything by or about Oscar Wilde. He was, for a time, an amateur of the Second Empire, and his collection of Napoleon Trois was the most comprehensive in the country. I read Philip Guedalla's *Second Empire* with relish, and dipping further into the library became a precocious expert on France beween 1851 and 1870, an unfashionable period of French history but an intensely romantic one. I read of Morny, Bazaine and the Mexican Adventure, of MacMahon and Marshal Le Bœuf who told his emperor on the eve of the Franco-Prussian War that the French Army was ready 'down to its last gaiter-button'. Indeed so expert did I become that during my viva at schools at Oxford I was congratulated by some dull don for not only listing the known mistresses of Napoleon III, but putting them in the right order. The most beautiful of them, Cora Pearl, was English. To this day I reread Michael Howard's *The Franco-Prussian War* every year, with its marvellous descriptions of the battles of Vionville and Mars la Tour at both of which the imperial armies came within an inch of victory. And the brave campaign of the doomed Général Chanzy, who in 1871 on the Loire gained the only French victory of the war.

Father also had a splendid collection of erotica with which I was much taken. This included the drawings of Félicien Rops and illustrated editions of de Sade. There was also a copy of Richard Aldington's *Death of a Hero* in which the author had filled in the asterisks with his original obscenities. There was an unexpurgated *Chatterley*, which I found unreadable, and the usual tattered copies of Henry Miller, smuggled past the Dover customs, whose eyebrow-raising lubricious accounts of his sexual conquests made a mockery of my celibacy among the Young Conservatives of Hampstead.

My father also collected pictures and at that time he possessed a Maurice Vlaminck flower picture, a Marie Laurencin, a better-than-average Lowry and a Piper among many others by less well-known artists. Sadly they are all now long gone. For a time he took up painting, but there his talent deserted him, his oils of the neighbourhood falling a good way short of those of the Camden Town school.

Father was a distant figure, emotionally shy, undemonstrative, cerebral and inclined to silence unless we were entertaining, when he sparkled. When called upon to perform he could be brilliant (his medical lectures were much admired), but he recuperated at home where he spoke little. It was like living with an actor. Yet he was mild-mannered, never angry or censorious. I can remember him coming home to dinner in the late forties at the time of the polio epidemics and terrifying us with stories of the iron lung. As a neurologist he must have seen many patients suffering from the disease popularly known as infantile paralysis. Thank God, two vaccines have largely eradicated it. The disease seemed to return with the summer and deep down I felt that I was destined to catch it. The threat of the virus hung in the air like a small but terrible cloud. But then I was a neurotic youth and would have thought the same of any medieval epidemic.

On the morning of Saturday 5 November 1949 I set out to walk to John Barnes, the department store next to Finchley Road tube station, but felt so ill I was compelled to turn back and make my way home. I went immediately to bed. I thought I had a bad attack of 'flu, and I can remember lying feverishly in a darkened room listening to the volleys of fireworks exploding over Hampstead. On the Tuesday morning I got out of bed to go to the lavatory and found that I could walk only with difficulty, my right leg had suddenly become much the weaker, and I knew the awful truth which my anxious parents had kept from me: I had polio.

It is hard to exaggerate how frightened people were of polio. Every summer since the end of the war there had been epidemics of a disease which seemed to strike at random but which almost always affected the young and vigorous. In August, swimming-pools would be closed as a precaution; the press would be full of speculation as to its cause; at one time it was believed that the virus was spread by excrement deposited on railway lines by passing trains. There was no cure; no way in which the paralysis, which occurred once the fever diminished, could be halted; it could lead to death by suffocation or, even worse, a life imprisoned in an iron lung. I was fortunate; the paralysis stopped at my right buttock, robbing me of the ability to run (I could not stand on tip-toe on my right leg) and withering the calf and thigh.

I was taken by ambulance to the National Hospital, Queen Square, and given a bed in Annie Zunz ward. I stayed in hospital for six weeks, the victim of intensive physiotherapy administered by a kindly but formidable Scotswoman called Miss Hurn. I fell in love with a nurse called Victoria Plum. She put me in a wheelchair and took me out to tea. I was much spoilt by the frequent visits of solicitous Hampstead friends, the Pats, Marions, Paulas and Sues, and for a time felt very sorry for myself. The army wrote me a letter telling me my services would no longer be needed and the Greenjackets left for Korea without me. I was lucky I was lame, but it barely showed. I did not need to walk with a stick. In time, I learnt to adapt to my handicap, about which I was at first unduly sensitive. In fact, I was little affected by it. I was careful to avoid being put in the position of being obliged to walk long distances and I trained myself to miss buses with equanimity. The Gay Gordons gave way to a night-club shuffle and I watched tennis rather than played it. I was nineteen when I was struck down: it was not until I was sixty and the disc controlling my right leg gave out that the disease finally crippled me. I did not know it but I had been given a forty-year reprieve.

7 La Vie en rose, Paris

In November 1950 there was only one way to enter Paris; through the smoky portals of the Gare du Nord. Only the rich flew into Le Bourget. A year to the day after falling sick with polio I took the *Golden Arrow* from Victoria and crossed the Channel to Calais. A great black pacific-type locomotive that should have been driven by either Jean Gabin or Michel Simon, pulled me swiftly from La Gare Maritime through the bleak chalklands of northern France to the dingy industrial suburbs of Paris. It was like a scene from *La Bête humaine*. I was filled with excitement. To pass the time before going up to Pembroke College, Oxford, in October 1951, and to make up for not fighting the Chinese hordes in Korea, I had been sent by my father to the Sorbonne to read a course encouragingly entitled '*Civilisation française*'. I had been given an allowance of 30,000 francs a month (£30; now worth £500) and the return half of my third-class train ticket. I wore a brown corduroy jacket which I had bought for ten pounds, having humped Persian lamb at the Hudson's Bay Company for three weeks in the summer. And I sported a variety of bow-ties. How better to attract attention?

The Gare du Nord was a smoke-filled cavern full of noise, staffed by dwarves in blousons and black berets frantically pushing trolleys. They had fierce-smelling cigarettes dangling from the corners of their mouths and engaged each other in raucous, non-stop conversation. In the pale autumn afternoon sunlight I took a taxi, red, box-like and badly sprung, which ought in 1940 to have saved Paris, and told the driver my destination. 'La Collège Franco-Britannique, boulevard Jourdain, Paris quatorzième,' I cried in halting Shrewsbury French. We drove across Paris from north to south, down same-seeming boulevards to a chorus of haphazard abuse and the sound of klaxons. The pedestrians were fleet of foot. The buses had open platforms at the back on which stood passengers, the women stout and serviceable, the men wearing strange hats with brims turned up at back and front. After Mr Attlee's austerity England the food shops were bursting at the seams, vegetables tumbling on to the pavements, the *charcuterie* hung with sausage. The chemists flaunted green crosses, which seemed a sensible idea, and the pavement cafés were safely glassed-in against the November weather. Waiters dressed in black wearing long white aprons stood to attention, trays at the ready. Who would not have been enchanted?

The taxi crossed the Seine at the Ile de la Cité and drove bravely up the boulevard Saint-Michel, past a large shop called '100,000 Chemises', and several street cafés that I was later to make my own. Everyone seemed to be wearing duffle-coats. We drove past the Luxembourg Gardens and, plunging into the southern suburbs, arrived eventually at the Cité Universitaire and my room. In it was a solitary young Frenchman who gravely shook me by the hand. I never did catch his name.

My inadequate French was not helped by my stammer; with a small vocabulary I found it impossible to juggle words. This and a general shyness made it hard to meet native girls, but there was no shortage of the English variety, or indeed Americans, who clustered round the course of *La Civilisation française* like bees round a honeypot. Jackie Bouvier/Kennedy/Onassis had spent, so it was claimed, the last academic year singing and dancing in Paris, turning up infrequently at the lectures, and being awarded at the end of the term with a *Certificat d'assiduité*, a large, ornamental piece of paper that was more imposing than the certificate awarded for those who had actually passed the examination. I cannot think what happened to mine. It was quite undeserved.

The Collège Franco-Britannique was one barrack among many others, dull, austere and uncompanionable. There was a communal students' restaurant of unrelieved awfulness; no one who has tried and failed to eat French institutional cooking can complain of its British equivalent. I swiftly abandoned it, and wandered the neighbourhood in search of *les restaurants de quartier*. During the day, that is before and after the lectures that took place within the Sorbonne, the English congregated at the Institut Britannique, a cultural establishment in the street next to the Sorbonne which provided warmth, newspapers and comfortable chairs. It made no demands upon us; there was a small library for the more serious, and sofas upon which the idle could recover from the self-indulgence of the night before. There were no posters of Mr Anthony Eden, only a discreet portrait of the king. Anthony Werner, a fellow student of White Russian origin (his father was a prosperous banker with a grand *appartement* at La Muette) with whom I fell into conversation, was convinced that there were many more English girls out there somewhere in Paris, living alone in dingy rooms or, if their parents were richer, lodging with several others in some smart house in the better suburbs under the strict supervision of an elderly Frenchwoman of irreproachable reputation. One such *maison* was believed to exist at 40 rue de Moscou in the 9th *arrondissement*. We nick-named it 'the Kremlin' and set about the task of liberating its occupants. But how best to make contact?

Tony Werner and I were both interested in politics; one or the other of us had the bright idea of setting up a branch of the Paris Young Conservatives. So severe a challenge to the institutions of the Fourth Republic passed unnoticed in France, but a report of the inaugural meeting was carried by the continental *Daily Mail*, and picked up by the British press.

Lord Woolton, the chairman of the Conservative party, sent us a message of support. Under French law we were obliged to register as a political organization, an act of a day which was met with bureaucratic incredulity. We were English and clearly mad.

We held the inaugural meeting at 4 avenue Rodin, an *appartement* in the 16th, belonging to Frank and Vera Laws-Johnson. Frank was my bank manager at Barclays in the rue Quatre Septembre; he doled out my thirty thousand francs, which enabled me to live like a prince for three weeks of the month and like a pauper for the other, and introduced me to his daughter Veronica who was also studying *La Civilisation française*. A sweet and friendly girl in love with all things Spanish (whence the Laws-Johnsons had come) she too had wind of 40 rue de Moscou to whose *incarcerées* invitations were sent in her capacity as the newly appointed secretary of the Paris YCs. I was elected vice chairman, and the branch's 'political officer'.

It was at the inaugural meeting that I fell head over heels in love. By some miracle the girls of the Kremlin (my mother would have thought them very 'nice' indeed) had been given permission to attend the function by their chatelaine, Mamzelle Vincent. They might not have been especially political (who was?) but they were desperate to escape a regimen of cultural visits, undistinguished food and exclusively female company. Well-brought up upper-middle-class girls of eighteen or so, I believe they would have joined the Young Communist League had it first offered a means of escape. I saw Prudence Marshall across a crowded room. She was tall, dark, coltish, slim and pretty with the most charming smile. She was a prep-school headmaster's daughter from Bromley, which added somewhat to the challenge.

It was a very 'proper' party. Vera Laws-Johnson had provided little delicacies that were wolfed down by the hungry. Frank had decorated the room with modest bottles from his famous cellar, and we danced decorously to the music of Veronica's record-player: Yves Montand singing '*Les Feuilles mortes*', Edith Piaf and the very best of Ella Fitzgerald. I had been 'in love' before Prue, and was to fall in love later with several others, and indeed to marry twice. But

Prue was, from the beginning, in a class of her own. Her nature was as sweet as her looks were good. She wore the fashions of the day; skirts just below the knee, tight sweaters and wide, elasticated belts. Sometimes, worried by a prettily tilted nose, she would run her finger down it while quoting extensively from T. S. Eliot. When her parents visited her in Paris she would wear tiny hats perched on the back of her head. She was fun.

As a child I was fond of Clare Allison, as a schoolboy there had been a maid of my aunt Beth's called Chrissie Hotchkiss of Clungunford who used to write me letters at Shrewsbury. In Hampstead, I had fallen for Susan Brown, Angela Goldberg, and later Marion Kidson, with whom I had biked around Ireland to the outrage of my strait-laced aunts. 'The exercise will do his leg a power of good,' said my wise parents. It did, but after several hundred miles I was still a virgin. I could never catch her up.

I had hankered after Pam Gosling, a good-looking girl who lived on the borders of Hampstead and worked for *Vogue*. She had paid occasional visits to 4 Harben Road to the strong disapproval of my mother who took exception to the fact that Pam was wearing green nail-polish. 'That girl will never set foot in my house again.' She did, and later played havoc with my susceptible Shropshire cousins.

How can I describe the sheer excitement of love? Perhaps there is no need to do so. My first task was to winkle Prue out of the Kremlin where she and her genteel companions lived like nuns under strict curfew. With Prue's enthusiastic connivance I wrote a letter to her on Institut Britannique paper to the rue de Moscou and signed it 'Uncle Mac'. I was visiting the city briefly: could I take my favourite niece out to the theatre (Molière?) and to a simple dinner (two courses). We might well be late as I had always wished to pay a visit to les Halles, the market then situated in the heart of Paris, a visit to which was the classical culmination to a night on the tiles. Would Mamzelle Vincent bite? Perhaps she was a kinder woman than we imagined for the answer was 'yes'. She was certain that Mamzelle Marshall would be in good hands. Prue communicated the good news by sending me a *pneumatique*, a curious form of post in which letters were blown across Paris almost instantly through a series of tubes. Bringing the good tidings, mine was promptly delivered to 22 rue de Château Landon, where I had a modest room.

We gave Molière a miss and went instead with two friends to the Bal des Anglais, a *boîte* in the 5th situated in a side-street running down to the Seine. I never saw it by daylight but at night it was bathed in a candy-pink light, a small floor surrounded by chairs and tables where we sat undisturbed drinking *cidre Normand* and dancing to the music of an accordion. Once an evening two apache dancers threw each other about the floor with all the abandon of a half-empty bottle of absinthe. It was not a tourist trap; we were the only foreigners, and we were made welcome because of it. '*Bonsoir, les Anglais!*' Today, it would be considered a cliché, but forty years ago we thought it *le vrai Paris*. Later, we walked over the shining river arm in arm, past a silent Ile St Louis and up le Topol (boulevard de Sebastopol), turning right into the bright lights of les Halles, the population of which turned out to be divided equally between market porters and foreigners of all sorts who sat cheerfully in the all-night cafés, sipping *soupe à l'oignon* for its restorative powers and toasting the porters in shared bottles of harsh white wine. It was the first time Prue had tasted wine. After Bromley and Brockhurst, Cheltenham Ladies' College and Shrewsbury school, this was the life.

Yet how innocent we were! We had eyes only for each other but we never properly made love. In the first instance we had nowhere to go; in the second, in the years before the Pill, we heeded maternal strictures to avoid pregnancy at all costs. Contraception was risky, and risible. I did not relish entering what I supposed would be the Parisian equivalent of a London barber's shop and asking to hearty Gallic laughter for *une capote anglaise*. Like nearly every other well-brought-up couple in the early fifties, we made do. This meant 'necking', a word that has vanished from our children's vocabulary. It consisted of passionate embraces, much French kissing (I had been taught the art by a Hampstead hairdresser), breast-baring and happy back-seat fumbling. It was frustrating but it was fun.

The Paris Young Conservatives waxed then waned. In the early days we held weekly meetings in the drawing-room of a flat owned by Tony Werner's father, the White Russian banker. We did not stand on ceremony. Tony was a serious fellow and would occasionally suggest a speaker, but he was always howled down. We were not into oratory. The proceedings were opened by planning to go dancing at Mimi Pinson, a prettier version of the Hammersmith Palais, which was up on the top left-hand side of the Champs-Elysées. At the weekend we would watch the tennis at Roland Garros, then eat cheaply at the *restaurants de quartier* on the rue de Passy before going to the pictures. In Parisian cinemas we soon learnt to tip the usherettes, and to join in the chorus, once the lights went up and the salesgirl appeared, of '*esquimaux gervais, chocolats, bons-bons acidulés*'. Tories we might have been but we would not have met with Geoffrey Finsberg's approval.

The winter turned slowly into a brilliant spring. The prevailing wind veering from east to south, the pavement cafés dismantled their shields of plate glass, and the chestnuts came slowly into bloom. Despite the return of the sun (and I have been colder and hotter in Paris than any other city of my acquaintance), a mournful Yves Montand continued to sing '*Les Feuilles mortes*', Autumn Leaves, a sad song from a poem by Prévert, that haunted Paris in 1951. I cannot hear a snatch of it played today without recapturing a feeling of careless rapture followed by the sadness of inevitable loss. When Prue and I met again in the late eighties and fell once more in love, we would talk about old times; comparing the vagaries of memory. She could not remember our meeting at the Gare du Nord when she returned from a visit home in April to be escorted to her new room in digs off the rue de Passy. I can see her now, suitcase in hand, emerging from the steam like a happier Anna. She could not even remember two furtive visits to hotels that we made. Motherly looking madames had scrutinized incompatible passports only to wave us upstairs with a smile and a blessing. '*Qui va savoir?*' demanded Prue in her best French. We lay together naked save for our knickers, a tribute to our anxious, ever-present mothers. We did not dare risk our great good fortune. In those days one was protected by love.

With Veronica Laws-Johnson and David Stern, we borrowed Frank Laws-Johnson's *cochon* (a tiny Renault) and drove south for a long weekend that May, crossing the Loire at Blois and driving down the straight poplared dusty white roads as far as Le Puy, eating picnic lunches, staying at small hotels with wishing wells, and then at Vierzon reluctantly turning northwards up the Rhône towards Lyon, abandoning for forty years the pleasures of Provence, and the hot, shuttered, silent, scented south.

We lived in a state of first love all that brillant summer, returning to England at the end of June. I did not return to Paris until the seventies when as MP for Aldershot the whips made me a delegate to the Council of Europe and the Western European Union. If the debates in the avenue Wilson were even duller than I expected, I would take the Métro and recapture the journeys of my youth when I lived in a box-room beyond the Gare de l'Est, and Prue in a room in an *appartement* near La Muette. I was certain that neither my children nor hers would permit sixteen *stations de Métro* last thing at night (Trocadero, Kleber, Chaussée d'Antin, Gare de L'Est . . .) to come between them and their heart's desire.

8 Going Up

I drove up to Pembroke College, Oxford, on my Vespa scooter early in October 1951. The Vespa had been an early twenty-first birthday present from my parents. One hundred and twenty-five ccs of Italian chic, and one of the first to be registered in Britain, for a time UMM 628 drew much attention. It was bright green, fun to drive, difficult to fall off, and capable of a top speed of forty-five miles per hour. It did something like seventy miles a gallon on a mixture of cheap petrol and oil. But no Vespa was complete without a girl on the pillion seat: in France or Italy girls were permitted by the authorities (elderly men with an eye for a shapely leg) to sit side-saddle, an elegance that was denied them by the Metropolitan Police. For safety's sake, Prue was obliged to sit astride my machine (named La Muette, in her honour) as if on a pit-pony.

I had spent the last of the summer driving down to Prue's house in Bromley from Swiss Cottage, crossing the river at Westminster and plunging southwards via the Old Kent Road, Lewisham High Street and Catford, *terra incognita*, through the seemingly never-ending drab, bombed, red-brick streets of south-east London, past the Bellingham estate, home of George and Henry, the Cooper twins, until and at long last I chugged up the hill into Bromley and Carn Brea, the prep school owned by Prue's father. Forty years ago the grand called Bromley 'Brumley', an affectation adopted by its then MP, Captain Harold Macmillan. Mr Marshall seemed unformidable – for a preparatory-school headmaster; once he slipped me a five-pound note to take his daughter to a dinner-dance in a local hotel. We went and I had change left over for a taxi home. Prue's mother, so I learnt years later, strongly approved of me, 'such a nice boy and an old Salopian', but my mother, viewing our *affaire* from the study window at Harben Road in the cold light of a Hampstead dawn (where Prue had passed an innocent night, uninvited) wrote to Mrs Marshall to complain that her son was seeing far too much of her daughter. I was, or so it appeared, too young for such entanglements. I knew nothing of this until many years later. My mother, of course, was quite right. I was not yet twenty-one, and was going up to Oxford. My future was before me. As for love, nothing so good could last for ever, as I was soon to discover.

Why was I going to Pembroke? There was no family connection; after attending the Christian Brothers my father had studied medicine at Bristol (he passed the requisite examinations at the age of fifteen), and none of the Shropshire Morrises had ever been to a university. I was first-generation public school; first-generation Oxbridge. Pembroke was the only college in the early fifties that did not require yet another examination. I had matriculated with both my certificates, higher and lower; that was deemed to be enough. There was also an interview, but my Old Salopian accent and a general deference stood me in good stead. Today, an aspirant would need straight 'A's; mine were simply required to be long rather than short.

Forty years ago Pembroke was a pretty college, anchored in the lee of Christ Church. 'Pemmy' men were, on the whole, rather dim, earnest types, much addicted to wearing college ties and scarves, prone to Saturday night drunkenness, absent from the wider university stage. They might have looked on me as a refugee from 'the House' (Christ Church) across the road. The master was Holmes Dudden who was bedridden, never making an appearance during the three years I was up. We were told he was in his nineties. His portrait, which hung in college, showed him to be a remarkably handsome youngish man in clerical garb, but in reality he was confined, presumably, to his rooms. The college was run by R. B. McCallum, the senior tutor, a delightful lowland Scot who taught politics and had written in 1945 the first of the general-election books that were to become a regular post-election event. He was an old-fashioned Liberal who once told me why he could never have joined Labour. 'The Labour party is not a party,' he explained 'it is a movement. I could never have joined a movement.' He did not like Dick Crossman who was a star guest at the Union, flaunting his black velvet dinner-jacket, his black suede shoes and his radical opinions. 'A dreadful man,' said McCallum. 'He has debauched his undergraduates.' I knew later what he meant. They had been corrupted politically.

No sooner had I parked my Vespa in the porter's lodge (it carried a small green light on the instructions of the proctors, and to the confusion of the police beyond Oxford) than I bumped into Michael Heseltine on the staircase. We had been given sets of rooms in the tower. I had not seen Michael since Shrewsbury where we had been in different houses. He wore his hair in a Swansea crop and save perhaps for his height was unremarkable; indeed he might at first sight have passed for a student in *Lucky Jim*. We made ourselves comfortable. I opened a bottle of sweet sherry, hung a print of Renoir's *A Girl on a Swing* over the mantelshelf, and displayed my copy of *France-Soir* which was delivered daily. It was the Sorbonne that had made me intolerable.

In October 1951, I held the advantage. I was two years older than Michael, had been to a foreign university, and wore several of my father's Savile Row suits together with hand-tied bow-ties. I even sported an old silk dressing-gown of my father's. Politically, too, I held the higher cards; had I not founded the Paris Young Conservatives, about which I had written a piece for the Undergraduate Page in the *Spectator*, and, before that, sat at the feet of Geoffrey Finsberg, Hampstead's rising hope?

We were both reading PPE; philosophy, politics and economics. I wish now that I had read history, but I was discouraged from attempting it by the prospect of a Latin exam in prelims. I had no wish to brush up my school certificate Latin. McCallum was an engaging politics and history tutor. Economics was taught by Neville Ward-Perkins, a youngish man who drove a Jowett Javelin, relied a good deal on Paul Samuelson's massive textbook, and sadly, died suddenly in the mid-fifties. Philosophy, a subject for which neither of us was temperamentally inclined, was the province of a dull man called McNab. I could never find the patience to get to grips with the linguistic philosophy that was then in vogue, much preferring the sound commonsense of Dr Johnson. If you see a stone and doubt what you see, kick it. But I should not give the impression of assiduity; Oxford was not for us a seat of learning, it was to be the springboard from which we would dive into the deeper end of a political career.

Oxford in the early fifties was full of delights. Aged parsons in greeny-black suits sat silently in corners of the Union Society's building, reading copies of the *Church Times*. American servicemen hung around Carfax on Saturday nights, patronizing the one dance-hall nearby in search of off-duty nurses from the city's hospitals. Girls from St Hugh's and St Hilda's gave us a glimpse of blue stocking. There were bikes everywhere, unsteady north Oxford wives of the kind to be found later in the novels of Barbara Pym, riding in search of a chop for supper, magisterial and mysterious figures in full academic regalia, and the bulldogs (whom we soon learnt to spot), the 'teeth' of the proctors, stocky parties in dark suits and bowler hats, capable, so we were told, of a surprising turn of speed.

I was quite rich. Not Christ Church, or Magdalen rich, but comfortably off. My father had taken out a covenant, blessed in those days by the Revenue, whereby I received eight pounds a week for seven years, a sum equivalent to the then industrial average wage. Michael had no such income, but his parents were generous. My year in Paris had accustomed me to eating out, and as the food in hall at Pembroke was atrocious, the chef having been trained under Fred Woolton in his wartime guise as Minister for Food, we ate out regularly, lunching off sandwiches in the Union bar, dining at Long John's, a restaurant somewhere between Worcester College and the station that was owned by one Captain Silver, who had served in the army under Colonel Heseltine's command. As a favour, he would reduce our bills by half.

In the early fifties, Oxford had two good hotels; the Randolph and the Mitre. At the Randolph (which still exists) the food was pretentious English and the prices high. The bar seemed to be the haunt of Lord Montagu of Beaulieu who was at the time either 'up' or 'sent down' depending on the severity of his prison sentence. The Mitre on the High is sadly long since gone. My favourite restaurant was White's in the High which has also long since vanished. It served a delicious dish which I have rarely found since – fried mussels in batter with tartar sauce. Very seldom indeed did we go to the Taj, the town's only Indian restaurant. I was always happy to experiment, being both thin and greedy; Michael, equally thin, was more cautious, a meat and two veg man.

Looking back to those days the food must have been pretty dreadful wherever we went, although I can remember discovering a new and delicious delicacy, rollmop herrings, the sort impaled on a stick which unroll to reveal vinegar-soaked white strands of onion. Curiously, they no longer have any appeal. We drank very little. A cheap wine very occasionally, or cider. For a week or so I tried to smoke Gitanes, but found them to be far too strong. Even affectation has its limits. In October 1951 Oxford was still reeling from the effect of the glittering generation of undergraduates who had come up after the war. Battle-hardened majors had made way for National Service lieutenants and boys straight from school. The talk in the Union bar was of the great men who had just gone down, Robin Day, Peter Kirk, Jeremy Thorpe and Ken Tynan: they had burnt so brightly we felt that we could not compete. Shirley Catlin, later Williams, was talked of as Britain's first woman Prime Minister; Margaret Roberts was never mentioned. The Union Society was a temple to precocity, its bar on the first floor the meeting-place of the ambitious, the debating hall itself the proving ground on which our own ambition would be tested to destruction. Its membership was large and subscription low. In consequence it was always in debt. Canvassing for election was forbidden by the rules but nothing could prevent the competing peacocks from displaying their plumage.

Jeremy Thorpe had been accused of canvassing for office and arraigned before a tribunal of his peers; not for the first time he would be acquitted. The young William Rees-Mogg, known to the irreverent as 'the oldest young man in captivity' was an ex-president of the Union. An owl-like person, he had brought down a full house by intoning at the start of a speech 'Mr President, I cannot conceive . . .'

Huddled over the single-bar electric fire in my rooms, safe from the autumnal winds, we charted our course. Michael and I would share out the offices of the University Conservative Association (OUCA) between us and then take the Union by storm. The college seemed small beer; the university was to be our stage. The presidency of the Union was Michael's avowed objective, although before October 1951 he had never made a speech in public outside the witness box. I had made several, usually to YCs; I had also adapted one or two of my father's lectures, for example, the story of the French mass murderer Marcel Petiot. But I lacked self-confidence, and was tethered by my stammer which could embarrassingly reappear in times of stress. Secretly, I avowed I would rise steadily in Michael's powerful wake.

My love affair with Prue came to an end in my second term, in February 1952. She had visited Oxford during the Michaelmas term, staying chastely at the King's Head in the Broad. In the December she came to my twenty-first birthday party at Quaglino's; her present to me a dark green velvet waistcoat with pearl buttons from Fisher's of Burlington Arcade. The vac I spent driving back and forth to Bromley where I earned the disapproval of her stern, old-fashioned grandmothers. 'Is Prue letting Julian kiss her?' one demanded of Mrs Marshall. She was, but that was almost all. I drove back on my scooter to Oxford for the start of term, up the old A40, through Gerrard's Cross and interminable High Wycombe (where I discovered a sweet-shop that sold clove-flavoured suckers to which I became addicted). In December I had asked Prue to come once more to Oxford for the weekend but her mother had put a stop to the expedition. 'You are chasing after that young man,' she warned her daughter. By way of consolation ('for the weekend that wasn't') I sent Prue a set of three wooden pigs, one of which has miraculously survived the intervening years.

In February, she came up to a party in North Oxford. I was asked, but to my chagrin she no longer had eyes for me. She seemed surrounded by a bevy of South African dentists. Dismayed, I went back to my rooms in Pembroke. Later she wrote to me saying we were far too young to be so involved. I was broken-hearted, suffering all the youthful pangs of unrequited love. Never have I been so unhappy. It took me months to recover from losing her; perhaps I never did, although I remember telling myself that never again would I permit myself to be the injured party in a love affair. Henceforth if anyone was going to be hurt it would not be me.

I threw myself into university politics. Michael and I attended all the meetings of OUCA and drew attention to ourselves with question and comment. This, we believed, would quickly lead to our election to the committee. We would then be able to rely upon the Conservative vote in Union elections; for the presidency was the object of the exercise. But we had forgotten 'the House'. The Oxford Tories consisted in the main of men from Magdalen and Christ Church, young sprigs whose fair hair flopped over their foreheads and who talked loudly of horses. They were called 'Paddy' or 'Robin'. They were the gentlemen and we were the players. Pembroke had no cachet, Shrewsbury was not Eton, and my father's suits (Stovel and Mason) and Michael's dialectic did not disguise the fact that we were bounders. We stood for election at the end of our first term but 'the House', the members of which have been described somewhere as spending their days either 'buggering, beagling or falling off horses', organized against us. Scores of young men in brown trousers came out to cast their votes; Old England had mobilized against the New.

The gentlemen were decent but not very bright. Lloyd George was not far out when he described the Tories as 'the stupid party'. We just went one better and announced at the start of the new term in January 1952 the formation of a rival progressive Conservative body to be called the Blue Ribbon Club. We were to be in tune with the 'new' Toryism of Butler, Macmillan and Macleod. We were in favour of the forces of light and against what we labelled 'black reaction'. The inaugural meeting drew a large audience, in the main from the humbler colleges; Michael was elected president and I was elected secretary, a relationship which has been sustained ever since. We were on our way.

Although Michael was younger than I, he was by far the more formidable competitor. Whereas I lacked confidence and was nervous of speaking in public lest my stammer reassert itself (stutterers are convinced that their inability to articulate will be taken by an audience as a sign of the speaker's stupidity), Michael seemed nerveless, although to begin with he was not a natural orator. He was also tireless in pursuit of his ambitions; no trouble was too great, no detail too trivial to neglect. His enemies might claim that he had an eye for the main chance, and the ruthlessness to match it, characteristics that his friends admitted but nevertheless welcomed as being of advantage to others besides himself. As he became more successful that year so his hair grew. He bought a couple of decent suits, borrowed some of my father's old ties and it was not long before he acquired that patina that the nation has come to know and love. But Michael had, and indeed still has, a saving grace: besides his decency and drive, he has a nice sense of the ridiculous and, in private at least, never took himself too seriously. He was a good companion.

What he never managed to afford was a motor car of his own, making use of mine for the better part of three years. I sold my Vespa in the summer of 1952 and bought a 1937 Model Y Ford from a Hertfordshire chicken-farmer. I can still remember the look of delighted amazement when, without a quibble, I gave him his asking price of one hundred pounds. I must have replaced every part of it at least once during the five years I drove it. It was black, uncomfortable and slow but reasonably reliable. It, too, was obliged to sport a small green light in order that it might be challenged by the proctors if spotted after eleven o'clock at night. This was an ancient regulation, included in some twenties' traffic act, which thanks to the connivance of the local garages was easily circumvented: the green light only came on when driving with side lights; with dipped headlights it ceased to shine.

My new chariot, NV 8508, enabled Michael and me to make a foray as far as Shrewsbury school, after I had suggested to the school authorities that we hold a debate on the 'site' about the future of the public schools. Incautiously, the school agreed, and the debating society (a new development that I did not remember from my time) was assembled to greet Ian Josephs, Michael and me who had driven in stately fashion to do battle. We had devoted little time to the preparation of our speeches: although I had already spent three long years preparing mine.

The debate was opened by Michael who must have been quite unrecognizable to those who had known him when he was at Moser's Hall. Besides the blond mane (and a decent suit) he was wearing a fancy waistcoat bought at some expense from Halls of the High, a clothes shop (it would now be called a boutique) for the richer undergraduate. Gone was the gauche schoolboy; in his place was a flamboyant undergraduate armed with facts, figures and a good cross-section of the older and better Oxford Union jokes. He asserted that the public schools were a breeding ground of class privilege, intellectually narrow and conformist and a gross encouragement to homosexual activities of a name-less kind. This diatribe was first listened to in silence, and then, as the younger element in the audience grew more confident, with laughter and applause. Anthony Chevenix-Trench, a housemaster who was later to become headmaster of Eton (where he was asked to retire as he had acquired the habit of kissing the bare bottoms of the boys he had flogged), was far from pleased: indeed he rose to rebut the charges with a face like thunder. He spoke (as far as I can remember) about character building which he attributed to cold baths, strenuous athletic activity and corporal punishment when merited. He sat down to a scattering of applause at the hands of the school's praepostors.

I spoke briefly to second the motion. I was wearing a green velvet waistcoat, and I was, because of the passage of time, something of an unknown quantity. I drew attention to Chevenix-Trench's passion for beating small boys (I think I referred to it as his 'hobby'), and then, having confessed that I had spent three and half years in preparation for such a debate, roundly attacked poor George Furnival, the school chaplain and a decent sort, if a bit wet, for doing irreparable harm to Christianity by boring the boys almost to death. (At Sopwith's we had two graces in Latin, two sets of prayers and one service in chapel a day, with two on Sundays.) I sat down to nervous applause. The chaplain then spoke poorly and at very great length. Michael and I, I regret to say, had gone a little over the top.

There was a short debate from the floor, and then the vote was taken. It was a draw. Amid scenes reminiscent of the worst excesses of the French Revolution (there was continuous uproar and some fighting), the vote was retaken, and the motion that we had proposed and seconded was carried by one vote. Furnival and Chevenix-Trench went off in a huff without as much as a farewell. Michael returned to Moser's Hall where he was to stay the night as the guest of his old housemaster; Ian Josephs and I went to a hotel. But that was not the end of the matter.

Flushed with success, I rang the Press Association and gave it a garbled account of our famous victory. The headmaster, Mr Peterson, was awakened in the middle of the night by various tabloid papers, and indeed The Times, and was asked for his comments. With the milk came the newspapers, which were to greet Michael Heseltine's rather tricky breakfast with Mr and Mrs Phillips. The Mirror's lead story was along the lines of 'Great Public School Votes to do away with Itself'. Michael, who was quite unabashed, proceeded to upbraid the Phillipses about juvenile homosexuality over the single sausage and elderly fried egg, a topic of conversation that drove Mrs Phillips from the breakfast table.

It was at this juncture that Ian and I arrived by car and rescued Michael from what had become a difficult situation. We drove back to Oxford in cheerful discomfort, leaving an umbraged Shrewsbury school thankfully far behind. There were to be ructions. We were threatened with expulsion from the Old Salopian Club, but so dire a punishment was never administered. I was accused of selling the story to the press; in fact, I was so green I did not know one could sell stories to the press. It had been a gift. When I returned to the school in the eighties to speak to the sixth-form I was reminded by Michael Charlesworth, a master who had been for very many years the unofficial conscience and chronicler of the school, of the outrage we had caused ('It even reached Australia'). I do not think Michael Heseltine has ever returned to Shrewsbury in an official capacity, and as for Ian Josephs (who had also spoken in favour of the motion), what more could one expect from an Old Carthusian? Today I might well have taken the stuffier view; forty years ago, it was a splendid undergraduate jape.

9 Salad Days

Oxford Vacs are longer than private school holidays but not as long as parliamentary recesses. For thirty-eight of my sixty-three years I have enjoyed holidays of a length that most people would envy. While at Oxford I frequently used to visit Michael's home in Swansea, a long slow drive in the Model Y through Cheltenham, Chepstow and Cardiff. He in turn would stay at 4 Harben Road. The Heseltines lived in a detached post-1918 house on the Gower road, the most salubrious quarter of what was a bleak and badly bombed Welsh seaport. The Heseltines were hospitable. Michael's father, Colonel Heseltine, was a director of Dawney's, a local steelworks, a kind and conventional figure who was to die suddenly in the mid-fifties from a coronary while mowing his lawn. Michael's mother, who is still alive, came from a prominent local family that had made and lost money in the coal trade; I can remember visiting her father in hospital, the donor of the thousand pounds in 1954 which was to put Michael on the road to fortune and fame. There was a younger sister invariably called 'Bubbles' who was later to share a flat with Prue and Pam Gosling. Mrs Heseltine was 'respectable' Welsh, a description that will at once be recognized by all who live in the principality. She once gave a tea-party for her friends at which Michael and I were duly present. Over sandwiches and three kinds of cake I asked, innocently enough, whether anyone knew Dylan Thomas. A deathly silence fell. At last Mrs Heseltine said chillingly 'we don't talk about Dylan Thomas in Swansea'. Perhaps I should have asked about Kingsley Amis?

The Heseltines' house was large, comfortable and architecturally undistinguished. It was bookless. A cupboard under the stairs was the showcase for one of the Colonel's hobbies – a collection of miniature bottles of liqueurs of all kinds and colours; there must have been a thousand of them. The garden had been turned by Michael into a part aviary inside which fluttered flocks of exotic birds. Later when he went into publishing Michael acquired the magazine *Cage Birds*, one of the many trade mags on which his fortune came to be based. We spent most of our time walking the cliffs and coves of the Gower peninsula, swimming in the summer and going to local hops with one or many of

Michael's girlfriends, or spending long afternoons in the Swansea cinemas. I had a taste for French films (unseen in Swansea), Michael loved westerns, especially *High Noon* which we must have seen together at least half a dozen times. I think he identifed with Gary Cooper. Whatever the occasion, whenever the song 'Land of My Fathers' was sung or played (which was often) Michael would shed a manly Celtic tear, much to my Saxon embarrassment.

The long vacs, mid-June until early October, were more of a challenge. A week in Shropshire staying at the shop at Onibury with Uncle Arnold and Aunt Beth, eating fat dry-cured farm bacon and drinking their mouth-pursing home-made cider, was a delight. In my first vac I spent long summer days exploring the country on my Vespa, still much the best way to do it, riding rough across fields to the tops of distant hills, and the evenings with my cousins Clive and Campbell, playing tennis with the girls of Ludlow on courts beneath the walls of the castle. Daisy, my cousin-cum-nanny, was at that time dying of heart disease brought on by an attack of rheumatic fever suffered as a child. She was bedridden in Rectory Cottage, cared for by Uncle Jack and Auntie May. Daisy had married unhappily during the war. For a time she had been a wartime guard on the Great Western Railway and could be glimpsed by her kin as she trundled back and forth between Shrewsbury and Hereford. I had loved her dearly, perhaps more so than my mother. We parted sadly; me on my scooter back to the shop at Onibury, she to an early death. She is buried in Wistanstow churchyard together with my mother.

Harben Road was comfortable, but I soon tired of rides on the tops of buses to undiscovered destinations such as Stoke Newington or Crystal Palace, few of which were in any way rewarding. The Pat Turners, Marion Kidsons and Sue Browns of the Hampstead Young Conservatives were holidaying with their families in Ventnor, or Burnham-on-Crouch, and the Conservative Association itself was shut down for the whole of August. There was no one left to sit at the feet of Geoffrey Finsberg. I cannot remember who or what put me up to it, but I went to the headquarters of the National Union of Students in Endsleigh Street in search of a vac job.

I was in luck. I spent a month or so of the summer of 1952 driving an elderly American couple around the British Isles. I was given a new Hillman Minx, my task to act as driver-cum-guide. We stayed at good hotels and visited uncounted beauty-spots, the history of which I was careful to mug up on the previous evening. They were simple Californians in a small line of business; they had hired me as 'a real Oxford man' with, they were later to tell me, 'an accent just like Cary Grant's'. They had no means of knowing that my father was just as much a native-born Bristolian as Archie Leach.

The summer of 1952 was good, but in 1953 I hit the jackpot. The National Union of Students wrote to me in the spring asking me whether I would be willing to drive four American girls round Europe in August and September. I said I would be prepared to do so. In August, I flew to Paris to meet them at their hotel near the Etoile. Calvine, Pat, Nancy and Denise ('Nisey') met me in the lobby, the pretty daughters of rich and indulgent Chicagoan parents. They were only too quick to tell me 'we will be living high off the hog'. It was not a phrase to which I was accustomed, but its meaning was plain enough. There was, however, one snag. The NUS had put me in charge of the money, allocating amounts for hotels (already booked in advance) and for breakfast, lunch and dinner. Petrol for the huge Danish-registered American Ford was no problem, but, as I was to discover, accounting for lunch and dinner most certainly was.

I was twenty-two, in my prime, more romantic than lustful. Europe lay at my feet. But what to do with four girls, as noisy as parakeets and as greedy as gannets? It would have been as difficult to fall in love with all four as it was to fall in love with one. There was safety in numbers. At lunch and dinner I was permitted to spend only a set amount on the five of us. It was not long before difficulties arose; Nancy wanted an expensive pudding, Nisey had a thing about Escalope de Veau Holstein, Calvine wanted two first courses and a pud. Pat, however, who was plump, usually stuck to the *prix fixe* menu. Faced with so many demands I surrendered, only to find that on my return to Endsleigh Street I was obliged to pay the difference. My pay was small, and smaller still after the accounts had been redone by a stern member of the NUS's staff. 'Never in all my life have I come across such accounting.'

Still, I would have travelled across Europe for nothing. We drove across a continent of almost empty roads, the only autobahns being Hitler's own. My year in Paris made me an admirable guide to that city, but it was harder elsewhere. It was my intention to mug up a city on the evening of our arrival, but I was often thwarted. Dinner went on too long, and I was exhausted by the driving. We sweltered in Rome (where we saw Peck and Hepburn filming *Roman Holiday*), drove across the Alps into Austria and then Bavaria, travelled up the Rhine to Bonn, Luxembourg and Brussels. The girls were either shrill or silent, depending on whether or not they had quarrelled among themselves. Like most Americans they were camera fiends, hungry for the picturesque, calling the Ford to a sudden halt to take pictures of donkeys, peasants and ruins. At The Hague they were especially exasperating; for some reason they all demanded to see the Peace Palace. I was tired, and my patience exhausted, I parked them in front of what I knew was the Hague waterworks, a formidable mock-Gothic building in the public-works style. It could have been owned by

57

Severn Trent. There was even a notice to the effect that it was a waterworks. 'That', I said 'is the Peace Palace.' They abandoned the car and solemnly took pictures of its many turrets and protuberances. It was a poor joke, but I have often wondered whether photos of the 'Peace Palace' can still be found to this day in some forgotten family album along Lakeshore Drive.

Oxford before 'the New Dark Age', as some right-wing Oxonians call the contemporary scene (when did it begin – in the sixties with the Beatles and the birth of secondary-modern culture?), was a self-contained world, isolated from events. Great Men would come from London to talk to us; occasionally we would drive to London in search of new pleasures. The undergraduates (never students) did not seem to obey Anthony Brown's dictum that we were 'much given over to drinking, gaming and much brutish pleasures'. The Pemmy JCR was noisy, the Bullingdon roared but I drank nothing but cider, and not much of that. I got drunk once during my time at Oxford, at a Tory dinner, on port. The depth of the hangover has put me off that drink for life. Neither Michael nor I put money on horses, a pastime that was left to Ian Josephs, which he did with success, while 'brutish pleasures' consisted of necking with girls in the back of my much-coveted and frequently double-booked Model Y Ford. Customers often emerged choking on chicken feathers. Ian seemed to have more success with girls than we did; perhaps being Jewish he was not quite so priggish and unworldly. In the vacs he hung around dances at the Old Chelsea Town Hall where he picked up au pair girls, some of whom he generously passed on to us. I will never forget three Norwegians, Aslang, Rutt and Borghilde, three Viking-ship figureheads. They too were apparently made of wood. We were idle, certainly, and more ignorant than we ought to have been for we neglected our books; it took us two attempts to pass 'prelims': if we had a vice it was that of ambition. We wanted to make names for ourselves. Looking back today, the happiest days of one's life certainly did not encompass Shrewsbury school or even Park's chaotic Brockhurst; the two early contenders would be my year at the Sorbonne and my second year at Pembroke.

The second year at Oxford was a time during which there was little to do but enjoy oneself. The examination schools were more than twelve months away. Prelims having at last been successfully overcome, I moved out of college and took rooms in the Botley Road in an artisan's house, an arrangement that included a hearty and traditional Sunday lunch. A typical day in term time would have included a full breakfast at my digs, a stately drive to the Union for coffee, a gracious attendance at a lecture by A.J.P. Taylor, then back to the Union for an undistinguished light lunch and much political gossip. In summer I would explore either on my Vespa or by car, driving beyond Chipping Norton, or south towards Wantage; dutifully taking with me a fat Samuelson with the very real intention of sitting quietly in a field reading economic theory. Swiftly and predictably I would be overtaken by sleep. In winter we drove up the Walton Road as far as Oxford's 'art house', the sole cinema which showed old French films. In the evening we would dine at either Long John's, White's or the Union. There might be a meeting of OUCA or the Blue Ribbon where we would listen politely to Mr Churchill's ministers and then drive them to the Randolph for drinks, or back to the railway station. My second Oxford year consisted of three hundred and sixty-five salad days.

Sometime in 1953 the Festival Ballet advertised in the *Oxford Mail* for undergraduates to take part in the chorus of *Scheherezade*. The bait was ten bob a night for three nights. Ian and I did our best to persuade Michael to accompany us to the New Theatre, but he was wary of making an exhibition of himself. Ian, who was sensitive about his height, was invited to play a eunuch; I was to be a guardsman, my fellow guards consisting of Australian rugger players, South African dentists and a quiet man from Keble. Our task was to rush on stage at the finale to massacre the sultan's harem. On the opening night we were waiting in the wings, the colonials as drunk as lords, clad in weird costumes with turbans, wellies and wooden swords. At last Mr Dolin's upraised hanky dropped and we charged on stage, laying about us to the urgently whispered pleas of the prostrate ballet girls and boys to 'mind our fucking feet'. There was a great slaughter made amid much drunken laughter and cries of 'Good on yer, mate'. (Could Rupert Murdoch have been one of the Australians? He was up during my time.) Two diggers clashed with wooden swords. I entered so fast that, having caught my foot in a flex, I tripped and in order to retain my balance ran straight out of the other side of the stage. There was pandemonium. The curtain was dropped; the extras were paid off and M. Anton Dolin himself was reported in the local paper as having said 'never again' to the prospect of hiring undergraduates.

Michael Heseltine, in particular, wished to perform, not on the stage of the New Theatre but at the dispatch box of the Oxford Union. The Library Committee, the Standing Committee, and the junior officerships were the stepping stones to the presidency of the Union. This, we fondly believed, would lead its occupant post-haste to a seat in the Commons, and a cabinet position. Had not the Duke of Newcastle rewarded William Ewart Gladstone with the gift of a pocket borough after a paper speech delivered early in his Union career? Hope sprang eternal.

The Union held its debates on Thursday evenings, proceedings presided over by its officers in tails, its guests – usually prominent politicians – wined and dined rather badly beforehand. There were three speeches 'on the paper' from either side of the motion, followed by speeches from the rival guests; the debate was then thrown open to the floor and concluded with a vote at a late hour. The high-spot of the term's proceedings was the presidential debate in which the rival candidates performed against each other, the vote taking place during the greater part of the following day. No canvassing was permitted. Term ended with the farewell debate in which the president invited his cronies to debate a motion of a more than usually frivolous nature.

It would be difficult to exaggerate the seriousness with which we took the Oxford Union. We slept in digs but spent our days, neither in healthy pursuits nor in scholarship, but sitting in the bar of the Union talking politics. I suppose I must have hoped to be carried somewhere up the ladder of promotion in the slipstream of Michael's all-consuming ambition, but I never got further than the top of the Library Committee election, and although I was once runner-up for the Standing Committee, I never won a place and so could not stand for any of the offices. I could not overcome my nerves. Frustratingly, when I returned as a guest at one of Michael's presidential debates I was on top form (the subject was the reunification of Ireland). I can remember Jeremy Isaacs telling me that I too could have become president; it was charming of him and some small consolation, although a little too like Marlon Brando's famous lament in *On the Waterfront*.

Among the other 'contenders' who else do I remember besides Michael? Gerald Kaufman; Kermit-like, acid-tongued, chip on shoulder, clever, witty and unloved. He was born bald. He was as one might expect a pillar of the Labour club. Geoffrey Samuel; a Pembroke man with whom I was very friendly, who in later years became headmaster of a comprehensive school in south-west London. Peter Tapsell; perhaps the most able Tory MP never to achieve even minor office, was a slimmer version of his Tory self. He was, in fact, a strong Labour supporter during his time at Oxford. On going down, he became a speech-writer to Sir Anthony Eden, much to our chagrin and surprise. He was clever, a touch pompous (he became more so with the passage of time), and no sufferer of fools. Paddy Mayhew; at the age of twenty he had a judge's manner and a duke's voice. Anthony Howard; who could speak as well as he could write, and who had a hand in scripting Michael Heseltine's presidential speech.

The rising hope of the more traditional Tories was Sir Andrew Cunninghame, a baronet who was sadly to die a young man. There were also Tyrrell Burgess, who rose to the top of the Union quicker than anyone else in my time (he made funny speeches and became an educationalist), an American called Howard Schulman and a fearfully fluent Indian called Rhagavan Iyer. Political Oxford was predominantly Liberal, although there were no distinguished Liberal undergraduates in my time. Perhaps it would have been hard to fill Jeremy Thorpe's shoes? The Liberal vote therefore was all-important, and was much wooed by the ambitious of all parties. The Left was divided into Labour and socialist clubs; the right-wing of the party, Kaufman, Howard, Isaacs and Bryan Magee, predominating. Magee, the philosopher, later to become first a Labour MP then a Social Democrat one, had a hand too in Michael's presidential draft. It was a left-wing script for a right-wing candidate.

The Conservatives were divided between the Gents – Mayhew, Robin Maxwell-Hyslop (an unpleasant eccentric who was later to become a Knight of the Shires) – and the Heselteenies (based on the Ovalteenies) that consisted of the Great Man, Oliver Crawford, Elgar Jenkins, Guy Arnold and myself. Michael attracted several nicknames including Michael Philistine and, owing to his Aryan good looks, Von Heseltine. He took them in his stride.

An article in *Isis* divided undergraduate Oxford into four categories: Hearties, which we were not; Tarties, which we most certainly were not; Arties to which we would claim affinity; and Smarties, which consisted almost exclusively of the men of Magdalen and the House – the brown-trousered brigade. Among the women undergraduates, the most coveted were Sarah Rothschild, and Phillippa Copley-Smith. Nemone Lethbridge edited a magazine called *Couth*, and Jackie Mason showed her favours, not in this instance by removing a glass eye and letting you hold it in your hand like Yvonne Lazenby, but by arranging a visit to Pentonville prison where her father was the Medical Officer. Both Michael and I spent time in the jail, a harrowing experience which has helped to keep us on the narrow path.

David Hughes, the novelist who was to marry Mai Zetterling, was a mutual friend. Anthony Thwaite, the poet, was an editor of *Isis* who published a short story of mine. Patrick Dromgoole was the most prominent figure in the Oxford theatre, while the young Maggie Smith, appearing often at the Oxford Playhouse, was the toast of Town and Gown. Clive Labovitch bought *Cherwell*, the rival to *Isis*, a newspaper produced weekly during term. In my last year I wrote for it as Union correspondent, and also about boxing, covering the inter-varsity match which meant travelling to Cambridge by train, an extraordinary journey across featureless country over the lines of at least four pre-grouping railway companies. (the GWR, the Midland, the Central and the old Great Eastern). Their tracks have long since been lifted. Elderly locomotives belched gouts of steam, stopping at half a hundred deserted halts, and I jolted all day among the reek of buttoned carriage-cloth, and sepia photographs of Grantchester, returning via King's Cross and Paddington. I cannot now remember who won the match. Had I not been lame, I would have sought a boxing half-blue.

In my third year Michael and I shared lodgings in St John Street, a smart Georgian, Cotswold-stone fronted house with a squat landlady to match. Pemmy had been left far behind. The bar of the Randolph was but three minutes away; the Union, five, and the Walton Street cinema all of ten. We lived at the centre of Oxford, our mantelshelves white with invitations. We danced to Tommy Kinsman and drove down to the station to meet the 'fornication flyer' from Paddington which brought girls promptly up from London by steam in time to change at the Mitre or the Randolph. Once, I remember, Michael was let down by some girl or other and promptly advertised in *Isis* for a replacement. He took the pick of the many applicants. It was a golden summer, or it seems so now from the perspective of forty years, with the limestone towers of the city touched by the rays of the setting sun. We happily ignored the inevitability of schools, the final examination in politics, philosophy and economics which was all of nine months away. I had done no work apart from some politics and nineteenth-century European political history, subjects which I read for pleasure; economics, the dismal science, did little for me, while philosophy I found to be totally incomprehensible. I made little effort to solve the riddle of linguistics. I was riding for a fall.

Our third and final year saw the culmination of Michael's Union career. He was elected treasurer and then president at the end of the summer term, an ever-indulgent Pembroke permitting him an additional term in residence. In my book *Heseltine, the Unauthorized Biography* (published in 1985 and described by Sir Robert Rhodes James, the eminent biographer, as the worst book he had ever read) I told the story of Michael's oratorical and entrepreneurial successes. One story can bear retelling; the account of how he turned the Union's cellars into a night-club and, by so doing, saved the Union (temporarily at least).

The Union was always broke. Michael and his friend Sarah Rothschild shared the gossip pages of the newspapers with Bernard and Norah Docker; he a Brummagem industrialist, she a former chorus girl. In an austere age they were famous for their diamond-studded Daimler. Norah was as vulgar as Barbara Cartland, Bernard as put upon as Denis Thatcher. Michael invited them to the opening of the repainted Union cellars, and although they must have been separated by at least forty years, Norah and Michael opened the dancing. When the music stopped, Lady Docker said to Sir Bernard (who was a good natured old trout) 'Bernard, this divine young man tells me the Union is short of fifteen hundred pounds for the cellars. Give him a cheque, do!' With some ill-grace, Bernard did exactly that, there and then, and Michael's reputation passed into Oxford legend.

My schools had an unhappy ending. I ended up with a fourth, the only thing I have in common with Sir Alec Douglas-Home. I got the highest mark (nineteenth-century political history) and the lowest (moral philosophy) in Pembroke. Michael, by the dint of much swotting, got a second. I had no excuse for I did no real work, hoping that all would come right on the night. Unlike in the theatre, it certainly did not. I was, I suppose, a shallow youth (my brother said 'callow'), spoilt by my limp and sub-Byronic good looks, who had met no real challenge, save that of lost love, since quitting Shrewsbury school six years before. 'Two years in the Greenjackets might have done you the world of good,' said my mother. I had not learnt how to work (it was years before I did so), and behind a glossy façade of scooters, bow-ties and Savile Row suits, remained a nervous and unconfident young man. My father, who got a first, was bitterly disappointed. 'At least you've got ambition,' was the only consolation he offered. That I had; I wanted to get into Parliament; I wanted fame, but had I the horsepower?

10 Winning with Harold

On the morning of Monday 12 October 1959 I drove into the Palace of Westminster in my brand new, dark blue Ford Popular. I had been elected the Tory MP for Rochester and Chatham on the previous Thursday, winning the seat from the sitting Labour member, Arthur Bottomley by 1,003 votes. Against the odds, and by clinging to Harold Macmillan's coat-tails, I had achieved my ambition. I was twenty-eight, married to Paula Baron, living in a rented flat in Blackheath with one small daughter. I was out of a job because the advertising agency for which I had been working as an account executive, Rayner, Webber and Styles, had collapsed during my three-week election campaign. But I had a parliamentary salary of £1,750 a year and the magic initials 'MP' attached to my name. I had arrived, or so it seemed.

In October 1959, there was still something of 'Chips' Channon about the Tory party. The great pre-war diarist would have felt at home. Today, the Conservative party in the House contains the party conference of ten years ago. Cheerful girls in hats who once moved conference motions in favour of corporal and capital punishment on behalf of the Young Conservatives of some Midland town, small-town solicitors, garage owners and estate agents with flat, provincial accents, are now among its members. Essex Men selected by Suffolk Women. As Mrs Thatcher (who was returned for the first time for Finchley in the same election) went up in the world, so the party came down.

Thirty-five years ago you could tell a Tory just by looking at him. Call the roll in the 1922 Committee and it was all Knight, Frank and Rutley. A Tory MP was well suited. The party still retained something of its pre-war sleekness; elderly gentlemen in Trumper's haircuts, wearing cream silk shirts and dark suits, Brigade or Old Etonian ties. They were all called Charlie; today, they all seem to be called Norman. In those days, everyone appeared to be related to everyone else. I was forever being accosted while sitting quietly in the Smoking Room (the far corner of which was occasionally occupied by the grander Labour MPs such as Hugh Gaitskell, Geoffrey de Freitas or Richard

Crossman), by nice old buffers who claimed to have known my father. They had not. I did not feel at home among so many Charlies.

This not uncommon misapprehension first surfaced when, having come down from Oxford, I applied to Conservative Central Office for inclusion on the official list of candidates-to-be without which I could not be selected for a constituency. My CV was a slim document: the Hampstead YCs, the executive of the National YCs (I had been defeated by Andrew Bowden for the chairmanship of London), the Paris YCs (raised eyebrows?), secretary of the Oxford Tories and president of the Blue Ribbon Club. There was also my modest career in the Oxford Union. It did not amount to much, save for a record of service among the party's youth. I was granted an interview with Donald Kaberry MP, the party's vice-chairman in charge of candidates. He was a bluff Yorkshireman, much later in life to be grievously injured by the IRA in its attack on the Carlton Club. I told him I wished to specialize in foreign affairs ('estate management but on a larger scale') and agriculture, about which I knew very little. Kaberry looked at me over his spectacles. 'Knew yer father,' he said. 'Damn' good man.' I tried to demur; it was clear that he had confused Dr Macdonald Critchley, the distinguished neurologist, with General Critchley, the Canadian adventurer who had introduced greyhound racing into this country, and for a time had run British Overseas Airways. He had also been a Beaverbrook-sponsored MP for some years before the war. Rashly, I waved the compliment away, but Kaberry was not to be deterred. 'Damn' good golfer, too,' he shouted. 'And his wife,' he added as an afterthought (she was Dorothy Fishwick). I then thought it wise not to strive too officiously for the truth; I sat silently, looking modestly pleased with myself. A fortnight later he wrote welcoming me to the list which would then be circulated to all Conservative associations in marginal or Labour-held seats looking for a standard-bearer at the forthcoming election. It was an important hurdle. I owed my success to 'Critch' and his greyhounds.

Today, someone in my shoes would be obliged to spend two hundred pounds of his own money in order to attend a weekend 'course' at a motel near Slough where he would be put through his paces. I went to one such undertaking in the early eighties, as a fly on the wall for the *Daily Telegraph*. Fifty aspirants were obliged to write essays, debate among themselves, deliver five-minute speeches on unrelated topics, and display a command of table manners essential for a future Tory MP. Chris Patten, then a promising back-bencher, acted as invigilator and examiner. He failed a quarter of them, but a Mrs Virginia Bottomley, not unpredictably, came top of the form. *Summa cum laude*. And it was Harold

Macmillan who once said that the only quality needed for an MP was the ability to write a good letter.

Within my first week or so in the House, while I was sitting in the Smoking Room after luncheon, reading a book, Charles Hill, the one-time Radio Doctor who had spoken for me in Chatham at the election, came up to me. 'Young man,' he said, 'it does not do to appear clever. Advancement in this man's party is due entirely to alcoholic stupidity.' I have scarcely opened a book in the House since.

I had been adopted as Tory candidate at Rochester and Chatham two years earlier. The seat was held by Arthur Bottomley who had won it for Labour in 1945, defeating a Tory called Captain Plugge, the founder of Radio Luxembourg before the war. (The good Captain pronounced his name 'Plooje' prompting a remark by a colleague whom he had no doubt offended 'Plooje? The "g" should be hard as in "bugger" which he undoubtedly is.') Nevertheless in Rochester there were fond memories of Captain Plugge who had the endearing habit of putting his most devoted supporters into charabancs and taking them to lunch at the Dorchester. On occasion, I was pointedly reminded of his great generosity.

Rochester with its castle keep and Norman cathedral co-existed uneasily with the saltier seaport of Chatham, where the Royal Naval Dockyard was the largest employer. The low pay of the 'maties', of whom there were some twelve thousand plus their families, was one of the reasons why 'Arthur', as he was universally known locally, had held on to the seat at every subsequent general election, frustrating the efforts of a series of Tory candidates, including Robert Matthew and John Campbell. Arthur, I was told, despite the narrowness of his majority, was 'unbeatable'.

The city of Rochester, which had a faded gentility revealed by two streets of fine Georgian houses, a corn exchange and memories of Charles Dickens, tended to look askance at its nautical sister, lacking city status and with its drunken sailors, chain stores and discreet knocking-shops. Built in the late nineteenth century it had row upon row of terraced working-class houses climbing steeply towards the chalk downs. It was as if Portsmouth had moved into bed with Chichester. To the west of the city, on the left bank of the Medway, was the unprepossessing town of Strood (which was mine) while to the east of Chatham was the Borough of Gillingham, large, lower middle class and characterless, save for the Sapper barracks, which was represented in Parliament in the Conservative interest by Freddy Burden who was in the rag trade and drove a Bentley. All four 'towns' were contiguous (they are all now administered as the Medway Towns), and, on a bad day, before the opening of the M2 and its splendid bridge by Ernest Marples in 1993, they would take an hour or more to traverse. As Paula and I were living in Blackheath Village, Rochester was just forty minutes down the A2, so there was no need to move into the constituency. I suppose that between 1957 when I was adopted, and 1966 when I retired having been defeated a second time, I must have driven down the A2 and back getting on for eight hundred times. I was a most assiduous attender.

As I have said, in 1957 I was, to my great pleasure and excitement, adopted as Tory candidate, beating a man with the unfortunate name of Raper in the final. I was twenty-six, and save for standing unsuccessfully in Stoke Newington and Hackney North at the London County Council elections in 1955, untried electorally. Still I was young and vigorous and, like most candidates in that position, prepared to promise the burghers of Rochester and Chatham the earth. I would attend every wine and cheese party, open every bazaar, visit every school and hospital; in short, I would be as energetic on their behalf (and mine) as the young Lyndon Baines Johnson was when running for a seat in the Texas Congress. I kept my word.

Local government in Rochester (Tory) and Chatham (Labour) had a faintly unsavoury reputation. It was perhaps shabby rather than corrupt, the scene of much municipal feuding and fighting. The most remarkable contest had taken place in the early fifties when, on a goodwill visit to the city's twin town, Abbeville, Aldermen Skipper and Tickner, having lunched extraordinarily well, came to blows in what the press was to call 'the battle of Abbeville'. It was the lead story in the *Daily Express*. The contestants were well matched: Skipper an elderly fifteen-stone newsagent of uncertain temper; George Tickner a cheeky local butcher. Happily for me they played little or no part in the life of the Conservative Association, although a source of much hilarity and disapprobation throughout the neighbourhood.

At Rochester during the election we were visited by the great ones of the party. A crucial marginal, in the jargon of the trade, we had to win the seat were the party to take up its rightful place at the helm of the nation's affairs . . . the rhetoric is catching. Super Mac himself passed through the Medway Towns by motor car, and for a mile or two I was permitted to sit next to him, not daring to speak. As we crossed the bridge into Rochester, he waved in the direction of cathedral and castle, murmuring 'very fine'. As I quit the car in Chatham he bared his very bad teeth in the curious way which was later to become so familiar, and said 'Beastly things, elections'. He stood for a moment on a portable platform asking several bewildered housewives not to let Labour ruin it. His plea was carried away by the September wind. I took over from him and waved him off down the Gillingham road into darkest Kent.

Charles Hill spoke at the Chatham Town Hall: twenty minutes of beef stew, served up in a rich gravy, demotic, funny and delivered with a marvellous self-confidence that turned every interruption to his advantage. In his prime he was the best platform speaker in the party, less cerebral than Quintin Hogg, more assured with the public than Harold Macmillan, less distant than Rab Butler. He was perhaps surpassed by Iain Macleod, who was to come down to Rochester later on in the Parliament to talk to a club of Tory businessmen, but Iain was never at his best keeping the wheels of Rotary turning. 'I thought my lot were dreadful until I met yours,' was his only comment. In an attempt to ensure victory, and to raise a little cash, the local Tories invited Sir Alfred Bossom, once MP for Maidstone and a survivor from before the war, to be drafted in as our president: he took the chair at the public meetings. Bossom was, of course, the man whom Churchill had said was neither one thing nor the other.

As is customary the local churches held a joint public meeting before which the four local candidates were invited to perform. There were no Liberals standing in the two Medway seats, so the choice lay between Arthur Bottomley and me; Freddy Burden and Gerald Kaufman (who had deserted the *Mirror* to stand as the Labour candidate for Gillingham). Burden and Bottomley sensibly pleaded prior engagements, so it was left to Gerald and me to fight it out. I cannot now remember what we said, but I do recall the action of the bishop, that formidable, one-legged holder of the Victoria Cross, Bishop Chavasse. As we processed slowly to the platform he took me firmly by the arm; when it was all over he solemnly marched me out in the same style, thus demonstrating clearly where the Church Militant stood in 1959.

At Rochester the culmination of four weeks' hard work was a surprise victory. A Labour majority of 2,000 had been overturned. It was due to the erosion of the dockyard vote: prosperity had reached even Chatham. We did not go to bed that October night. I had made it, and against the odds. I was cock of the Rochester walk. Whatever the future it was no mean thing to have had 'MP' after your name. And I had beaten Michael Heseltine to it.

The 1959 Tory election victory was universally attributed to Harold Macmillan's skill in expoiting the return of the nation's self-confidence after Suez, and its return to prosperity. It was a personal triumph not to be rivalled until John Major won against the odds in 1992. Harold Macmillan, in consequence, was at the peak of his popularity and power. The grandson of a crofter (the famous photograph stood on his desk at Birch Grove), married to the daughter of a duke, and the scion of a famous publishing house (the Cavendishes used to refer to Harold snobbishly as 'the publisher' in the years of his political exile before the war), Macmillan was a very untypical Conservative, socially progressive at home, and very much the realist abroad.

Towards the end of October 1959, Peter Emery, a man of about my age who had won the Reading seat at the election from Ian Mikardo, arranged a dinner at the East India Club for the newly elected to meet the Prime Minister. I forget what we had to eat – very probably mulligatawny and chips – but I shall never forget the effect Harold Macmillan made on thirty or so guests. We dined in one room and then moved to another, where some us literally sat at his feet. Macmillan was the ideal speaker for the intimate occasion: splendid after dinner, witty, elegant of phrase, skilled at flattering his audience, taking us apparently into his confidence. He was especially beguiling with the young. He told us 'revolt by all means; but only on one issue at a time; to do more would be to confuse the whips'. This from a man who had had the party whip taken away from him in the thirties. 'Do not be impatient with the majors in the party; all regiments have need of majors . . .' I took his advice on the first point, but not on the second. I have made fun of the majors in print for years.

It was my first close-up of Macmillan's peculiar gestures: the nervous fingering of his Brigade tie; his curiously hooded eyes which would suddenly open wide, and the famous baring of the teeth. He told us that no one who had not experienced Oxford before the Kaiser's war could know '*la douceur de vivre*'. At that time Oxford's only industry was a marmalade factory. He told us of his experience in the Great War, and of his hatred of conflict. He suggested tentatively that European unity might keep the peace, and he wondered how long Britain could carry the burdens of empire. It was to become a familiar and attractive theme.

The 1959 intake was later to be described by Rab Butler as 'the worst in my experience', but it did include Margaret Thatcher, James Prior, Nicholas Ridley and Humphry Berkeley. I must admit, however, that it did have perhaps more than its share of those who could talk nonsense with distinction. One of the fifty-niners actually ended up in jail. What effect the Macmillan magic had on my colleagues I cannot tell. Speaking for myself, I fell promptly under his spell. I was impressed by his style and convinced by his content. Here was someone on whose behalf I could draw my sword, however short. Thirty-four years later I lunched with Ian Gilmour and we agreed that we had both been more in tune with Harold Macmillan than any of his successors.

I was soon to learn how much he was disliked, even hated, by many Conservative MPs. The party has long suffered from its irreconcilables. Imperialists hated Baldwin, the supporters of Churchill and Anthony Eden were beastly to poor Neville; in turn the Chamberlainite wing of the party suffered unhappily under the long rule of Winston Churchill and his successors. Did not Churchill say to Macmillan that had it not been for Hitler neither of them would ever have got to Number 10? The pattern has continued under Ted Heath whom the party found incompatible; under Margaret Thatcher when she was opposed by the so-called 'wets', and the Thatcherites' work to undermine John Major on the grounds of his so-called 'betrayal'. Whatever else we might be, we Tories are not a band of brothers.

Macmillan's enemies considered him to be 'pink', and the old things with whom I would sometimes find myself sharing a table at lunch or dinner, were bitter in their condemnation. They alluded darkly to 'Bob and Lady Dorothy' (a longstanding relationship between Lord Boothby and the Premier's wife about which I knew nothing at the time), and more openly to *The Middle Way*, the book Macmillan wrote in the thirties advocating a halfway-house between capitalism and socialism. When I protested – mildly enough, for in those early days I knew my place – I was told that Attlee himself had believed that one day Harold would lead the Labour party. The members of the Suez Group were particularly bitter, but their hostility was as nothing when compared with Nigel Birch's or Enoch Powell's.

Thorneycroft, who had been Chancellor at the time of the famous triple resignation in 1958 (the 'little local difficulty' to which Macmillan, who was about to embark on a Commonwealth tour, so crushingly referred), was comparatively restrained. But in the first years of the Parliament when Macmillan's reputation was at its zenith, adverse criticism of this kind was muted; people talked behind their hands. It was, with the passage of time and the coming of political misfortune, to become a chorus of complaint.

I will admit I found the Chamber terrifying. It took a long time for my self-confidence to grow, and until it did so I was handicapped by my residual stutter. In conversation I had developed a skill in word substitution, but on the floor of the House, or more particularly at question time, it did not suffice: in consequence I tabled questions for written answer, and spoke infrequently from the back benches. I made my maiden speech in May 1960 in a defence debate. I spoke for ten minutes somewhat critically of the government's nuclear policy, and was followed immediately by Manny Shinwell from whom compliments of any kind were rare. My speech had two consequences: Gerald Kaufman, not yet an MP, having failed to win Gillingham, described it in the *New Statesman* as 'a farrago of nonsense'; but in *Punch*, Christopher Hollis wrote a glowing account of it. I was delighted, and at Hollis's prompting we met in the House for a drink. He was a large, elderly man who had been an independently minded Tory MP, and a prolific journalist. He was clever and well-disposed. He was also homosexual. Had I been more mature I might have benefited from his friendship, but as it was I brushed him off as swiftly as I decently could. Kaufman's was probably the less-biased opinion.

If my stammer was initially a handicap in the Chamber, I could always fall back on my pen. John Biffen who was not yet in the House suggested to Tom McKitterick, the editor of the *Political Quarterly* in 1961, that I write a piece about the Tory party. I did so; it was a success and I began, tentatively at first, to write on current politics for the broadsheets and the weeklies. Little did I realize that I was making a rod for my own back. I began to pay a price for having a sense of humour for its possession leads you to take pleasure in the discrepancies of human nature; it leads you to mistrust the protestations of the famous and to look for the unworthy motives that they can conceal. The disparity between appearance and reality diverts you and you are apt, when you cannot find it, to create it. A sense of the ridiculous is something to which you should give scope, but the humourist, however laboured, has a quick eye for humbug (and there was plenty of that in politics); he does not always recognize the saint.

Once again I had been quicker off the mark than Michael Heseltine. It took him a term or two to overtake me while up at Oxford, and he did not enter the House until 1966. In 1959 he had fought a Labour-held seat in South Wales where he lost to Jim Griffiths. In 1964 he drove up the newly opened M1 night after night to Coventry (as I did to Rochester) in his Jaguar 2.4, the model made famous many years later by Inspector Morse. He was rich, by my standards, having dabbled successfully in property development with Ian Josephs, but he was not yet an MP. We saw a lot of each other, and I entertained him often in the Strangers' Dining Room. When he got married in 1962 to Anne Williams, the beautiful daughter of a Welsh solicitor whom he had met when she was working in an art gallery in the West End, I was invited to be his best man. The wedding took place at the Savoy Chapel and the reception, not unnaturally, at the Savoy Hotel. *Tout* Swansea, and *toute la jeunesse dorée politique* were on parade. In my speech I made mention of the elegance of Anne's fine legs, and what an addition she would be to his platforms; it was a crass comment and Michael in his reply answered in kind. Elspeth Howe, who was standing behind a curtain, unsweetened by champagne, was heard to remark 'what a couple of shits'. She might have been, on balance, right.

I suppose my trouble was that I was, in the eyes of all right-thinking Tory MPs 'almost a gentleman'. Michael Heseltine once said to me that he passed for white (the reference was to Tavistock, the seat that he won in 1966), and we were both first-generation public school and Oxford. Michael Jopling when he was chief whip in Mrs Thatcher's government said of Michael that 'he is the kind of man who had to buy all his own furniture', a remark quoted by Alan Clark in his *Diaries*. So did I. I began my married life in October 1955 with nothing more substantial than a bogus water-clock and a second-hand wardrobe. We were, to that extent, two of a kind. But there was an important difference: Michael made money; I earned it – by my writing. Tory MPs in the early sixties were lawyers, company directors, *rentiers* and ex-senior officers living on their pensions or their wives' incomes. A few owned land; many were the sons and grandsons of MPs, in Paul Channon's case inheriting directly his father Chips's old Southend seat. Some were undoubtedly cads; but we were bounders.

There was one other journalist on the Tory benches, Charles Curran, who was a polemicist of an old-fashioned kind. He wrote a column in the *Evening News* in which he attacked socialism and all its works. His was not my style. The piece on the Tory party in the *Political Quarterly* in which I described the 1922 Committee as 'the parliament of the skimmed milk' attracted the attention of both 'the colleagues' and editors, and I began to be asked to write for the newspapers. Brian Inglis, the editor of the *Spectator* asked me to write an occasional 'Westminster Commentary' which I did with some glee. On my election my father sent me a smart executive leather briefcase and gave me some advice: I should specialize. I chose defence, prompted by Alastair Buchan's book *Nato in the Sixties* which I read and reread during all-night sittings. The late fifties was the time of the Sandys White Paper which had signalled the end of National Service, and greater reliance on the so-called British independent nuclear deterrent. I was convinced by Buchan that it might be unwise to rely over-much on what was called in the jargon 'first use'; and by Nigel Birch, Antony Head and Fitzroy Maclean that it would be a mistake to do away with conscription (we were to be the only major Nato ally to do so). Our fear – and it was widely shared at the time – was that the Soviets would attack with conventional forces, defeat the weaker Nato armies, and thus leave the West with a choice between nuclear suicide and surrender. Those of us who opposed the government's defence policy preferred to strengthen our forces-in-being and win the war, were there to be one, without having recourse to nuclear weapons. We cast doubt on the effectiveness of the deterrent. This is no place to rehearse the arguments which can today be of little interest; it is enough to say that my stance did not endear me to the party whips. Nor did my writings, which were in great part about defence. I shudder when I think of how many worthy pieces

I wrote entitled 'Whither Nato?' for as many worthy journals, national and international. I made a few guineas but cracked few jokes in the sixties.

It cannot have been long before Mr Martin Redmayne, the government Chief Whip, decided that I was 'on balance' perhaps not a good thing. In today's terms I might even have had something in common with Rupert Allason (alias Nigel West) – except that I did not take refuge from three-line votes in the Bahamas. In fact, I was an assiduous attender, but clearly 'unsound'. I had views, and had occasionally poked fun at 'the colleagues'. The more charitable might have put this unwisdom down to my extreme youth, but Redmayne was in an unforgiving mood. This could have been due, in part at least, to the episode of the suit, which I think is worth recounting yet again. I was rung up by Michael Heseltine who had just become the owner of a rag-trade magazine called *Man About Town*. It was his intention to turn it into a glossy but perfectly respectable men's magazine, and he asked whether I wanted a suit. As Sir William Teeling MP had recently opined to my mother-in-law, Betty Baron, that I was 'the worst-dressed MP' at a dinner-party at their flat in Bryanston Court, I snatched at the opportunity. The spread was predictable enough – a suit for a lawyer, a suit for a doctor, a suit for a Member of Parliament, etc. I forget the name of the tailor, but I was first fitted for a splendid black, double-breasted suit (with a white waistcoat), and then finally photographed leaning on an umbrella. The picture can be seen on the back of the hard-cover edition of my *Westminster Blues*, sadly long out of print. I thought no more about it until two or three months later the revamped magazine appeared with my carefully posed pictures in it. I took one horrified look at the feature and waited for the balloon to go up. It rose determinedly.

The matter was raised at the Thursday evening meeting of the '22 by some old buffer who complained, somewhat peevishly, that 'the fella's modellin', Major Morrison'. Later that evening I was summoned to attend upon Martin Redmayne in his office. He was seated behind an enormous desk which was bare save for a copy of *Man About Town*. I was not invited to sit down. Redmayne picked up the magazine between finger and thumb and asked 'Are ye hard up?'

I should have said 'yes'; had I done so, I doubtless would have been sent to Alice Springs, as a remittance man paid a pittance from some fund long established by Conservative Central Office. Instead I denied the charge. I was dismissed from his presence having been told that what I had done was 'not the thing'. I knew then that my chances of becoming Assistant Postmaster General in Harold Macmillan's government had vanished. Instead the post was given to

Ray Mawby, MP for Totnes and the party's only genuine worker (he was an electrician), an exquisite act of patronage on Redmayne's part.

If Tory MPs were well suited they were also well shod. Double-barrelled Knights of the Shires doubtless had their shoes hand-made. For four days a week the uniform was a dark jacket and striped trousers (very occasionally a dark blue suit); on Friday, Private Members' Day, when government business was not taken, and in consequence the House was thinly attended, the whips wore weekend tweed suits and brown brogues. Not long after my maiden speech I was standing in the crowded 'No' lobby waiting to vote at ten o'clock on a three-line whip when I glimpsed Sir Jocelyn Lucas, whose twin claims to fame were that he bred Sealyhams and looked remarkably like the Prime Minister. He moved remorselessly in my direction, breasting the wave as if he were Captain Matthew Webb. Was he about to congratulate me on my maiden speech, or to ask me to dinner? He grasped my elbow, hissed 'You're wearin' suede shoes' and promptly vanished. He never spoke to me again. What would he have made of Kenneth Clarke?

But it was the real Harold Macmillan who, in the early sixties, dominated politics. I saw him once standing just inside the St Stephen's entrance of the Palace of Westminster gazing at the war memorial for MPs killed on active service. He was accompanied by Knox Cunningham, a very large Ulsterman. He beckoned me to him and asked how I was doing. I asked why the list of MPs killed in the Great War was so much longer. Macmillan replied 'In the first war, the sons of gentlemen joined their regiments. In the second, it was the crews of Bomber Command who suffered most. They were grammar-school boys. There were no grammar-school boys in the Tory party before the war.' Clearly the process of social change in the Tory party is a continuing one.

11 The Wider World

No sooner does the ambitious MP of whatever party begin to attract attention to himself than invitations to travel abroad land upon his secretary's desk. The only foreign country I knew at all well was France. But once I had taken my seat as the Honourable Member for Rochester and Chatham, I, too, was in demand.

In 1960 Granada Television sent me to Sharpeville to make a *Searchlight* programme about the massacre. For a fee of one hundred pounds each, the team (which included Sir Ivor Jennings, the constitutional historian, Tom Hooson, the chairman of the Bow Group and the Labour MP John Dugdale, who later became my pair) took tea with Dr Verwoerd, the Prime Minister, at his Dutch-style residence at Cape Town and dined with Helen Suzman, the prominent Progressive MP. She was a very sassy lady, charming and courageous in her outspoken attacks upon apartheid. I came back with two overriding impressions: the sheer beauty of the country (rivalled only in my experience by the highlands of Ethiopia) and the chasm that separated the whites, living in fortified private houses even thirty years ago, and the primitive squalor of the majority of the blacks. 'The Boers will fight,' said Professor Jennings magisterially. 'They have nowhere else to go.' He will probably be proved right. But it was *Searchlight*'s producer, Tim Hewat, whom I remember best. A frenetic and foul-mouthed Australian, who for some unaccountable reason held strong views on Lord Eden's love-life, or the lack of it, he summoned Jennings before the camera with cries of 'the idiot board for Sir Ivor', and more winningly described his native land as 'the biggest sergeants' mess in the world'. Larger than life, he was replaced some years later by Clive James.

On 11 August 1961, Michael Heseltine and I flew to West Berlin on what we told our friends was a fact-finding mission. We spent the Saturday touring the divided city escorted by the British Army whose four-power rights included entering East Berlin at will, visiting the refugee camps in the Allied zones and admiring the sculpted head of Queen Nefertiti in the Berlin museum. The centre of Berlin on the eastern side had not yet been rebuilt and the piles of rubble looked like a wartime newsreel. It was all very Harry Lime. We gazed on the ruins of the Führer's bunker and into the windows of East Berlin's biggest department store in which were displayed dozens of metal salad shakers. We dined together in our hotel and went to bed reasonably early. We were awakened at four a.m. by our escort who told us the Russians were building a wall between East and West, and that World War Three was about to begin. This was somewhat more than we had bargained for.

We spent Sunday 13 August driving in a British Army jeep throughout Berlin, east and west. Soviet T54 tanks were lined up beneath the trees of the Unter den Linden, and Russian and East German soldiers, the Vopos, were busily engaged blocking off streets, erecting barricades, and manning strong points. We drove at a smart pace, a Union flag fluttering from the jeep's aerial. Apart from soldiers and police, not a soul was to be seen. Over in the Western sector, huge crowds soon gathered at the Brandenburg Gate, the symbol of the divided city, and shouted abuse at the Russians. In the early afternoon we walked the length of the gate along a strip of no man's land, on our right hand the Russians, on our left a thin line of West Berlin police spraying the crowd with hoses in order to discourage their advance eastwards. It was as if, for a moment, we were alone in the cockpit of the world. For our pains we were soaked with spray. Later we watched, from a discreet distance, the head-on confrontation between American and Russian tanks at Checkpoint Charlie. For fifteen minutes the two tanks faced each other, gun muzzle to gun muzzle. It was the moment when the world held its breath. As soon as we had drawn ours, we were driven swiftly to Tempelhof Airport and flown home, immensely relieved to quit Berlin before the balloon went up.

The same year I was invited to visit Israel as the guest of its government. This was part of a more general public-relations campaign; 'promising' MPs of all sorts and sizes were liable to receive such invitations. I was pro-Israeli anyway, influenced by the fact that Paula, my wife, was of Jewish origin (I can never read Charles Snow's *Conscience of the Rich* in which the young Lewis Elliot is accepted into a Jewish family, without being reminded of my own courtship of Paula Baron).

Once again I toured the country, lunched with the young Shimon Peres and was given the obligatory tour of the museum of the Holocaust. I was not quite certain why, as I needed no convincing of the facts of Nazi atrocity. More enjoyable was my trip to a tank park, where five hundred Sherman tanks were mothballed, standing in long, silent, menacing rows. An Israeli captain asked me to choose a tank at random: I did so and a soldier ran to it, leapt inside, and pressed the starter button; the tank's engine fired immediately, and the vehicle disappeared in the direction of the East Bank. 'In this way, we survive' said the captain. It was certainly an impressive demonstration. I was driven to Eilat on the Red Sea, King Solomon's mines and finally to Sodom, on the shores of the Dead Sea, whence I sent picture postcards to a handful of my male friends bearing the legend 'Wish you were here'. Only David Walder, the Tory MP for the High Peak, got the joke.

What was most coveted among the up-and-coming in the House was a Smith-Mundt scholarship to visit America. I let it be known that I had yet to visit the Land of the Free, and, lo and behold, I received a summons to attend the US cultural attaché in Grosvenor Square. He was an earnest, bespectacled man, only too eager to tell me the detail of my prize. Six weeks in America, going where one wished, a handsome *per diem* in dollars, and the gift of twelve books of my choice. I could not believe my good fortune. As I was interested in defence ('security' in American), I asked to visit Cape Canaveral, and the headquarters of Strategic Air Command in Omaha, Nebraska. The cultural attaché then read me something of a lecture on the virtues of the American way of life, talked of its high technology and its ancient civilization. Had I a final question? I had. Was it safe to drink the water?

I flew to America in January 1963 in a Pan-Am Boeing 707. Today I hate flying, with its squalor, tedium and endless delays; thirty years ago I was young enough to enjoy every minute of what was a personal voyage of discovery. At the airport in New York a customs officer looked at my suitcase and asked whether it contained a pork pie. I said it did not. 'What do you do for a living?' he barked. Nervously I said I was a politician, forgetting that in America the word is a term of abuse. 'We've got too many of them as it is,' he grunted, waving me through. I was in New York only long enough to be welcomed by a girl from the State Department who gave me a comfortable dollar advance and a detailed itinerary. I took the shuttle down to Washington where I was met by an old girlfriend of John Biffen's.

My hostess, who slept with a revolver next to her bed and drove an elderly Wolseley motor car, arranged for me to meet Senator Willis Robertson, who at the age of about eighty was the junior senator from Virginia. We went to his office on Capitol Hill. He was white-haired, courtly and looked like Walter Pidgeon; behind his enormous desk was a large Confederate flag. He rose majestically to his feet and said 'Sir, I want to apologize to you for all that the United States' servicemen did to your women during the war.' What could I do but accept?

I left Washington for Charlottesville by train, the staff of which semed to consist entirely of elderly Negroes of the sort that stayed loyal to Scarlett O'Hara. After Charlottesville I flew to New Orleans, the home of Ignatius P.

Reilly, where I breakfasted at Brennan's, dined at Antoine's and sailed down the bayous to the Gulf of Mexico. My next stop was the Manned Space Centre at Houston, Texas, where the astronauts were beginning their training. I still have the photograph taken at the time: I am surrounded by eleven of the best-integrated men in America, many of whom went on to conquer space. The moment before the picture was taken, I had noticed an announcement pinned to the wall which proclaimed the visit that morning of 'Lord Julian Critchley', a promotion that took me into the highest ranks of younger sons. After the flash I told them that they had been assembled under false pretences, at which ten of them sloped off, leaving me with the astronaut on duty. I had visions of the *Daily Mail* picking up the story 'Obscure Tory MP passes himself off as the son of a duke . . .'

A. J. P. Taylor is quoted in Alan Watkins' *Brief Lives* as saying that he never visited the United States 'because they have neither good food nor good architecture'. He was a curmudgeonly old thing. On food, he has a point: some of the fast food is nasty, and the salad dressings are a trap for the unwary (note 'Italian' = French), but in private houses one can eat every bit as well as in England, and in restaurants the seafood is invariably good. Americans do have a distressing habit, however, of drinking hard liquor in quantity before meals and then sitting down, half-cut, to glasses of iced water. Wine was not as fashionable as it has since become. As for architecture, Washington alone can claim Dulles Airport, Pei's extension to the National Gallery and the Metro. And what about the handsome classical plantation houses from the time of the modern country's birth in the mid-eighteenth century?

At Phoenix, Arizona, where I stayed with a neurologist friend of my father's, I was allowed two days 'out of schedule'. This break from my hosts' remorseless hospitality was very welcome. I took the bus across the desert to the Grand Canyon where I arrived after night had fallen. I slept in a cabin and when the sun was up walked in a dressing-gown to the rim where I sat for perhaps an hour gazing at what is, I am sure, the ultimate spectacular: a slash in the earth thirty miles across and a mile or so deep, the Battenberg cake-like strata taking the eye down to the distant gleam of the Colorado river. The far rim was encrusted with snow; the temperature on the river a mile below must have been tropical. I only wish I had had the time to descend the canyon on muleback, or even to have ridden the river on a rubber raft, but my schedule was unyielding; I took the bus back to Phoenix and a plane to Las Vegas. I found the 'wicked city' boring; day turned into night, and squads of blue-haired widows in luridly coloured Courtelle trouser-suits endlessly playing the machines.

I suppose I have visited the United States twice a year since my grand tour, my last being in 1983. During twenty years, I have lectured at Middlebury College, Vermont, as guest of its president, Olin Robison, tramped round Williamsburg and picnicked at Wolf Trap to the strains of Richard Strauss. I have breakfasted at the Watergate, had mid-morning coffee with Nixon in the White House, lunched at the Senate, and dined in the *bijou* restaurants of Georgetown. I have stayed at half a hundred cheap hotels, the most alarming being in New York where you are urged to lock and double lock your door and open it to nobody, not even your mother. Most of all I have listened to, and been lectured by, those academics, bureaucrats and politicians – the so-called 'defense community', whose numbing logic and fractured prose I followed for more than twenty years. Recently, I found the titles of my twelve books, the gift of the American taxpayer: there was no Hemingway, Wharton or Henry James; they were the works of Kissinger, Schelling and Herman Kahn.

I returned from that first trip, richer by many dollars and much experience, to find Hugh Gaitskell dead, our application to join the Common Market vetoed by de Gaulle, and George Wigg hot on the trail of the Minister of War, Jack Profumo.

12 Departures

I have always found politics to be a spectator sport. The 1959 Parliament had its share of characters, perhaps rather more than today. I spoke infrequently, wrote more often for public consumption and travelled widely. Politically, I became an extreme moderate; adversely critical of the government's defence policy with regard to nuclear weapons, but an enthusiast for the Prime Minister's 'wind of change' in colonial policy and, thanks to listening to Roy Jenkins' advocacy, a supporter of British membership of the European Economic Community. Thus the whips disapproved of my stance on defence; the great majority of 'the colleagues' did not share my passion for integration and retreat. My name was absent from the first list of promotions to junior office (it contained the names of Christopher Chataway and Margaret Thatcher), something to which, over the years, I was to become accustomed. For nearly thirty years I have sat on the back-benches scrutinizing the soles of the feet of those invited to climb the ladder of promotion.

Among Tory back-benchers, Gerald Nabarro was certainly larger than life. A short, stocky man with sleek black hair and an enormous handlebar moustache, Nabarro possessed a loud voice, enormous cheek and a hide made of India-rubber. He was only a back-bencher but a media celebrity. It seemed as if one had only to switch on the TV or radio to see his hairy face or hear his booming sergeant's voice. A former non-commissioned officer, he had made a lot of money making cardboard boxes, and his fleet of Daimlers, NAB 1, NAB 2 and so on, were as famous in their time as Norah and Bernard Docker's gold-plated Daimler had been a decade before. A Jew with all the confidence of an Old Testament prophet, Nabarro had declared war on the anomalies of purchase tax, and his question-time offensives had demolished the reputation of many a junior minister. Politically, he was the Man in the Street, a noisy populist without whom no *Any Questions* (Freddie Grisewood in the chair) was complete (a typical panel of the day would have consisted of Gerald Nabarro, Michael Foot, the journalist Nancy Spain and the Bishop of Crediton. I once came across him on a summer's afternoon at the Severn Valley Railway near

Bridgnorth. He was wearing overalls and a shiny railwayman's cap and standing in the cab of an ex-GWR 0-6-0 locomotive. He blew the whistle in greeting and invited us to tea at his house in Broadway, that Worcestershire village that even Americans think is just a little too quaint to be real. While waiting for the kettle to boil, I counted the number of pictures, photographs and cartoons of Nabarro displayed in his study. They totalled sixty-three.

Nabarro was a buffoon, but a formidable one. He stood out in Macmillan's Tory party like a bird of paradise among the pigeons of Trafalgar Square. There was an extraordinary postscript to his career. It was a mystery that might have been written by Conan Doyle. On 25 January 1972 Nabarro was fined £250 and banned from driving for two years at Winchester Crown Court where he had elected trial by jury. The judge said the jury had found him guilty of a deliberate and hazardous piece of driving 'with a determination to get past a queue of slower vehicles'.

Witnesses had described being forced off the road when he went the wrong way round a roundabout, and recognized the moustachioed face of the driver. Nabarro had asserted all along that he was being driven in his 4.2 Daimler NAB 1 by his secretary-cum-driver Mrs Margaret Mason. He was asleep in one of the passenger seats. Mrs Mason gave evidence that she had, in fact, been driving and that she had no recollection of any untoward incident. Nabarro, who happened to be the chairman of the St Christopher's Motorists' Association – which provided chauffeur-driven cars for banned drivers – went on the radio after the trial asking for other witnesses to come forward. Several did so, and the Court of Appeal, in what was said to be a unique case involving a motoring offence, ordered a retrial. The appeal, which was not heard until October 1972, partly because Nabarro had been sick, acquitted him. Nabarro died just over a year later.

Nigel Birch could not claim to be immediately recognisable. A tall, stooped, balding man with a reddish face, he had been Secretary of State for Air in Sir Anthony Eden's government. More importantly, perhaps, he had resigned in 1958 from the Treasury along with Thorneycroft and Enoch Powell. He had suffered the rise of Harold Macmillan's reputation with grace, biding his time. By 1962, the Macmillan magic was beginning to fade. The Prime Minister dismissed a third of his cabinet overnight, thereby making a martyr of his Chancellor, Selwyn Lloyd, whom he replaced by the more expansionist Reggie Maudling. Birch wrote a memorable letter to *The Times*, 'For a second time the Prime Minister has got rid of a Chancellor of the Exchequer who tried to get expenditure under control. Once is more than enough.'

In 1963, when the Profumo scandal broke it was Birch who emerged as the willing Cassandra. I shall never forget his speech in the Profumo debate on 17 June 1963. I sat immediately behind the Prime Minister on a seat above the gangway traditionally occupied by the party's loyalists. Birch spoke from below the gangway. It is not exaggeration to say that Birch's speech destroyed Macmillan. He contrived to be contemptuous of Profumo, but much more contemptuous of a government which had not seen through him: 'I must say he never struck me at all as a man like a cloistered monk, and Miss Keeler was a professional prostitute. There seems to be a certain basic improbability about the proposition that their conduct was purely platonic.'

In fact, Miss Keeler was not a professional prostitute, but in any case she was not of interest to Birch. For him the real culprit was Macmillan for permitting it all to come about. He did not suggest that the Prime Minister had acted dishonourably, but 'on the question of competence and good sense I cannot think that the verdict can be favourable'. It was time, continued Birch, twisting the knife in the wound, for Macmillan 'to make way for a younger colleague'. Birch's peroration was from Browning's 'The Lost Leader'. 'Let him never come back to us' the quotation began, and ended 'never glad confident morning again'.

As Birch delivered his final line, Macmillan turned towards him, his face contorted with pain and anger, an indelible impression on my memory. For Birch the Profumo affair was no 'little local difficulty'. Revenge was sweet. Birch was a political assassin in the class of Geoffrey Howe. But in Nigel's case my sympathies lay with his victim.

In 1962, before Profumo was rumbled, I was invited to spend the weekend with Esme and Nigel Birch at their manor house in Flintshire. Save for a weekend spent in a cottage in the grounds of Lord Waldegrave's great house near Wells in Somerset (discussing writing a Bow Group pamphlet on defence with Len Beaton and David Howell; the young William was still at school), my Flintshire visit was the only example of traditional 'pre-war' hospitality that I received. If country-house political weekends still existed in the sixties, leaving aside the Astors, Cliveden and nude bathing, to which I was happily not invited, I took no part whatever in them. But in Flintshire the Birches were hospitable and Nigel rather surprisingly cooked a splendid dinner on the Saturday evening himself. We agreed about nuclear weapons but not about 'Harold'. Birch could not abide him.

Nigel Birch was a superb parliamentary performer. He spoke for less than ten minutes, making every word count. He was always incisive with none of the garrulity of the Left, and his contributions to debate were listened to with rapt attention. He clearly took immense pains with his speeches (he had notes but never referred to them), and his wit, as we have seen, could be savagely wounding.

Ernest Marples was a card. I am told that even the wind and weather of more than thirty years has not yet managed to erase the slogan 'Marples Must Go' from one of the primitive Lego-like bridges on the first stage of the M1 motorway. Ernest Marples was Minister of Transport in the first part of the sixties, while in the fifties he had been Harold Macmillan's deputy at the Ministry of Housing; together they had been responsible for building 300,000 houses a year, many of them on desolate estates built on hillsides on the outskirts of northern industrial cities. They were not the homes fit for heroes so often promised the working class, but Marples (and Macmillan) could claim credit for an achievement of sorts.

'Ernie' Marples was short, self-made and cocky, a foil to the urbane, even laid-back Harold Macmillan who took a party conference delight in lauding his junior partner's accomplishments. As Minister of Transport, Marples built the first motorways, leaving the railways to be decimated by Dr Beeching. Marples also permitted British Railways to scrap its fleet of steam locomotives long before the bulk of them had earned their keep. In short, and in showbiz terms, Marples was 'big'. I once travelled to Blackpool with him, sharing a compartment with other conference-goers. At noon, Marples opened a Fortnum's hamper, and took from it a bottle of red wine, on the jet-black label of which was written in letters of gold the one word 'Marples'. He had a house in Fleurie, he told us, where he grew his own Beaujolais. We were not, however, invited to taste it. On another occasion he invited me to lunch at his penthouse flat overlooking Eaton Square. His wife served at table; at least the guests assumed it was his wife although Ernest never bothered to effect an introduction. In consequence the guests, who included Rab Butler, were forever half-rising in their chairs out of common politeness. After the salad came a tray of cheeses: Marples urged Butler to try the Camembert, which the Home Secretary gravely did, only to find that it was made of rubber and squeaked. At which Marples, always the cheeky chappie, fell about with hysterical laughter. Rab remained grave. Still, Marples was a character, light years away from the Sir Tufton Buftons of the party. I shall seek out his memorial the next time I drive up the M1; the bridge is, I believe, some way north of Watford Gap.

In my early days in the House I was a regular attender at the weekly meetings of the 1922 Committee. The committee, of which all Tory MPs are members, has been variously described (usually by me) as a theatre either of cruelty or of the absurd. But on most Thursdays nothing very much ever happened. The secretary read out the minutes, sitting on a raised dais before a huge tapestry rather alarmingly entitled 'The Death of Harold', and the chairman, Major John Morrison would then ask for 'matters arising'. The whip on duty would then read out the business for the next week stressing the urgency of the summons to attend. My friend David Walder, who was elected for High Peak in a by-election in 1961, invented 'Walder's Law' in which the first three people to speak from the floor on any matter whatsoever were invariably mad. David was right; I cannot remember who they all were (Anthony Fell? Ronald Bell? Harold Soref?) but Major Morrison's injunction did seem to encourage the dim and the dotty to hold forth, and at some length.

The individual back-bencher does not count for much; to carry his point he needs the signatures of a hundred of his fellows; but the '22 does matter; the anger of two hundred or so back-benchers when focused upon a man or an issue can destroy the reputation of a minister (Leon Brittan), or force a resignation (Lord Carrington); it can also gravely weaken the standing of the Prime Minister of the day. After the débâcle of Suez, Harold Macmillan restored the reputation of his party and government by a bravura performance on the floor of the House, which enhanced his standing in the country, and, less obviously, by his end-of-term appearances at the '22. Macmillan's election victory in 1959, when he was returned with a larger share of the vote than Mrs Thatcher enjoyed at any of her three election victories, and with a Commons majority of a hundred, was the reward for his efforts. Macmillan always treated the '22 as if it were a university historical society: his speeches, which usually contained a reference to the Great War and its appalling casualties, were eloquent attempts to place Britain in the context of its decline in power. His audience, many of whom had enjoyed 'a good war', respected Macmillan's personal bravery (there was a phrase, common in the Brigade of Guards until the thirties 'to be as brave as a Macmillan') and felt flattered by his approach. I felt something of this veneration in the first two years after my election, 'Harold', as the old things invariably called him, had had not one but two good wars: he had style; his views were a touch unconventional for a Conservative, it was true, but, most important of all, he had saved the party's bacon. The more priggish did not like his carefully cultivated vulgarity, 'there ain't going to be any war', and his cry of 'You've never had it so good'. (In fact Macmillan never actually used those words, but it was an accurate summary of his achievement.)

By 1962, economic difficulties, the retreat from Africa (presided over with enthusiasm by Iain Macleod) and Macmillan's advocacy of Britain in Europe had served to erode the Premier's standing within the party. The Tory Right never had time for him, and as his political difficulties grew in magnitude – the Night of the Long Knives; 'stop-go' and then the Vassall and Profumo affairs –

his support within the party drained away. He would attend upon the '22 with difficulty, nervously fingering his Brigade tie. Somehow the old magic did not work as well as it once had, and his mannerisms no longer beguiled. The more curmudgeonly thought they were being sold down the river. Even as left-wing a Tory as Humphry Berkeley took to calling him 'the old actor-manager', and there was something of the Donald Wolfits about the Prime Minister.

Macmillan was once asked what was the most difficult part of being Prime Minister and he replied 'Events, dear boy, events.' By the beginning of 1963 'events' were dictating the government's agenda. I sat in the Chamber, high up on the government back-benches, scrutinizing the backs of the heads of my fellow Tories for signs of intelligence, and watching with some fascination Her Majesty's Loyal Opposition. Hugh Gaitskell was the last high-minded leader of the Labour party. I was lucky enough to hear Aneurin Bevan's last major speech in the Chamber in December 1959 months before his death from cancer. He warned the packed government benches, recently reinforced by the newly elected, that the prospect before us was one of 'hours and hours of exquisite boredom'. He was only partly right. I had been brought up to believe Nye Bevan a bogeyman. Had he not dragooned the poor doctors into the National Health Service, and called the Tories 'lower than vermin'? Yet now he seemed to me a benign and witty old man.

Whom did we hate? It has become a cliché to assert that one's political enemies are not to be found across the party divide, but within the ranks of one's own party. Labour and Liberal MPs were our 'opponents', and it was perfectly possible to make friends in all quarters of the House. It is an elementary error, and thus a common one, for political 'hatreds' to be focused upon those who hold extreme views: simple Tories hated Michael Foot, or Marcus Lipton; simple socialists loathed John Biggs-Davison or Julian Amery. The same could be said for relationships within the parties: right-wing Tories had no time for left-wing ones like me, while moderates despised the raucous simplicities of someone like Captain Henry Kirby. But I believe the truth to be rather different: extremists are often rather fun, and the correlation between their views and their character does not often exist. I think Michael Foot is a marvellous old man, but not one with whom I would often agree.

Someone whom I did dislike intensely was George Wigg. He was an old humbug who pursued a malevolent vendetta against John Profumo. A tall, donkey-eared, long-faced, lugubrious old rogue with more chips than Harry Ramsden, Wigg, having been thwarted by Profumo in a parliamentary exchange over missing British servicemen in Kuwait, was determined to even the score. Wigg was an old soldier, a role that he played up to the hilt. A pre-war regular, he rejoined the army on the outbreak of war and became a half-colonel in the Royal Army Education Corps, the only unit in the British Army, it was said, entitled to include the general election of 1945 among its battle honours. In the early sixties, before he attached himself to Harold Wilson – whom he served with dog-like devotion ('wiggery-pokery') until Wilson, tiring of him, kicked him upstairs – he was a defence specialist, using his army contacts to good effect. We became reluctant allies because the Fitzroy Maclean/Birch/Head views on the need for greater emphasis upon conventional forces coincided with Wigg's. As the storm brewing around John Profumo's head thickened (the House was full of rumour and counter-rumour) George Wigg raised the affair publicly in a debate held late at night on Thursday 21 March 1963. I sat and listened to his speech. Wigg called for the setting up of a select committee to investigate the 'missing witness', Christine Keeler, so as to dissipate the rumour that the authorities, in order to protect Profumo, had spirited Keeler away to Spain on holiday to prevent her from giving evidence at the trial of a West Indian called Edgecombe who had fired shots into her flat.

Wigg went on to say 'and to protect the honour of the minister concerned [Profumo] freed from the imputations and innuendoes that are being spread at the present time'. Wigg always maintained that there was nothing personal in his campaign, but some weeks before his speech on 20 March I had stood next to Wigg in the Commons urinal. He whispered to me that he had uncovered a scandal concerning the Minister for War, who, Wigg claimed, was 'a massive homosexual', a remark which in retrospect must be the daftest slander ever uttered. I had no wish to become involved in the row over the Profumo affair, however obliquely, so I held my tongue, but it served to convince me of Wigg's insincerity. Wigg's speech, in which he made full use of parliamentary privilege, was followed by speeches on similar lines from both Richard Crossman and Barbara Castle.

The next morning Profumo made his fateful personal statement in which he lied to the House. The House was packed and Profumo, as is the custom, was listened to in silence. I wanted to believe him: the campaign against him was hateful in its gleeful intensity, with the Labour party using the cover of security (Profumo and Ivanov, the Soviet Military Attaché had apparently shared Keeler's favours), to strike an attitude holier than thou, while the gutter press (and William Haley's *Times*) had a field day mixing prurience with probity in a way to which we have long become accustomed. I had never spoken to Profumo and, unlike Nigel Birch, knew nothing of his activities. He had, it appeared, convinced his colleagues of his innocence on four separate occasions:

they took his word which should have been good enough. Clearly, it was not, and in consequence the Macmillan government was struck a savage blow. The Prime Minister, who was curiously unworldly in matters of sex, simply took the word of a gentleman. Martin Redmayne, the government Chief Whip and a lifelong Conservative, should have known better than to do so. It also now appears that information on Profumo, gathered by the intelligence services, was not passed on to the Prime Minister's private office.

Apart from Brigadier Jackie Smyth VC, another back-bencher, I was perhaps the only loyalist. I travelled to Hampstead to speak to the Young Conservatives. 'The Prime Minister must not be driven out of office by two tarts,' I cried – it was reported in the next day's *Guardian* – but sadly he was. As for Wigg, I shall include an uncharitable postcript. In 1976, Wigg was charged with kerb crawling near Marble Arch. The Wells Street magistrate concluded that it was Wigg and not the police who was lying, but Wigg was acquitted solely because the magistrate considered 'kerb crawling' did not constitute an offence.

Emmanuel Shinwell was not a man with whom it was wise to trifle. Chairman of the Labour party, a back-bencher then in his late seventies, he was the most difficult of customers. He had grown a carapace against all disasters (such as the 'Shinwell Winter' of 1947/48), but had blossomed, if such a fruitful word could be applied to Manny Shinwell, when Minister for War. He had moved over a long lifetime from the far left to the right of the Labour party (save on Europe). He was a supporter of Nato, and in the early sixties had no time for Labour's unilateralist wing. He was the military's favourite Labour politician. Born in the East End of London in 1884, the son of a tailor, he was brought up in Glasgow, retaining something of the Red Clyde until his death at the age of 101. He had none of the pomposity and false heartiness of the cheap politician. Under Macmillan, I do not think we exchanged more than a few words; twenty-five years later when driving home late at night, I spotted Shinwell waiting for a cab in New Palace Yard. I gave him a lift back to his flat near Regent's Park. He was uncharacteristically mellow: he told me that in 1924, when he was first made a minister, there were no such things as ministerial cars, and that he had therefore walked to Buckingham Palace. On his arrival at the gates he accosted a policeman with the words 'I am Emmanuel Shinwell. I am the Parliamentary Under-secretary for the Mines in the new Labour government; I have come to kiss hands with the Sovereign.' 'Fuck off,' said the constable. I expect Shinwell had dined out on that story for half a century but it served to cheer me on my way.

I had a soft spot for the Tory Knights of the Shires. There was something splendid about them: Sir Hugh Monro Lucas-Tooth; Sir Samuel Storey, Sir William Arbuthnot, Sir Charles Mott-Radclyffe, there were not enough round tables to accommodate them. They were not striving for office, as every Tory MP does today; most were content to serve in Parliament as an extension of their sense of social obligation. Most, if not all, had served in their regiments during the war, and some had been awarded what was described somewhat cryptically as 'a good MC'. I wondered if there could be such a thing as a 'bad' Military Cross. I read *Eastern Approaches*, and, in consequence, much admired Fitzroy Maclean. He told me that he had served with both Randolph Churchill and Evelyn Waugh in Yugoslavia. This I knew, but I had not heard his Evelyn Waugh story. It appeared that a message reached Fitzroy in his cave that Waugh wished to see him. The request was granted, and after a journey lasting several days across wild and mountainous country Waugh arrived, saluted, and said that he wished to be posted home. 'Why?' asked Fitzroy. 'Because none of my fellow officers is my intellectual or social equal,' was the reply. Needless to say the request was denied and Waugh was obliged to retrace his footsteps.

Fitzroy was one of our most distinguished fighting soldiers of the Second World War. Had not Ted Heath called an election in February 1974 we would have travelled together to Russia, retracing in part his footsteps in *Eastern Approaches*. Among other literary Tories, I also read Jasper More's *A Tale of Two Houses*, the story of how his family regained their ancestral home in south Shropshire. Jasper was a 'library squire' with perhaps the most perfect manners of anyone I have ever met. The Mores had represented south Shropshire, on and off since the Commonwealth, and my maternal ancestors must have touched their caps to many a More. In the seventies, I spent a weekend with Clare and Jasper at Linley, the first 'Morris' to be entertained at the great house.

When one is young, all-night sittings are something to be taken in one's stride. I spent them in the library (private offices for MPs were not provided until the seventies), dozing fitfully to the sound of corporeal explosions, or rummaging through the shelves where I would discover books like *How I Rowed across the North Sea Singlehanded* by Sir Spencer Summers. Such tales of derring-do were the antidote to a young man's contempt. Handsome girls with degrees were forever climbing ladders, and as the summer dawn broke we would eat bacon and eggs on the terrace. But what one can do comfortably at thirty, one cannot do at sixty. Today I would feel as if I had travelled sitting up all night in a third-class railway carriage from Calais to Cannes – and my refreshment department can no longer rise to bacon and eggs.

I did not go to the party conference in Blackpool in 1963, which has since been a cause for regret. I missed Hailsham's throwing down of the gauntlet; 'Rab' Butler's and Reggie Maudling's disappointing speeches, and the whole fuss and furore that surrounded Harold Macmillan's retirement. He wished to lead the party into an election in 1964, but prostate trouble (he was told he had cancer but the diagnosis was wrong) obliged him to withdraw. His favoured successor would have been Quintin Hogg, but when that horse fell he *transferred* his support to his Foreign Secretary, Lord Home. Along with many of the younger Tories, I wanted Butler, the architect of much of post-war Conservatism, to succeed and wrote, as requested, to the Chief Whip, stating my preference. I eventually received an acknowledgement, long after the choice was made. I was outside the 'magic circle' looking in. In those days Tory leaders 'emerged', rather than being elected. And who now shall say whether recent results have justified themselves?

Sir Alec Douglas-Home (or Lord Home, if you prefer) has achieved near-canonization. Universally loved, if not always respected for his expertise in economics, his brief period in office provided a postscript to the Macmillan years. Abandoned by Iain Macleod and Enoch Powell on the grounds that he was a social anachronism, and despised by his Chancellor, Reggie Maudling, who told me some years later that Alec never understood a word he was saying (Macmillan, he asserted, fully understood the relationship between economic and social problems. 'I used to cry on his shoulder,' Reggie told me), Alec nevertheless healed, for a time, the divisions that are endemic in the Tory party. We are a right-wing party inside which the moderate and traditional wings contend for the leadership. Alec was a 'traditional' Tory but he did, however, give Ted Heath his head, with instructions to do away with resale price maintenance, a reform that mightily enraged the shopkeepers of Rochester and Chatham, and that could – in the opinion of some – have cost us the close-run October 1964 election.

I have one vivid memory of Alec. I was strolling up St James's past Locke's, the hatters, when I glimpsed the Prime Minister, as he then was, walking alone up the other side of the road. He had been in the Carlton Club. As he walked up the street, passers-by solemnly raised their hats and, in return, Alec gravely acknowledged their salutes. Two points come to mind: in the mid-sixties men still wore hats; and 'security', which today protects the *prominenti* from assassination, was then quite unheard of.

Were the sixties a golden age? They were, for me at least, an age of travel. The election, long postponed in the hope of an eventual upturn in our fortunes, had to take place in October 1964. I knew that my majority of 1,003 was vulnerable to the smallest swing back to Labour, and therefore that defeat awaited me. During the year I took advantage of three parliamentary visits: to Ethiopia, to the Yemen and to Australia. The delegation to Ethiopia was led by Sir Charles Taylor, once the 'baby' of the House, and included Harry Walston, the Labour peer who farmed the better part of Cambridgeshire, and James Allason, the father of Rupert. James was a nice old thing, decent but dull; one wonders how he could have sired so flamboyant a son. We arrived in Addis in the wake of the first conference of the heads of African states. Sir John Russell, our ambassador, told us that the tarts of the city had refused to sleep with any of them on the grounds that they were black. The Ethiopians are Amharic, with light skins and fine features: the soap-powder hoardings in the city gave us the idealized picture of themselves. The women were particularly lovely.

On the evening of our arrival, we were included in an invitation to a dinner given by the emperor in his palace to mark the anniversary of his country's liberation. We went *en smoking* and, having gingerly skirted a mangey lion that was chained to the palace gates, took our place on a small table in the far corner of a huge tent. It was not a great gastronomic experience – the dish of the country is *quat*, a kind of unleavened bread, smothered in a sauce which is horrible, and the drink consisted of two small bottles of Bass, each wrapped in a white napkin. As a spectacle, however, it was splendid. The uniforms were partly Ruritanian, partly Rider Haggard, one could not be sure whether Stewart Granger was playing *King Solomon's Mines* or *The Prisoner of Zenda*. Whatever else it was, it was more fun than the annual dinner of the Rochester Rotary Club. Savages in sky-blue uniforms, ambassadors with plumes and naked slaves with drawn swords all clamoured for our attention. There were no women. Haile Selassie (whom I had once glimpsed while he was in exile in Shropshire) gave us an imperial wave to which we bowed low in return, and we were provided with a mounted escort back to the local Hilton. They were dressed as I imagined the Hussars of Conflans, but without shoes.

The next day the delegation was divided into three groups in order to visit different and distant parts of the country. I went south to Diredawa and Harar along the railway line to Eritrea up which Basil Seal climbed in *Black Mischief*. Happily, we went by car. The towns were dusty and brilliant with bougainvillaea and packed with Ethiopian troops ready to do battle with the Somalis over the disputed province of the Ogaden. On our return several days later to Addis, Lady Russell, a Greek who had been 'Miss World' in 1937, presented us all with silver coptic crosses.

We spent a rest day before returning home, at the Imperial Guest House some way out of Addis where we were quick to put our feet under the table.

The leader of the delegation, Sir Charles Taylor, a *parfait*, genteel Knight of the Shires, lit upon a cache of noble claret, Lafite and Latour from the twenties, which we drank to the accompaniment of goats' cheese and unleavened bread, sitting in the garden, watching an enormous sun set behind the distant Abyssinian mountains. I was living, and drinking, well above my station. On my return, however, I promptly went down with dysentery. There was a postscript worthy of Basil Seal. I wrote a piece for the *Financial Times* about Ethiopia only to be summoned to see Rab at the Foreign Office: Russell had complained that I had taken advantage of his hospitality.

In the company of William Yates, Tory MP for The Wrekin, a jolly eccentric who wore Arab dress on polling days, Humphry Berkeley, Tory MP for Lancaster who went largely unloved by the Knights of Shire and Suburb (he was too acerbic and left-wing) and John Dugdale (the pleasant Labour MP whose 'pair' I duly became), I went to the Yemen in the wake of the overthrow of the sultan. At the Foreign Office briefing a supercilious young man, of the sort once found in publishers' offices or working for Berry Bros and Rudd, informed us that we would find the Yemen to belong to 'the twelfth century; not the eleventh, or the thirteenth, but the twelfth century'.

He might well have been correct. As we entered the gates of the walled city of Sana'a, there was a display of severed heads mounted upon pikes. We had flown from the then British base at Aden in a Yemini Airlines Dakota, the windows of which were continuously sprayed with oil from its starboard engine. We were met by the ex-sultan's motor car, an enormous and ancient vehicle within which there was a metal device which, at the push of a button, propelled the sultan out of the back seat and into a standing position. This we kept for Yates, a fanatical Arabist (Berkeley called him Mohammed el-Yatees) and the leader of the delegation.

We slept in the town's principal guest-house, sharing accommodation with a Russian colonel whose task it was to keep the rudimentary airfield operational. He spoke no English. Bill Yates fed us with various pills and instructed us on the formalities. In the afternoon we were the guests of the coup's leader, a bearded young Yemini in the pay of Colonel Nasser. Standing on a low balcony we were introduced to a mob of several hundred irregulars, armed to the teeth. On being told that we were British MPs there were cries of anger and shots fired into the air. Bill Yates was then introduced to tumultuous cheering (and more shots). He was 'a friend of the Arab nation' and his reputation was such as to cover Berkeley and me, who were pro-Israeli, in a blanket of general approval. There was then a parade, a march-past and finally a charge in our direction, the front rank of rebels stopping at our feet. I gazed nervously into the eyes of one armed tribesman who turned out to be wearing the uniform jacket of a guard in the old Great Western Railway. As the tribesmen all wore skirts, Dugdale promptly congratulated the leader of the coup on the quality of his women soldiers. Happily, I do not believe the remark was fully understood.

Australia was more mundane. The Ministry of Defence invited a party of defence specialists to see a Blue Steel missile being fired from a V-bomber at the missile range at Woomera. Among the party was the writer/soldier Alun Gwynne-Jones, later to become Lord Chalfont and Wilson's Minister of Disarmament. He turned out to be an immensely congenial companion with whom I was more than happy to share my Fortnum's hamper. Sadly the missile aborted when the countdown reached '2', and our embarrassed hosts, conscious that we had spent many hours in a Bristol Britannia turbo-prop flying from Wiltshire to Canberra via Cyprus and the Maldives, put us into buses for a five-day tour of the Snowy Mountain irrigation scheme, complicated engineering and tunnelling works in which the courses of rivers had been reversed. We clambered cheerfully aboard and spent five idle days admiring the girls (all girls look good when glimpsed from the back seat of a bus), eating the excellent lamb and drinking the unknown wines of the country.

Thirty years later we British have become the victims of Australian cultural imperialism, addicted to *Home and Away* and *Neighbours*, our institutions rubbished by Rupert Murdoch and his newspapers. In 1964 I loved what I saw of Australia, the huge skies, the distant clumps of European trees that marked a farm or homestead, and the geniality of the natives. A week in Australia was not enough; I fear that today it would seem a lifetime.

It is no fun fighting to defend a seat in Parliament. MPs hate elections; candidates, on the other hand, love them, for if luck is on their side they too could inherit the magic initials, a modest income and the chance of instant fame. My Labour opponent was Mrs Anne Kerr, a handsome if unsuccessful actress and an extreme left-winger, who had been adopted as candidate by one vote. The Chatham Labour party, consisting as it did of dockyard maties, had grave doubts about her views on defence. They had good reason to do so. She had attended Mayor Daley's riotous re-election in Chicago where she had been tossed into a paddywagon by the cops to the cry – much reported in the British press – of 'get that broad out of here'. Would it make a suitable slogan? She was, however, a statuesque candidate and ultimately a successful one. Ted Heath spoke for me at Chatham Town Hall where he was heckled by umbraged Tory shopkeepers. After a bitter battle, and an unpleasant declaration of the poll where I was surrounded by exultant Kerr supporters, I went down by 1,013 votes, a majority ten more than mine had been. The campaign was a rehearsal of the arguments between unilateral nuclear disarmament, in which Anne Kerr believed, and the multilateralist case that I espoused. But the voters were not much interested in such political niceties. At elections, the swing governs all.

The day Parliament dissolved I walked alone through a deserted Palace of Westminster, knowing full well that defeat was practically inevitable. I took a long, last farewell. What had I achieved in five years? I had gained a certain notoriety, several fat books full of press-cuttings and a passport full of stamps. The Tory whips had come to think of me as 'unsound'. It would not be easy to get myself adopted for a safe seat were I to lose Rochester: just how difficult I was about to find out.

13 The Lean Years

I had lost my seat in Parliament and with it the bulk of my income. I had a living to earn. Ex-MPs are unenviable creatures: cut off from their careers by the people's will; unhappy spectators of events that once were so familiar; without privilege within the Palace of Westminster, save to linger unescorted in the Members' Lobby. I have noticed former colleagues doing precisely that; men grown old, waiting hopefully for the crumbs of recognition. That was not for me.

Besides which I had other problems. I had fought the election alone for I had left my wife Paula in the spring of 1963, on my return from America, and had been living with Heather Goodrick, who had left her husband – a British-born doctor living in Seattle – two years before. Heather was a close friend of Paula's, they had been at Cheltenham Ladies' College together; in 1962 she had turned up at our flat at Blackheath and we had befriended her. My marriage had long been an unsatisfactory one, despite the birth of our daughters Julie and Susannah. For both of us it had been an unhappy time. I had discovered Paula's infidelity with our next-door neighbour in the summer of 1960, but after a lonely period on my own in digs in Kensington (and for a time in a 'dormitory' run by John Biffen in the Fulham Road) I returned to her that Christmas and Susannah was duly conceived. Sadly, the marriage still did not flourish and the triangular friendship of Paula, Heather and myself soon broke the frayed bonds of matrimony. I fell head over heels in love with my wife's best friend. It was the stuff of bad novels or poor 'Wednesday Plays', of the kind once so popular on BBC1, but I was ecstatically happy. I shall not 'do an Osborne' and write unkindly about my wives as the playwright did in his autobiography *Almost a Gentleman*; my faults were no doubt as grievous as theirs, and the small change of failed marriage is of interest to no one but ourselves. I recount the fact of my divorce, which came through in 1965 after ten years of marriage, and my second marriage to Heather Goodrick née Moores in April of the same year at Kensington Registry Office, purely as background to my own story.

I was determined to get back into Parliament but the question was how. Given the size of Harold Wilson's majority (four, shortly to be reduced to two) another general election was bound to take place quickly. Should I seek readoption in Rochester or look for a safer seat elsewhere? As my divorce was pending, I had no choice but to stay put. Divorce was a serious matter among Tories thirty years ago. Not so much among Tory MPs, who, if they were of the grander sort and found a woman trying, soon swopped her for another, but the Party activists, drawn from the more 'respectable' citizens of Rochester, still looked askance at marital infidelity. The inhabitants of Chatham with its naval tradition did not seem to care quite so much; they considered my love-life to be my own business.

My pending divorce was not the only problem. My independence had been none too popular with members of the local party, while my support for the abolition of resale price maintenance in what was very much a shopkeepers' seat had not endeared me to the Rotarians of Rochester. And the *Chatham News* was hostile owing to my support for the Common Market. The executive committee of the local party met and duly recommended my readoption, but I then had to appear before a Special General Meeting of the Association.

The ride promised to be a rough one, and ballot papers had been prepared in anticipation. A crowd of two hundred forsook the TV for what promised to be a more exciting evening's entertainment. I spoke, but it was not my tongue that saved me. An unknown in the audience rose to his feet at the start of the meeting and attacked me personally ('party representatives need to set a high moral tone . . .'). As if by magic the atmosphere changed, friends rallied to me and no vote was taken. In his book *The Selectorate*, Peter Paterson wrote of my readoption; 'Thoroughly petit bourgeois and narrowly unrepresentative of the community at large, riled no doubt by some of Critchley's policies and attitudes, and possibly worried by the imponderable electoral effects of his divorce, which had just become public, the committee nevertheless recommended his readoption as the prospective candidate.' And at the larger meeting of the two hundred I was lucky in my enemy. I had lived to fight again, although the chances of beating Anne Kerr so soon after her victory the previous October were none too good. Wilson was biding his time. One result of the Rochester meeting in 1965 was that a part at least of the folklore of candidate selection was buried: 'that the selectorate, particularly in Conservative Associations where women predominate, invariably take an illiberal attitude over the private lives of politicians'. Tim Yeo probably feels differently.

I had three sources of income: the publicity account of Rosenthal China in London, the *Glasgow Herald* (whose defence correspondent I became) and freelance journalism. Heather had a small income from several family trusts. I had worked for Rosenthal for several years. The headquarters of the firm was in Selb, Bavaria, and the company opened an extravagant showroom in the Brompton Road where they sold their range of contemporary porcelain. The boss of the international undertaking was Philip Rosenthal whose infrequent visits struck terror into his German, London-based staff. They would line up to greet him on his arrival as if he were Frederick the Great. He was an arrogant man about whom I was told by the London manager 'You may mention the number of mountains Mr Philip has climbed, but not the number of women he has married.' It was as good a brief to sell modern china as any. The job amounted to sending photos of cups and saucers, pots and plates to the home editors of national newspapers and glossy magazines and then entertaining them to lunch.

In 1965 I turned down an offer from Gavin Astor's *Times* to become its defence correspondent in place of Alun Gywnne-Jones who had, at the bidding of the Prime Minister, become Lord Chalfont and the Minister for Disarmament. There was, unfortunately, a proviso; I could not stand for election. I preferred to fight Rochester again at the next election (which could not be long delayed). I feared that if I stood down, it might be the end of my chances of election elsewhere. In the event the job went to Charles Douglas-Home, who was later to become the paper's editor, and I accepted David White's invitation to write for the *Glasgow Herald*. He was the newspaper's London editor, a charming, white-haired old man to whom I would present my copy three days or so a week. I never set foot in Glasgow. The *Herald* had a reputation for not only supplying Fleet Street with its Scots sub-editors, but much of its writing talent as well. Frank Johnson once told how when he first worked for the *Telegraph* he asked for an increase in salary, only to be warned half-jokingly by Bill Deedes that 'there are lots of clever young men on the *Glasgow Herald*'.

Anyway, with money from four sources and with two families to support I could just about make ends meet. My income from all sources was in the range of £2,500 a year. Out of this sum I was, of course, obliged to pay Paula alimony and maintenance; indeed, at the time of writing she still receives £1,500 a month from me – thirty years after our divorce. The sixties might well have been swinging, but they were lean times for me.

In the early sixties I had joined the Bow Group, an organization of the more cerebral Young Conservatives, founded some years before by the likes of Geoffrey Howe who was at that time slim enough to mount buses that would convey him and his friends deep into the East End, to the Bow and Bromley Conservative Club. It was an unlikely venue, but the 'Beau' Group (as it was nicknamed by the press) soon won the reputation of a left-wing Tory pressure group inside which people like Patrick Jenkin, David Hennessy and David Howell won their spurs. Heseltine joined but did no pamphleteering. The reputation I had gained as a maverick back-bencher enabled me to stand for and win the chairmanship of the Bow Group in the spring of 1966. I beat Hugh Dykes, later to become the MP for a Harrow seat. I made it my custom to entertain the Group's speakers to dinner at my club, the Carlton, before the meeting. All went well until I entertained Jo Grimond. The meal passed without incident but a day or two later I received a summons to attend upon Lord Grimston, the chairman of the club, who had sat in the Commons for Westbury. The appointment was for one o'clock (there was no mention of lunch), and I was regrettably but unavoidably late. Try as I might I could not find a taxi and there was no direct bus route. Grimston had gone but his disapproval had been made very plain. I asked my friends for their advice. Leon Brittan thought the whole affair absurd; but David Windlesham did not: 'You should never entertain at your club someone whom you could not put up for membership of it.' The Carlton is, of course, a club for Conservatives. I expect he was right, but somewhat ironically Ted Heath, by then the Leader of Our Great Party, entertained Kosygin to lunch at the club the following week. I quit the Carlton with its fine staircase and poor food (the menu was enlivened only by the choice of whose Prime Ministerial portrait one sat under: I chose Balfour) and joined the Garrick instead. There the staircase was almost as handsome, the collection of Tinsel pictures upstairs unique and the members decidedly more fun. I could never bring myself to buy the tie though.

The Bow Group, which has tended to be first-generation public school and Oxbridge, swung to the right politically in Mrs Thatcher's golden days; under John Major's less-ideological regime, the flavour of the Group has become suitably bland. In my time as chairman, the favourite term of approbation was 'X has gravitas', which suggests we were pretty insufferable. Mind you, gravitas is a condition to which I have long secretly aspired; I fear the lack of it has been my undoing. Patrick Jenkin, who was a very grave young man, once went so far as to accuse me of levitas. We ran into each other on the platform of Westminster Underground station, Patrick was clearly enraged and it was not long before I realized why. *Crossbow*, the Group's quarterly, had just been published and on its cover was a picture of a pretty Young Conservative wearing nothing but a man's shirt, an outrage for which the magazine's editor, Mr Leon Brittan, had been responsible. Patrick's parting shot, before the train doors closed mercifully upon him, was a request for 'plain brown envelopes in future', a remark which helps to put the 'swinging sixties' into perspective. But I wonder why he blamed me?

The favourite topic of Bow Groupers in my day was candidate selection, for we were all desperately on the make. Why else put pen to paper? We would bump into each other in the dingy offices of Conservative Associations, seated, to the smell of cat, on the hardest of chairs, waiting for our summons to sing and dance. I had done so in Rochester in 1957, and was to perform on several occasions in the late sixties before Aldershot finally gave me a standing ovation. How we must have patronized the local worthies with our references to *Sybil* and *Coningsby* and by our careful disregard of their prejudices. The aspirant candidate has a choice: he can do as I did, that is to try not to stoop to conquer; or he can act as a megaphone for his audience's views. Put a group of Tories under one roof and they do tend to revert to a state of nature. Geoffrey Dickens, the twenty-stone Conservative MP for a seat in Lancashire (as an amateur boxer he once went nine rounds with Don Cockell) showed me the notes for his speech before a selection committee. They read: (1) Twenty years of ceaseless fight against socialism; (2) Hanging and flogging; (3) Mrs Thatcher. I cannot claim that my year in office was especially distinguished. I discouraged the Group from holding its annual ball at the Hurlingham Club on the not unreasonable grounds that dancing was one thing that the Group did not do well. We held a weekend conference in Oxford. I organized the requisite number of meetings and encouraged Simon Jenkins to take over the editorship of *Crossbow* once Leon Brittan's time was up. He did so and the covers became much plainer. No longer were they cheered by pictures of pretty girls. There is a lobster salad side to our European Commissioner. I was succeeded in office by John MacGregor who, almost thirty years later, was to be burdened with the denationalization of the railways.

At that time Michael Heseltine, having lost money in the early sixties, was recouping his fortunes through the Haymarket Press which he owned jointly with Clive Labovitch. In 1964 he had fought and failed to win the Labour seat of Coventry North but in the 1966 election he had succeeded Sir Henry Studholme as the Tory MP for Tavistock. I duly went through the motions of fighting Rochester for a third time but the swing towards Labour was too strong for me. After a hard-fought three-week campaign with Heather at my side, Anne Kerr was returned with a majority of 2,000. We had stayed for the duration of the election with Frank Bannister, the treasurer of the local party, living over his garage business in Chatham. To console myself I swopped my Mini Cooper for a Reliant Sabre at a marginally reduced rate of interest, and drove swiftly up the A2 to London for the last time. I have never been back to the Medway Towns. We were then living in a top-floor flat at 50 Chepstow Villas, Notting Hill Gate, a house that the Heseltines had mortgaged from the Scottish Widows. Michael, newly elected, and on his way up, had passed me coming down. History was repeating itself.

After my second defeat at the hands of Anne Kerr, who went on to be a sharp thorn in the side of Harold Wilson (sharper, perhaps, than I would have been), I abandoned hope of returning to Westminster until the next general election. Rochester was a marginal seat, a swinger, liable to be won by the victorious party at an election, and the name of the game was to pick up a 'safe' seat, a parson's freehold. (Rochester, its boundaries redrawn, was won for the Tories by Peggy Fenner in 1970 only to be lost in 1974.) Anne Kerr was married to Russell Kerr, the Labour MP for Feltham, who one of my ex-colleagues described to me as being 'not only a communist, but an Australian communist to boot – and they are the worst of the lot'. He might well have been right. Kerr was a drunken boor who hung around until the seventies; Anne, who died before he did, after a career of futile notoriety, was found dead in a position of prayer beside her sleeping husband's bed. She, too, was drunk. According to the inquest she had more than five times the permitted level of alcohol in her blood. She was a sad woman, handsome in a Spanish way; La Pasionaria of the Chatham Dockyard. Arthur Bottomley whom I had defeated in 1959, was promptly returned for Middlesbrough, and served in Harold Wilson's cabinet throughout the seventies. A nice old boy, he is now safely in the Lords.

When we returned home to the flat at Chepstow Villas after my second consecutive defeat, Michael Heseltine invited me to become editor of *Town* magazine, the star of his publishing stable. I was more than happy to accept. Anthony Howard, for many years a close friend of Michael's, later told me that he too had been offered that particular chalice, but had taken care to refuse it. *Town*, in which four years before I had so unwisely modelled my suit, was a glossy men's magazine both flashy and respectable. Soft-porn came in with *Mayfair* and later, less soft, with Guiccone's *Penthouse*, but that was still five years away. Heseltine's *Town* was a blend of men's clothes, sport and current affairs in which the girls were still the kind my mother had hoped to find living next door to her. It was flashy in that it aspired to speak for the 'swinging sixties'; risky, because the frequency with which it had changed its editors suggested either a meddling hand or, more likely, financial insecurity. But it was a challenge and I stepped smartly into the shoes of a better-paid editor (Dick Adler) who had been sacked to make room. And there was always the fact that I had lost the Rosenthal account, and that when it came to paying, the *Glasgow*

Herald was as mean as any West Coast Scotsman. The salary at *Town* was £3,000 a year.

Editing a monthly magazine has much in common with working on the staff of a Sunday newspaper like the *Observer*. There is not the unremitting pressure of working on the dailies. Haymarket Press had its offices on the first floor of a modern block on the Edgware Road, in a quarter of London then Jewish, later to fall to the Arabs. The calendar had to be watched carefully, different pages going to press in each of four weeks, and the editorial budget had to be shared among its art and editorial contributors. The magazine had always enjoyed a good reputation for its visual excellence: indeed, in 1984 the magazines of the sixties were the theme of an exhibition held at the Institute of Contemporary Arts. Its covers and some of its photo-journalism was given pride of place. Parsimony had begun, however, to effect the quality of the editorial, although I bought pieces from Jill Tweedie and Jeffrey Bernard, both of whom were then relatively unknown. I sent Cyril Ray, the doyen of wine writers, to cover the recently opened Playboy Club. We met for a drink beforehand at the Carlton where we were lucky not to run into Lord Grimston, for Cyril was very left-wing. At the Playboy Club, surely the quintessential sixties institution, we nervously sipped the soup that had been ladled into our dishes by cantilevered Bunnies looking like the figureheads on a fleet of storm-tossed men o' war. Hugh Hefner, wearing sunglasses, made a little speech; we ate ribs of beef and drank Chambolle Musigny premier cru, all on *Town* magazine. It made a good piece, and began a friendship with Cyril (I never got as far as calling him 'Ray', which was reserved for his intimate friends) who persuaded me to contribute to several of his annuals, the *Complete Imbibers*, volumes which are now collectors' pieces.

Despite my defeat at Rochester early in 1966, the year proved to be a good one. I was chairman of the Bow Group, which everyone took reasonably seriously, and editor of a fashionable magazine that no one I knew took seriously at all. Heather and I were certainly not well off for what money we had was divided between two families and much of our time was spent on the sad entertainment of the two small daughters by my first marriage. Paula put no barriers in my way, and we drove them most weekends to my paternal uncle's house at Hadlow Down in Sussex. When not in the country, being entertained by Drs Doris and Michael Critchley, we did the rounds so well trodden by the recently divorced: visits to the London Zoo, Hampton Court and to *One Hundred and One Dalmatians*. Guilt and divorce go hand in hand especially when there are small children involved, and there is the risk of overcompensating, which puts a strain on one's new partner. As for Paula, I was sorry but not sad for I considered she was young and attractive enough to make her own way. I had made the mistake – for which she, too, had to pay – of marrying far too young.

I saw surprisingly little of Michael. I do not remember ever being invited back to the Commons for lunch or dinner. He would, on occasion, pass me either on the stairs at Chepstow Villas (the Heseltines kept the small town garden for themselves) or in the corridors of 82 Edgware Road. If he seemed worried, he had good cause to be. *Topic*, his news magazine, had been a disaster; *Town*, so he told me years later, had never made a penny in its life, and he was in all probability still paying off debts incurred while dabbling in property. But his fortunes were eventually to improve. *Management Today* was to prove a winner, and a clutch of trade magazines soon started to make a deal of money. In the meantime the monthly contributors' budget for *Town* was cut for every issue, and after a bright enough start I was reduced either to writing much of each issue myself or printing pieces commissioned by my predecessors and discarded by them. *Town* slowly shrank, and much of its colour advertising was either carried free, or heavily discounted.

As the rate of descent quickened we did discuss whether or not our girls should appear naked. By 'naked' I do not mean the sort of gynaecologically explicit pictures which are commonplace today in the top-shelf magazines but the sort of romanticized nudity which can be found in the advertisements carried by *Vogue* or the Sunday supplements. But there is, or was, a Swansea side to Michael, a Valleys prudishness which reinforced his anxiety lest his political career be damaged by the charge of pornography. A copy of *Town* with a girl on the cover had been brandished at an election meeting in some south Devon market town, much to the candidate's embarrassment. To his credit or not, Michael did not permit me to make the magazine more sexually attractive to the young executive (indeed, he was forever complaining about whatever sex there was in the magazine); in consequence, the writing was on the wall.

Several factors had combined to erode our friendship. The fact that I was beholden to him out of the House and in no position to share or even sustain his own political progress within it; and of course his own financial worries, which he did not share with me. The old intimacy had gone. Anne did not much like me; Michael did not take to Heather, and Heather did not like either of them. The fact that we shared a house did not help.

In the event I tried to become the editor of the *Listener* – it went to Karl Miller, and Michael began a discreet campaign, always at second hand, to force me from *Town*. The dirty work was left to his managing director, Lindsay Masters. He employed the tactics of exclusion and discreet hostility. After eleven months as editor I was finally sacked and given a month's money. Brian Monyhan was put in my place. Six weeks later, in the early summer of 1967, the magazine folded.

It was the most humiliating perod of my life. In just over two years I had lost my seat, my job and my oldest friend. Heather and I were obliged to sell our flat back to the Heseltines and move to a ten-pounds-a-week rented cottage in Shamley Green near Guildford. The cottage was a prettily converted single-storey barn which belonged to the Bransons, Richard's parents.

It was William Rees-Mogg who came to the rescue. Editor of *The Times*, he wrote to say how much he admired my efforts to make a success of *Town* and asked me to become a regular contributor to the paper, writing a twice-weekly column of television criticism (part of a threesome that included Michael Billington and Henry Rayner) and a monthly political column for the Saturday paper. It saved our lives. In the early seventies I interviewed Michael for the *Illustrated London News*, and asked him whether he had ever made a mistake. He replied 'Yes, sacking you.' A politician's answer?

Life in the Surrey Hills had its compensations. I had been living in London, either at Blackheath Village or Notting Hill Gate, for the better part of twelve years and was glad to quit London for the country. Shamley Green was then a *bijou* village, its green surrounded by fine houses, occupied by retired admirals and late middle-aged members of the professional classes. Mr Branson was a barrister, his wife a former dancer. There was a village shop and an hourly bus to and from Guildford which was patronized by the small rural underclass. To pay back-taxes I was forced to sell my Reliant Sabre at a knock-down price to a garage situated under the elevated section of the Western Avenue. Thus we went *en exile* to stockbroker's Surrey by courtesy of public transport. We had a three-month-old daughter, Melissa, who had been born under Heseltine's roof. In summer the cottage, with its large garden, was idyllic, and the Bransons kindly and unobtrusive.

The Times took its television criticism very seriously indeed, its arts pages edited by John Lawrence who had an eagle eye for solecism. I was paid fifteen pounds a notice: some weeks there would be three such reviews, which had to be written late at night against the clock (the better progammes worthy of review usually came on late) and then telephoned through to 'copy' before one a.m. The political column (twenty-five pounds) was a much more leisurely undertaking. With some other freelance writings, we were able to survive on some seventy-five pounds a week, a proportion of which went to Paula and my two older children. The advent of the Barclaycard in 1968 enabled me to borrow seventy pounds with which I bought a fifth-hand Austin seven.

Heather had returned to her husband in Seattle at the end of 1962. I spent some days with her early the next year towards the end of my Smith-Mundt scholarship, and persuaded her to return to live with me in London. We were married in the spring of 1965, midway between the two general elections. She was a Moores, a member of a family richer even than the post-war Barons, although Paula's Aunt Elsie (Mrs Robert Tritton) was probably as rich as any of the Moores, and a good deal smarter. The contrast between the Barons and the Moores was an interesting one. Paul and Betty Baron, my first in-laws, lived in a flat in Eaton Square when I was courting Paula. Betty was his second wife. The early Barons were Russian Jews who had fled the country via Odessa for the United States at the turn of the century, only to re-emigrate to Britain. Their fortune was made by Bernhard Baron whose name can still be seen on a wing of the Middlesex Hospital. He founded Carreras, the makers of Piccadilly and Craven 'A' cigarettes, well before the Moores' football-pool and mail-order empire. That splendid art deco building, the Black Cat factory, still stands en route to Camden Town. By the time I met them, the Barons, who included Sir Edward and Lady (Bertha) Baron (flat in Portland Place, country house near Sunningdale) as well as Elsie Tritton and countless others, were café society, and far from being orthodox Jews. When Paula and I were married at Caxton Hall in October 1955, the registrar greeted the 'congregation' with an effusive familiarity; many of them having been his customers in their time. I felt then that the warmth of his greeting constituted something of an ill omen for my own marriage. 'Good to see you, again, Mr Paul', and 'How nice to see you, Mr Theo'. The reception was held in Eaton Square with Betty Baron the belle of the ball. As a wedding present we had been promised a fridge. It took a year to come.

Paula and I once drove down to Godmersham, Aunt Elsie's country seat near Canterbury, for lunch. The house was exquisite and boasted a summer-house in which Jane Austen had written *Pride and Prejudice*. There was a small Renoir in the downstairs lavatory and several more elsewhere in the house, which was something of an Aladdin's cave. (Its contents would be auctioned by Sotheby's in the eighties and raise over £5 million.) Elsie was the widow of Sir Louis Baron and, upon his death, had married a charming old fop of an antique dealer called Robert Tritton. Before lunch, he asked me to answer his telephone: I did so, and an old man's voice said 'Willie, here'. It was W. S. Maugham.

The Moores were native Britons but of no less humble origin. John Moores, the firm's founder (who died in September 1993 aged ninety-seven) left school at sixteen to become a Post Office messenger. He picked up the idea of football pools from its unsuccessful inventor and by the thirties had made the first of his three fortunes, the others coming from mail order and the Littlewoods chain stores. Just how rich the Moores family has become can be shown by a table published in the press in 1993 when the Queen announced that she would pay tax: two names appeared in the table of wealth above that of the Sovereign; Betty Grantchester and Donatella Moores, daughter and granddaughter of Sir John. I doubt if ever the Barons, even in their pre-war heyday, could have matched that.

John Moores lived relatively simply in a four-bedroomed pre-war house in Formby on the Lancashire coast. He had a cocktail cabinet and some good modern art. The first generation never really escaped its working-class roots, and there is little doubt that 'Uncle John' with his remarkable initiative, stern patriarchism, and puritan attitude to money (not to its amassing but to its spending) was by any reckoning a great man. His children adopted the syle of the *haute-bourgeoisie*, but apart from Betty do not seem to have inherited his flair. They are a quarrelsome lot. Nevertheless, there seems little chance of the old Lancastrian saw 'From rags to riches and back to rags in three generations' applying to the Moores family. Once the company goes public they will become even richer.

Two vignettes: I last saw Paul Baron when I was editor of *Town* in 1966. I had remarried the year before, and I had not seen him for several years. He was a small, stocky, dark, dapper man who wore navy-blue double-breasted suits. He looked like a violin-case carrier in an Edward G. Robinson film. The Barons had sold Carreras to Rothmans, and Paul had lost his directorship. He had come to ask me for a job. He had always been pleasant to me and it was sad to see him so humbled. He died in his sleep a year later. In the early years of my marriage to Paula we would dine not infrequently with Paul and Betty at their flat in Bryanston Court (immediately above the apartment once owned by Wallis Simpson) and her Aunt Bessie. Betty I found tiresome, a trifle 'grand' and overbearing, very protective of her daughter Sarah, Paula's half-sister who was later to marry Alastair McAlpine, the author, collector and courtier. Paul never had much to say, but we were united in praise of the cook, Lola, who had once worked for the Argentine ambassador. The Barons' table was an eye-opener: the food was of a quality I had not previously enjoyed served in surroundings that made Harben Road seem shabby. The Barons must have been fighting to keep the wolf from the door, but they did not show it.

In the eighties, Heather and I were invited to a ninetieth birthday party given for 'Uncle John' by his daughter-in-law Luciana, the estranged wife of his younger son Peter Moores. The venue was yet another flat in Eaton Square, but unlike the Barons' first apartment of thirty years ago, situated on the north side of the square. Sir John Moores, as he had become (he had been a generous subscriber to Conservative party funds, giving the party £30,000 in 1979) was, not unnaturally, the centre of reverent attention. Three or perhaps four generations of Mooreses stood in line to present themselves or their small children to the patriarch. It was a little like Marlon Brando receiving tribute in *The Godfather*.

The cynical reader might now be wondering what financial advantage I derived from my proximity to the rich. The answer is simple: from the Barons, none; although Heather did receive relatively small but welcome amounts in family trusts, the great proportion of which went towards school fees for our two children, Melissa and Joshua.

Living in our dacha in Shamley Green, writing about telly at night and politics by day, going up to Waterloo by cheap day returns once or twice a week, I had not lost sight of what remained my objective, the prize of a safe Tory seat, and with it my ticket to Westminster. Besides writing pieces for *The Times*, and anyone else who would pay, I wrote begging letters to chairmen of Conservative Associations who were in search of a candidate. Had not *Crossbow* published a list of all those poor old buffers over sixty who still sat in the Commons for safe Tory seats? They were, as far as we were concerned, all in intensive care. I watched as one by one, friends and enemies who had sat with me in the Commons were picked for safe seats, but the postman stayed away from my door. Then in the summer of 1968 I had a letter from Reigate in Surrey asking whether I would appear.

We were still without a car so, wearing a new check suit bought on tick from Simpson's of Piccadilly, I took the train from Guildford to Reigate along the old South Eastern Railway line that runs from Reading to Tunbridge Wells. The Reigate selection process was one of the very first 'open primaries' ever held by the Tory party. The shortlist was decided by interview and from the last six (Howe, Chataway, Peter Thomas, Anthony Meyer, David Walder and myself) Howe and Chataway were picked to meet in the final, which was to be filmed by Thames Television's *This Week* and reported by me for the *Sunday Times*. The contest, which was an intriguing one, was to be decided by the votes of the paid-up members of the Association, and the contenders were evenly matched. Geoffrey Howe had been in the House for two years and on the front-bench, losing his seat in 1966; Chataway had been a junior minister in Harold Macmillan's government. They were the most promising of the younger Tories, Howe right-wing, at least on economic matters, Chataway excessively 'moderate'.

They were given twenty minutes each followed by questions, and their wives five. Six hundred people, most of them women, made up the audience.

Howe won, but only on points. He was thoughtful and his appeal to the party activists – 'people who care about our country and want to do something about it' – was well judged. Chataway was the more sophisticated but visibly nervous. Perhaps the occasion was too much for him? The wives provided a telling contrast. Anna Chataway was possibly too 'West End' for the mid-Surrey middle class, but Elspeth Howe got it right. 'What politicians need is a certain sort of love,' she declaimed, and there was not a dry eye in the house. The open primary has never been properly followed up. Years later I tried to persuade the SW Surrey Tories (we were living in Farnham) to open up the selection process that saw the adoption of Virginia Bottomley as their candidate but they refused, saying that such publicity would be unfair to the contenders. What nonsense! The national publicity resulting from the exposure of such esoteric political practices would have been beneficial, and the fee paid by television a handsome one. Too much that happens within our political parties goes on behind closed doors; it is little wonder that constituency politics remains the activity of a rapidly diminishing minority.

I think it was Phillip Whitehead, the producer of *This Week* (for whom I fronted a programme on boxing), who asked me to invite myself to lunch with Harold Macmillan at Birch Grove in order to ask him whether he would appear on Independent Television. I travelled by car to Birch Grove, a modern country house the back of which abuts the Bluebell Line, a preserved steam railway often to be glimpsed on television. Macmillan greeted me gravely, and we lunched together. I noticed on the grand piano, among the clutter of signed photogaphs of heads of state in silver frames, a copy of Mosley's autobiography, which had just been published. To make conversation, I asked Harold what he thought of Oswald Mosley. Immediately, he came to life: 'Ah Tom Mosley, quite the most able man I have ever met, but quite mad. He came to me once and said "Harold, I'm thinking of putting my people into black shirts." "Tom," I replied, "you must be mad. Whenever the British feel strongly about anything, they wear grey flannel trousers and tweed jackets." ' I failed to persuade him to abandon the BBC, but returned with a signed copy of the first volume of his memoirs.

After Reigate I had to wait six months until I received another letter, this time from the Rugby Conservatives, a seat which Labour had won from the Tories' Roy Wise in 1964 and held two years later. While this was no better than Rochester would have been, it seemed my only chance. After the interview, when I beat the young Jeffrey Archer (who was later to be adopted for Louth), I was invited to contest the final.

Towards the end of 1968, my Uncle Michael and Aunt Doris decided to live and work in Algeria and offered us the use of their house in Hadlow Down. They were to spend five years abroad, and we accepted their invitation. Hyders was a large, early-Victorian house set in a large and splendid garden with a tennis court. Although far grander than the Bransons' cottage and free of rent, but not rates, it was at the end of the Uckfield line to Victoria and hence less convenient for London. My uncle threw in his elderly, left-hand drive, Wolseley. We left Sussex by the sea for Rugby by our new car in the teeth of a blizzard. It was a nightmare six-hour drive first up to and across London and then up an arctic M1, blinded by swirling snow and the frozen slush thrown up by heavy lorries. I arrived at the hall five minutes before the proceedings were due to begin, neither fed nor watered. My speech went well but the battery of questions was all about race. 'Should not the blacks be repatriated?' Such questions were greeted with cries of 'Enoch was right' delivered in what might be described as a Middlemarch accent. I had retained enough of my liberalism not to equivocate, and I did not give to many the answers they sought. I lost, but then so did the Rugby Tories in June 1970.

After so narrow an escape, or massive misjudgement as you will, I next received a letter from the Wimbledon Tories who were looking for a successor to the redoubtable moralist and low-churchman Sir Cyril Black. I had no great confidence in the outcome. I was summoned to an interview by some local party functionary who, looking hurriedly through my biographical details, spotted the word 'divorce'. 'That won't do for Wimbledon,' he said grimly. A fortnight later it was reported that he had left home with the au pair girl. But Wimbledon, like Reigate, opened up the final to the press, although not to television, an event which I attended for *The Times*.

This time it was a battle for hearts and minds between Michael Havers who was later to become briefly, Lord Chancellor, Ian Gow and my friend David Walder who had lost High Peak in 1964. The rumour was that it had all been sewn up in favour of Havers in advance, the Tory party in the House being chronically short of competent lawyers. David Walder was never at his best on his feet, and his laconic response to the question asked by an eager housewife 'What are your views on drugs, crime and pornography?' which was 'I'm against them' was deemed to show rectitude but not enough relish. Hellfire and damnation would be expected of Sir Cyril's successor. David was swiftly eliminated. Ian Gow, who was to wax under Mrs Thatcher until his murder at the hands of the Provos, was last on the bill. He delivered a fundamentalist speech of such a dizzy eloquence, out-Blacking, as it were, even Sir Cyril, that the ranks almost broke as a small claque greeted Gow's revivalism with cries of 'A-men'. Happily the audience soon settled down, a vote was taken and Michael Havers duly adopted. Ian Gow went on to win Eastbourne and in 1979 became Mrs Thatcher's 'Great Chamberlain', her devoted Parliamentary Private Secretary.

Although living in what amounted to internal political exile, I was not denied the opportunity to travel freely abroad. This was due to Otto Pick, a young Liberal of Czech origin who had fled his country a second time after the communist coup in 1948. He had become the general secretary of the British Atlantic Group of Young Politicians (Bagyp), a cross-party grouping of the young and promising to which the Foreign Office gave a handsome annual subvention. Its purpose was to recruit, confirm and convince young politicians in favour of the North Atlantic Alliance, and similar bodies had been set up in all the Nato countries. As a defence specialist, I needed no convincing of the case for collective security and I welcomed the chance Bagyp gave us to travel to congenial places at public expense and to 'meet with' (the flavour of such meetings was American) our opposite numbers among our allies. The British contingent included Dick Marsh who was soon to become a cabinet minister, Dick Mabon, an engaging Scottish doctor who defected in the eighties to the Social Democrats, and John Austin-Walker, now the Labour MP for Greenwich. Fellow Tories included Nicholas Scott, Keith Speed and Stratton Mills, at that time an Ulster Unionist MP. The American delegates included several with whom I made good friends: Olin Robison, later to become the president of Middlebury College, Vermont, and a Soviet specialist, Spencer Oliver, a Democrat *apparatchik*, and Hodding Carter, Jr, who was later to achieve fame as a television commentator. Among the Germans perhaps the most distinguished was Peter Corterier, later to be a minister in the Schmidt government and today the general secretary of the Nato Parliamentary Assembly.

We had scarcely been living at Hadlow Down for nine months, when my aunt and uncle returned precipitately from Algeria. My aunt had reversed her car out of the garage and inadvertently run over my uncle, injuring him grievously. We were, of course, obliged to go on our travels once more; this time renting a pretty cottage from a parson at Cousley Wood, near Wadhurst, on the borders of Kent and Sussex. No sooner had we settled in and set up the Victorian half-tester double bed yet again than I heard from Aldershot. Sir Eric Errington was retiring; would I permit my name to go forward? I learnt later that all former Tory MPs had been invited to do so. Aldershot I saw as my last chance; by then most of the hundred or so Tory MPs who had lost their seats at the two previous elections, had been suited. I asked Philip Goodhart, an old friend and MP for Beckenham, for his advice. It was to this effect: too many aspirants make the mistake of making a predictable political speech attacking Harold Wilson and sliding over the discrepancies in Tory politics, when what the selection committees really want is local knowledge and concern. How wise he was.

At his bidding I rang the editor of the local paper and journeyed for the first time to Aldershot, where I spent a day with him. I was briefed, and a couple of days' work enabled me to speak to the executive committee of the local Tories with some authority about the constituency, its problems and its peculiarities. It worked. I was marked top in three separate stages and beat Colin Turner, who had sat for Woolwich, in the final. I had been chosen for a safe seat. And I had not even served in the army, unlike several of my rivals who claimed to have 'crawled over every inch of it'.

I had the impression I would not have been Eric Errington's choice, but he was kind, permitting me to buy him a large lunch at the Garrick. In the 1966 election, so I was told, Eric had addressed a public meeting in Fleet, a dormitory for retired officers of middle rank. Age had sadly taken its toll (Errington had been high on *Crossbow*'s list of the infirm) and during that campaign he was escorted everywhere by two stalwart Young Conservatives whose task it was to help him to his feet at public meetings. An act of levitation took place, after which Eric began his speech by saying, 'Mr Chairman, I have difficulty getting up but once I am in the erect position I am as good as ever I was . . .' By all accounts, and over the years I heard several, his audiences of colonels and their ladies would collapse with laughter. I have dined out on my Errington story, and I should add a wry postscript. In the 1992 election I was similarly handicapped, although I relied upon crutches to become 'erect'; but I took great care not to repeat Eric's opening sentence. After the election the local Tories presented Eric Errington with his portrait in oils. My last glimpse of him was driving off to Anglesey in the rain, his picture trussed to the roof of his shooting-brake.

It was not until much later that I heard that there might have been a hiccup in my selection. Midway through the selection procedures, Central Office had asked the Association to drop everything and adopt John Davies, the chairman of the CBI who had announced his wish for a political career, but had been politely refused. Another prominent Tory, Mrs Anne Peters, asked for the inclusion of the young Winston Churchill, which was also refused. She then asked the president of the Association Sir Richard Gough-Calthorpe whether he knew I had been divorced. 'I do, and so what?' was his reply. I had my share of luck.

What then are the qualities needed for adoption as a Tory candidate? I am tempted to say persistence but there is a little more to it. Even so, Geoffrey Howe and Leon Brittan between them must have appeared before at least fifteen selection committees before winning their spurs. Political progress is a subject worthy of a book on its own; indeed Peter Riddell of *The Times* has written one called *Honest Opportunism* that was published in the autumn of 1993. It does not much matter whether you are on the left or right of the Conservative party for we are not yet, despite 'Thatcherism', an ideological party. Local Tories are still, if only just, members of the non-political political party, and they much prefer courtesy and conventionality. There is, however, a tendency to what I call 'Critchley's Law', that is to choose as successor a person with radically different views and/or qualities to the sitting MP. Aldershot have picked Gerald Howarth, an ex-MP, who carried Mrs Thatcher's handbag after her defenestration, as the next Conservative candidate for Aldershot. He was, in fact, her last PPS. We have few prejudices in common, but we do share a sense of humour. I needed one, and so, undoubtedly, will he.

Wives are also important. A nice old colonel from Fleet, called Alex Bennett, once asked me if I knew why I had been chosen. Nervously, I said no. 'It was your wife,' he said. 'Damned fine woman. And she was the only one of them to stand up when we asked her a question.' Heather, like Paula, had been to Cheltenham Ladies' College. So, too, had Prue.

I was adopted as Aldershot's candidate in the winter of 1969. It was like winning the pools. It has thus been over twenty-four years since I was subjected to the necessary impertinences of candidate selection. I had few qualifications, save a quick tongue, a public-school accent and a well-mannered wife. I had never commanded men in battle, run a great company or made (as opposed to earned) money. I just wanted to get into Parliament; apparently, it was enough. After many vicissitudes, and six years in the wilderness, I had fallen on my feet.

14 Return to the Commons

As I have said before, candidates love elections; MPs do not. In June 1970 I was a candidate fighting to inherit a safe Tory seat. Banished was the angst that had been my constant companion in three Rochester campaigns. Places like Odiham, Crondall (pronounced by the grand 'Crundall') and Hartley Wintney did not seem, at first glance, to contain a single Labour voter. The tile-hung pretty houses were covered with wisteria; in every gravelled drive, a Triumph Sodomite. It was a brilliant summer, and the temptation to quit Aldershot with its cheap shops, gasworks and brutal and licentious soldiery, was overwhelming.

Twenty years ago a much smaller population in and around Aldershot meant a larger constituency, its boundaries embracing the greater part of north-east Hampshire as far west as Rotherwick and Eversley, and as far south as Long Sutton. After six years of Harold Wilson's government, the local Tory party lacked for nothing. The fighting fund (which was raised at one election to have money in the bank to fight the next), was full to overflowing, and an army of party workers decorated both sides of the A30 with a hundred 'Vote Critchley' posters. With Sir Richard Gough-Calthorpe at its head, the Aldershot Conservative Association could muster a battalion of retired officers and their wives, the largest contingent coming from Fleet, a curiously dull early twentieth-century planned town where retired colonels and their ladies hung like an army of bats in the mouth of some Goanese cave. The 'ladies' of Fleet were under the command of Mrs Anne Peters, a formidable widow-woman of alarmingly right-wing views. She had badly wanted the Young Winston as candidate, but frustrated in this she transferred her affections to me. She was quick to ask me to draw the raffle.

The Conservative Club was in the middle of Aldershot itself, a large thirties two-storey building with a much-coveted car park. While sitting on the most valuable site in the town, it was, in fact, a working-men's club with a Tory top-dressing, an annual subscription of five pounds and its halls and corridors hung with slot machines. There was unappetizing pub grub, and a large coloured photograph of the real Winston, a silent spectator of beer and snooker. There was always a garrulous sponger or two in the bar, encouraging for all his worth 'the next Member' to refresh his glass. Weakly, I complied. The local party office was upstairs, and the club was a generous subscriber to party funds at election times.

'Aldershot Man' was a retired non-commissioned officer who had gone into business in a small way; his favourite topics of conversation were capital punishment ('hanging's too good for them') and the diminishing fortunes of the local football club. He had little time for Eric Errington ('we never see him'), a failing that I pledged myself secretly to emulate. I put myself out to be congenial company, relying more often than not on my knowledge of boxing to break the ice. Boxing is the working-class sport *par excellence*, and I could blind them with science. Had I not seen Woodcock knock out Gus Lesnevich and sparred with the great Jimmy Wilde? (I would also later entertain Henry Cooper to lunch.)

It is no big deal to fight a safe seat at a general election. The great of the party do not waste their breath in constituencies where the result is only too predictable, and what public meetings I held were modest affairs. Three or four meetings a week for three weeks were held at eight o'clock in village or school halls, fifteen minutes of 'onwards and upwards' from the candidate (Errington was an incredibly poor speaker; I shone by contrast), for thirty or so people, followed by thirty minutes of question and answer. In 1970 the only subject that seemed to rouse the Hampshire upper middle class was Rhodesia. The tide of black rule in Africa, summoned up in the view of some by Iain Macleod himself, was so emotive a subject that even the Labradors in the audience were moved to discordancy. I kept the straightest of bats. As for the press, even the local papers gave the election scant coverage. To fight a by-election must be hell, such is the exposure; to fight a safe seat at a general is the quiet way into Westminster.

In those days the Conservative Association could afford a full-time party agent, a bright young man called Frank Richardson whose cheerful round-the-clock competence kept the show on the road. We were later to lose him to a career in public relations. He saw to it that every morning at ten o'clock I mounted the back of an open Land Rover, borrowed from a friendly farmer. Beribboned like a bullock I was driven off by volunteers to spend the rest of the morning canvassing the streets of Cove and Farnborough. We would be met at some dusty corner by a group of the faithful, cards in hand. My lameness, which was in those days barely noticeable, prevented me from running from door to door, leaflets in hand, the sort of exercise on the part of candidates much encouraged by Peter Walker and Conservative Central Office. Instead I stood winningly at garden gates, hoping for a smile of encouragement on the part of some bewildered housewife. 'Wilson out,' I murmured. Canvassing held two perils: the political opponent determined to keep one talking and the family dog which on no account must be kicked, whatever the provocation. I admired babies but did not kiss them, drank endless cups of milky Nescafé and crept exhausted, supperless, to bed. Aldershot was no Rochester, but knowing no different I amazed my helpers with my energy. I fought a seat which had never returned any candidate other than a Tory as if it were a marginal. It was what I was used to.

A general election campaign reaches its climax at the count. The candidates and their wives circle the floor, watching while the counters count, for the first signs of how the voting has gone; friends come up with transistor radios bearing the results of other contests, the pattern of only one of which (in our case Guildford) will be enough to tell you all you want to know. The rows of bundled hundreds of ballots lengthen along the top table, each snake a different colour. Thirty minutes or so before the final announcement by the Returning Officer, the result will be known, and the counters, a proportion of whom will have worked for you, will be celebrating or commiserating as the case may be. The Liberals will take their defeat badly; Labour, which comes third in Aldershot, invariably behaves well. There is one thing in politics that serves to unite Labour and Conservative and that is a dislike of the Liberals and, more particularly, their election tactics. We have seen a recent example of them in the East End of London. All too often they show a complete lack of scruple, incline towards personalized attacks and show poor sportsmanship once the result is announced.

Victory banishes all fatigue, defeat numbs the senses; whatever the end of it all, almost the best part of the whole 'beastly business' is the return home, a stiff drink and the TV, to sit and watch the fate of friends and enemies. It is fun to see the results coming up with their inevitable crop of surprises. It is the end of an ordeal by exposure.

My return to the Commons in the wake of Ted Heath's somewhat surprising victory was marked by two newspapers. 'Crossbencher' in the *Sunday Express* claimed that together with Pat Hornsby-Smith I was destined for office: *The Times* carried a photograph of Heather and me together with Norman Fowler and his first wife, Linda Christmas, standing outside St Stephen's entrance. The caption read 'Two *Times* journalists take their seats'. Fowler had been the paper's home affairs correspondent while I had been a TV critic. The *Sunday Express* was wrong as usual. The idea that after six years out of the swim I would be immediately offered a junior post in Ted's government was as wrongheaded as most of that great paper's editorial opinion seemed to be. I had been brought up on the *Sunday Express*, my mother used to take it at Harben Road, the predictable prejudices of the young John Junor (was he ever young?) adding Scots bile to the wet gloom of a Swiss Cottage Sunday afternoon. My father read the *Telegraph*.

As I had feared the Commons was not what it had been six long years ago. The salary had doubled, and there was an allowance for secretaries and stamps, but twenty-seven Tories were missing, seventeen of them Knights of the Shires. Gone were such luminaries as Sir Walter Bromley-Davenport whose brief sojourn at the whips' office has passed into legend. In those days the whips were posted at the various exits to discourage MPs from sneaking off home after the ten o'clock vote. Walter pursued an errant Member, caught up with him and booted him up the arse. The arse belonged to the Belgian ambassador. War was averted, but Bromley-Davenport was promptly replaced as whip by the young Ted Heath. Such are the vagaries of fate.

Among the other twenty-six, listed under 'vale', were Colonel Claude Lancaster, a dapper mine-owner, Sir Charles Mott-Radclyffe and my favourite, Sir Hugh Monro Lucas-Tooth. I never spoke to him, although in my first incarnation I had shared a table with him at lunch. He was at that time, and somewhat untypically, a junior minister at the Home Office; a long, lean, lugubrious figure, with a subaltern's moustache. He was beautifully shod. Real Tories wear hand-made shoes. But it was his names that grabbed me. Could it be true? Four names and a title; he was surely far too grand for suburban Hendon which he remotely represented. Perhaps I should have modelled myself on him? Sadly, it was too late.

Nigel Birch, Macmillan's assassin, had gone to the Lords, having complained in debate that Harold Wilson and his cabinet were the worst ever to have 'moistened' the government front bench. Sir Edward Boyle had given up his seat to take up a University appointment. I met him one evening in the Carlton a year or so after Margaret had seized power in the Peasants' Revolt of 1975. He had no time for her, but it was about Reggie Maudling that he wanted to talk. He told me that the morning after Reggie's defeat by Ted Heath for the party leadership in 1965, he had gone into the Smoking Room before lunch to find Maudling behind a glass of Scotch. 'What is there left for me to do save to sit here and get pissed?' was Reggie's greeting. 'Which was precisely what he did,' said Edward. Maudling, who had come so close to the highest office, was then in his late forties. Boyle and Maudling, who were among the most illustrious and congenial of the post-war Tories, were both to die of cancer. I saw them last in the Members' Dining Room, gallant but emaciated almost beyond recognition.

It did not take me long to get back into the parliamentary swing. I would drive through the gates of New Palace in my second-hand Rover (I have always bought British) having left Farnham at nine o'clock in the morning, thereby avoiding the early morning rush hour. Having parked my car in the first circle of the underground car park (the fifth circle is quite properly reserved for Members' secretaries), I hung my sword in the place provided in the Members' Cloakroom, glanced at the tapes where the news of the death of a well-loved colleague receives equal billing with Aldershot's relegation to the fourth division, and made my way to the Post Office in the Members' Lobby to collect my mail.

It was usually early enough in the day for me to stand in line patiently with MPs' secretaries, handsome girls with Harrods bags from whom there are no secrets. Happily, their sense of discretion about what MPs might or might not be getting up to is highly developed. Secretaries tend to become MPs' second wives, and should therefore be treated with circumspection. I have had a series of devoted secretaries over the years, none of whom I have married. In the sixties, Susan Bagshawe who went with me to *Town* and left in protest when I was sacked; Sarah Wood who served Nigel Lawson, John Biffen (whom she later married) and me so well throughout the seventies; and Angela Bayfield who took over from Sarah in the eighties and who, working not in the Palace but from her home near Farnham, has held the fort admirably ever since. I did employ my wife as secretary for a time, but it was a great mistake. One can make demands on secretaries that one cannot make on wives and vice versa. Researchers are more tricky, as poor Harvey Booth found out to his cost in January 1994. I employed Morrison Halcrow, once the deputy editor of the *Telegraph* (he was sacked by Conrad Black). Morrison is an old friend and who could be more respectable than a middle-aged Scotsman? The Palace of Westminster is today packed with a motley crew of researchers; blue-stockings and bimbos. In 1970, it was enough to have a secretary paid for by the taxpayer.

In 1970 there were no select committees covering a particular subject (they were to be invented in 1979 by Norman St John Stevas when he was Leader of the House), only standing Committees on Bills which met on Tuesdays and Thursdays from 10.30 to 1 p.m. My tendency to be energetic rather than industrious could well have been my undoing; I avoided service on such committees, appalled by the prospect of such boring detail, but on reflection I made an error. Service on committees is one sure way of impressing the party whip with one's knowledge and capacity; the occasional speech in the Chamber, although remarked upon as a matter of course by the whip on the bench, may not be enough to build a reputation for both loyalty and competence. I had been seduced by the example of Peter Emery who, as a newly elected MP in 1959, was put on the Scottish Grand Committee as an English makeweight, much against his will. He turned up one morning unannounced in full Highland dress, including dirk and sporran, that he had hired from a theatrical costumier, an act that gave great offence to Scots of all political persuasions. The government whips, however, thought it a spendid wheeze, and Peter was duly excused service.

Although the parliamentary salary had barely kept pace with inflation, I was given a room in an Upper Committee Corridor which I shared with Peter Viggers. In 1959 I had been banished over the road. My new quarters were built on the roof; they were hot in summer and cold in winter and rarely cleaned, but the room did contain a free telephone, desk, armchair and stationery, including franked envelopes of various sizes. These facilities, bequeathed by Harold Wilson, enabled me not only to manage my constituency correspondence, which was never very great, but to continue my journalism as well. At the time I wrote regularly for the *Illustrated London News* which was edited by James Bishop, a former *Times* features editor. The *ILN* had stopped appearing fortnightly, and had shrunk to twelve editions a year (it is now a quarterly). It was missed in clubs, dentists' waiting-rooms, and in the United States, where it was much at home in the smarter East Coast drawing-rooms.) I also wrote regularly for the *Telegraph*, and occasionally for *The Times*.

I was also the editor of an obscure magazine published by the Atlantic Centre for Teachers, called *The World and the School*. The Teachers' Centre had offices in Wimbledon Village, and was directed by Otto Pick. It was funded in part by the Foreign Office and in part by the Ford Foundation, and for several years while the money lasted we produced both *The World and the School* and *Crisis Papers*, the very best sort of Nato propaganda. It was an undemanding and congenial task made all the more pleasurable by the Centre's cheerful habit of organizing conferences abroad in attractive places like Cascais, near Lisbon, Bordeaux in France and Elsinore in Denmark. I became a conference buff, a combination of chauffeur and lecturer, aping in a modest way the Call Girls of Arthur Koestler's splendid novel of that name. I was elected president of the Atlantic Association of Young Political Leaders (a related body) and, once again thanks to the Free World's public coffers, we would meet in Bonn or West Berlin, where we would be lectured by generals and patronized by diplomats. And my modest editor's salary paid the mortgage on our new early-Victorian

1   *Top*, Julian Critchley portrait, taken in Members' Dining Room, 1989

2   Julian Critchley's grandmother, Jane Morris, and her six children outside the front door of Rectory Cottage after the death of George Morris on the railway in 1902

3   Eight-year-old Julian on his bike, followed closely by mother, in the lane outside the Rectory Cottage, Wistanstow September 1939

4   A bashful Julian Critchley in shorts, Barrow Gurney Naval Hospital, August 19

5 John Park, newly-appointed Headmaster
of Brockhurst, in 1942

6 'Killer' Critchley, Shrewsbury's best middle-weight (centre)

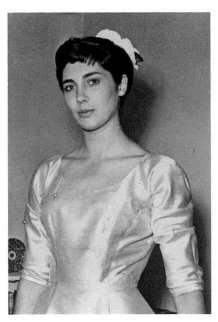

7 Prue Marshall in the early fifties, as a bridesmaid to Pam Gosling

8 Julian Critchley and Paula Baron before their engagement in 1955

9 Julian Critchley hanging from a Royal Navy chopper, 1960. 'I wish it was round his bloody neck!' commented one loyal Chatham constituent

10 *Top*, 1963 visit of 'Lord Julian Critchley' to the Manned Space Centre, Houston, Texas, where he met the 12 best integrated men in the USA, most of whom were to conquer worlds (third from right, bottom line)

11 Julian Critchley with his second wife, Heather, with Norman Fowler and his first wife, Linda Christmas, outside the House of Commons in 1970

12　Julian Critchley on a rare visit to No. 10 Downing Street in 1971

13　Julian Critchley on the stump, Aldershot, February 1974

14 Critchley with John Rogers MP and 'Bobby' Riley drinking champagne on the Boulevard Saint Germain in 1978

15 Julian Critchley dining in 1988 with the remnants of the 1959 intake ('quite the worst of my experience', R. A. Butler). The woman in the middle is Mrs Thatcher

16 Prue in Provence, 1989

17 JC in his attic office at Bridge Square, Farnham, in 1991

house at the top of Castle Street in Farnham which Heather and I bought in 1970 for £13,000. In the autumn of that year our son Joshua was born.

Farnham had the advantage of being outside the constituency boundaries, but only a mile and a half from Aldershot. It is a pretty town, pickled in aspic by the affluent, every door a different pastel shade. It lacked nothing except a branch of Marks and Spencer. In the town we could be anonymous; there was no need to shop with a fixed smile of greeting, the *rictus politicus* which can transform an MP from a man in the street to the man with a message. I remember going to have drinks with a *grande dame* who lived at the bottom of Castle Street. 'Tell me,' she said, 'why do you wish to represent a seat in the east of Hampshire when the western part is so much smarter?' I asked how could she tell. 'By the number of admirals per village,' was her splendid reply. And as a piece of social observation it was true; it is hard to drive down the Meon valley without knocking over an admiral's widow.

15 La Politique de Vacances

After a morning spent writing, there was always lunch to look forward to in the Members' Dining Room. It is now well known that we practise gastronomic apartheid: the Tory party sitting at small tables at one end, eating bloody beef and eggs in aspic; the People's party at the other, wrestling with gammon steak and pineapple. The Liberals and the Clerks of the House have separate tables. There is a cold buffet and a roast. The food, while never reaching the culinary heights, is very much the kind that mother used to make; comfortable dishes like steak-and-kidney pie, and haddock and chips. The wine in 1970 had not recovered from Robert Maxwell's rape of the cellars five years previously. Maxwell had been elected the Labour MP for Buckingham in 1964 and in order to keep him quiet the Labour whips had made him the chairman of the Kitchen Committee with a brief to balance the books. 'Never such innocence again', to quote from Larkin. Maxwell had 'sold off' the cellar, which had been accumulated over the years as a result of the efforts of the Wine Committee, an exclusive body of elderly Tories. In its stead, Maxwell brought in Grant's of St James's. Many years later, but before the old rogue's suicide, I sought out the records of the transaction, only to be told that they had long since disappeared. I can only hope that he never laid hands on the Members' pension funds.

The better part of lunch was the company. Or to be more accurate it could be the better part, depending on the luck of the draw. There were people to be avoided at any cost, colleagues whose sole topic of conversation was the extent of their ward boundaries and the political composition of their local authority. Ray Mawby ate with his mouth open; others, less hungry, rarely closed theirs, piling gossip upon gossip and regaling the table with anecdote. Sir John Vaughan-Morgan was grave and Norman St John Stevas gay. But the most amusing companion of them all was my friend David Walder.

David had been returned in 1970 for Clitheroe in place of Frank Pierson. A large, rather plain man in his early forties with thinning fair hair, he wrote novels about love among the Young Conservatives (he had a 'thing' about girls playing tennis in Aertex shirts), the parliamentary selection process (thus raising many an eyebrow among the silly old things) and Wellington's campaigns in Spain (*The Fair Ladies of Salamanca*). He had been a cavalry officer with service in Malaya, and was a barrister. Later he wrote history, books about the Russo-Japanese War and the Greco-Turkish War of 1920. He was thus many-talented; he had a roving eye which must have been a trial to his nice wife, Elspeth, and a remorseless sense of humour.

I went with him to Germany on a Defence Committee visit, which included – for the first time – a day spent by two MPs as guests of the Bundeswehr. David had a fantasy that he was the illegitimate grandson of Field Marshal Von Waldersee of the Kaiser's army, a point which he made to the colonel commanding the Panzer brigade with whom we were lodging. The colonel was mightily impressed, and promptly substituted a rather better lunch for the one that had been laid on. It is only fair to say that the colonel was himself the son of a field marshal, but of Hitler's army. There was much fellow feeling. We were joined by a squad of senior officers and there was a good deal of saluting, heel-clicking and the noise of opening hock. I was the innocent party in this outrageous deception (lunch lasted three hours), my enjoyment only in part marred by the fear that David in his cups would complete his Von Waldersee story, which he had so far, in my hearing, never failed to do. Thankfully he did not, for his account could have wounded the susceptibilities of so many gallant officers, few of whom were sober and one of whom was armed. Von Waldersee was, in David's version at least, found dead in bed in his house in Berlin, dressed in the costume of a female ballet dancer.

David was immensely good company, cynical and irreverent, and no respecter of the great and the good. I had lunched with him in the early sixties when we had been joined in the Members' Dining Room by Peter Kirk and the young Margaret Thatcher. It was, I think, the first time I had met her. I doubt if we three men managed to get a word in edgeways. I can no longer recall what it was she talked about, but I do remember David's comment after she had gone: 'She's like the chairman of my women's advisory committee writ hideously large,' he said. David, who was to die suddenly in 1978 after a second heart attack, would not have thrived under Margaret; he was never 'one of us'. But under Ted he was made a whip, a position he held until the government's defeat in February 1974. I was asked to write his obituary for *The Times* in which I wrote that, given time, he would have made a formidable Chief Whip.

The Westminster day, more often than not, has a double climax: question time (Prime Minister's questions are on Tuesdays and Thursdays at 3.15 p.m.) and the ten o'clock vote which can be the end of a long day. The gap, if one does not live in London, and in the seventies I commuted from Farnham, is not an easy one to fill. The back-bench party committees, invented after the war to 'keep MPs out of mischief' (the words are Harold Macmillan's), meet from four till six, but they could not guarantee entertainment, being all too often the preserve of those of the colleagues who could neither speak effectively nor remain silent with dignity. My office, which appeared attractive in the mornings, became less so in the long watches of the afternoon.

These *longueurs* provided ample opportunity for me to consider my chances of promotion. I had been an MP for five years, but had been out for six. I had thus missed the years of opposition, the routs and rallies which might have enhanced my reputation. I was thirty-nine, energetic, if not especially industrious, and presentable. I was also a keen supporter of the Prime Minister, Edward Heath; or, to be more accurate, of his policies, particularly those with regard to Britain's entry into the EEC. I had had no dealings with Ted Heath, and it was not until many years later that I got to know him at all well. My area whip was Sir George Young, the 'bicycling baronet' of the popular press, who told me years later that I had never caused him a moment's concern. Given the reputation I was to win as an anti-Thatcher back-bencher during the eighties, I must have been just one party loyalist among many. How best then to shine? To attract the good opinion of the then Chief Whip Francis Pym?

There's the rub. This I clearly failed to do, for David Walder, when he was promoted to the whips' office, was to tell me that Pym did not consider me to be a Conservative. He may well have been right: when serving in her cabinet, he did not consider Mrs Thatcher to be a Conservative either, classing her, as I did, a Manchester School, free-trade Liberal. Perhaps Pym, a dull and dapper little man, thought me to have been a Hampstead Liberal? Many of my views and attitudes were closer to Flask Walk than to Smith Square, and have remained so. It was not, however, a matter I thought I could happily discuss with him. And his prejudice was, rightly or wrongly, to block my promotion in the years of the Heath government. Being an MP is good for one's vanity, bad for one's sense of self-respect. Was I not wasting my time, my sole task being to sustain the government in office while acting as welfare officer for the more pushy of my constituents?

I am, of course, being wise after the event. It was not until 1973 that I learnt from David that I was not, from Pym's point of view, 'one of us'. In the meantime, I looked forward to every government reshuffle and was continually disappointed. I make no apology for my ambition, for as Henry Fairlie has written 'ambition is the engine of the public good', and I dearly wanted to become a junior minister and to rise in office with my peers. To have been in

Parliament without holding office, was, I thought, rather like having been in a war without hearing a shot fired in anger.

Writing today, twenty-five years on, I wonder if I was, in fact, more fortunate than I deserved. Having read in Alan Clark's splendid *Diaries*, that self-proclaimed record of 'lechery, malice and self-pity', just how much he hated his time as Parly Sec at the Department of Employment, I now realize just how lucky I was. I don't think I could have stood the boredom of uncongenial work, stultifying routine and the necessity, on occasion, to stay up all night as well as voting the ticket. A black Austin Princess, and even a black driver from the ministers' pool, would have been but small consolation. Promotion, had it ever come my way, would probably not have been to an office of my choice. In the early seventies, I would have enjoyed the Foreign and Commonwealth Office, and especially the Ministry of Defence, for defence was my special subject, but 'experts' are rarely placed in round holes. Expertise, the whips would say, is not really necessary. In their view, that is what civil servants are for. It is the minister's task to take decisions. It is, I suppose, possible that had Heath won in 1974 I might have been offered something (Pym would no longer have been Chief Whip), but Ted Heath has never said so, and there is no means of knowing what might have happened. By the time Margaret came to power, my disaffection was obvious; from 1979 onwards, office was out of the question.

In 1972 I was offered what amounted to a consolation prize, although I did not recognize it as such at the time. John Stradling-Thomas, the deputy Chief Whip, asked me whether I would like a tax-free income. What he meant was an invitation to join the British delegation to the Council of Europe and the Western European Union. These, he explained over a glass in the Smoking Room, were 'assemblies', that is non-elected bodies of Parliamentarians drawn from the member countries of both international organizations. They met several times a year in congenial places abroad, members were paid a subsistence rate of seventy-four pounds a day and there was a plethora of committees. The WEU was a defence organization in which, suggested Stradling-Thomas, I could play a lively part. As I was at the time relatively hard up with two wives and four children to support I accepted his invitation. I was to trip the light fantastic abroad for the next eleven years. 'Welcome to the delegation,' said Sir John Rodgers, the Tory MP for Sevenoaks. 'You will find the food better, and the oratory largely incomprehensible.'

In July 1972, Hansard published the list of Tory MPs appointed by the whips to the Council of Europe and the Western European Union. Our leader was Churchill's son-in-law Duncan Sandys, who was soon to be succeeded in that post by Simon Wingfield Digby, a Dorset squire of no great distinction. The team included John Peel, Dame Joan Vickers ('*La truite bleu*' as she became universally known in Strasbourg owing to her bright blue hair), Percy Grieve, a pleasant barrister whose fluent French delivered in a laid-back 'Oxford' accent, earned him the nickname '*Ici Percy*', Ian Lloyd, a dull industrial chemist, Sir John Rodgers, a nice old thing with a taste for gossip, intrigue and champagne (he was much later to become our delegation leader – one of his favourite sayings was '*Une femme sans fesses est comme un manteau sans poches, on ne sait quoi faire avec les mains*'), Hugh Rossi, a pleasant north London MP of Italian origin who was the delegation's whip, and last but most certainly not least, the Lord St Helens, who had told me in my first incarnation, in the guise of Michael Hughes-Young, Harold Macmillan's deputy Chief Whip, that the party 'would not wear' my becoming Parliamentary Private Secretary to Bernard Braine. So much for the first step on the ladder. (Later, in some *estaminet* near the station in Strasbourg, he was to deny all knowledge of the incident.) Michael was a sad figure; recently bereaved, his favourite story at lunch or dinner was to recount his exploits in the Guards Armoured Division during the liberation of Brussels in 1944. 'Shot in the arse by a jealous husband' was his cheerful boast. Thank God, he never showed us his scars.

The above were full members; the Tory 'substitutes' (it was a distinction without much of a difference) were, besides myself, Jim Scott-Hopkins, later to become prominent in the European Parliament, John Hill, a Norfolk squire, Arthur Jones, Sir Brandon Rhys-Williams, a dotty intellectual who sat for South Ken, Denis Walters, close friend of Ian Gilmour's, and Norman St John Stevas, at that time a back-bencher with a taste for helpful interruptions at Prime Minister's questions. By December 1972, all substitutes except for me were replaced by the following: Jack Page, Patrick Wall, an intense right-winger who wore a wig, Ken Warren, whom I had known in the London YCs, John Farr, a dull Harborough squire, John Hunt, once Mayor of Bromley in a good year, and Michael Roberts, who was later to collapse and die while making a speech at the dispatch box. What a way to go! Viewed as a whole, the Tory delegation was a *cru bourgeois*, with the exception of Duncan Sandys who could claim to be a first growth 'village wine' of a particularly good year. The Labour party fielded Michael Stewart, the former Foreign Secretary (among others), and the Liberals David Steel.

We flew by British Airways charter five times a year: to Strasbourg on three occasions, May, September and January; and to Paris on two, December and June. On every occasion we spent the better part of a week during the day either in committee or in plenary session; at night, we caroused in the cafés, restaurants and *boîtes* of both cities. As we filed out of the aircraft, rosy with taxpayers' champagne, clasping in our hot hands the gift of a small bottle of scent, Ma Griffe (not every one of which reached home), we were ready to build the new Europe. It was *la politique de vacances*.

If the composition of the Tory team had something of the flavour of a second eleven, it had not always been so. In the great days soon after the war the leaders of the party went to Strasbourg. Churchill, Eden, Macmillan, Boothby; their yellowing photographs can still be found in the more remote corridors of the Palais de l'Europe, their faces flushed by *les vins d'Alsace* in the congenial company of Alcide de Gasperi, Paul Henri Spaak and Robert Schuman. They would have travelled by train from the Gare de l'Est in Paris, pulled by a great, black, Pacific-type locomotive, gathering speed through the suburbs and the darkening countryside, lulled by the gentle tinkling of ice on glass. And how well they must have dined these great men, cosseted by the best chefs of the French railway, comforted with napery, encouraged by noble claret. They would have arrived at Strasbourg, the mellow victors of Hitler's war, to be met by the mayor, the préfet, and the municipal band. *Vive Churchill! Vive l'Angleterre!*

We took taxis in from the tiny, deserted airport (which doubled as a French fighter-base), driving swiftly through the southern suburbs of Strasbourg, the hoardings ablaze with Krönenberg beers, and even La Vache qui rit, crossing the canals into the old city to l'hôtel Sofitel which is situated in a small square next to an austere Protestant church. The hotel was *de grand luxe*; so much so, as we soon learnt, that in the recent past a Knight of the Shires had telephoned to the concierge with a request for '*deux oreillers*', only to receive, *à sa porte*, two *filles de joie*. There had since been a change of '*direction*', prompted by the police.

The Sofitel was a luxurious modern hotel with none of the transatlantic anonymity of its sort. Our leader had a suite; his followers were responsible for their very expensive rooms. Even at seventy-four pounds a day I could not manage comfortably; not if I wished to have cash in hand to return home with little delicacies: pots of foie gras, bottles of Poire William and packets of dried morels. I promptly moved to another hotel, the Gutenberg in the Place Gutenberg next to the city's one-spired cathedral. The hotel had been a favourite of the Germans: I was told of 'the Wehrmacht'; Geoffrey Finsberg, who led our delegation in the eighties, said 'of the Gestapo', and had refused to stay there. I had no such qualms. The hotel was perhaps unique in France in that it celebrated the Second Empire, with pictures of Napoleon III, his empress, and his marshals; patriotic memorabilia which no doubt had been stored away safely between 1940 and 1944 when the city had been reabsorbed into the Reich.

I made Room 8 on the first floor into my own. It had a huge bed, hung with yellow faded drapes on which buzzed the imperial bees, an armchair, loo and bidet, in which I lodged a bottle of Riesling, cool and ready for emergencies. It was noisy, particularly on Saturday nights, but I was usually lulled to sleep by the bells of the cathedral. My retreat from the Sofitel was greeted by much huffing and puffing ('the delegation should stick together'), but my example was soon followed. In time only the leader kept his suite. I would return to the restaurant in the Sofitel three times a year for a solitary dinner – very welcome after so much official and unofficial entertainment – when I ate frogs' legs the size of ballet dancers' thighs and *œufs à la neige* washed down by country wine. To dine alone in a good restaurant is one of the more underrated pleasures of life.

I fell in love with Strasbourg, the city which Ernie Bevin declared, when told that its inhabitants spoke French between nine and five and German at home, should immediately become the capital of the new Europe. There are in effect four Strasbourgs – the old town, huddled around the cathedral, much restored in its charming south German black and white, entirely surrounded by water; the official and university quarter built mainly under the Second Reich, with its heavy, Wilhelmine architecture; the streets running down towards the main station which resemble any French provincial town with its Place de la Gare, a semi-circle of cheap hotels, garages and cheaper shops; and the northern leafy suburbs, home of the well-paid Eurocrats, reached by long avenues lined with plane trees, fronted by fortress-like blocks of flats. Richard Cobb, who writes more winningly about France than anyone else I know, claims that all French provincial towns have a 'boulevard de Strasbourg', almost always a long, gloomy thoroughfare leading out of town, fronted too by unwelcoming blocks of bourgeois apartments and small *épiceries*. At the end of such a long avenue in Strasbourg itself was the Palais de l'Europe.

In 1972, it was a prefabricated structure erected opposite a small park in which there was a rather half-hearted zoo and a pretentious restaurant much patronized by the Council of Europe for *les vins d'honneur*. In May I would take a baguette and sit on a bench beside a lake; once I stretched out on the sward, basking in the sun, only to be awoken by a tiny Frenchman in an official-looking cap, blowing frantically on a whistle. In France it is absolutely *défendu* to lie on the grass.

The Council of Europe was a body with a high moral content, inclined towards the passing of emergency resolutions in favour of good causes.

However, it carried little weight. One of the first things the Assembly did upon my arrival was to admit Liechtenstein into the comity of nations, after which a funny grand duke arrived to award funny medals to the moving spirits of the enterprise. In the early seventies, the mayor of the city was Pierre Pflimlin, one of the Fourth Republic's many ex-Prime Ministers. He was then in his late seventies, a distinguished figure much in evidence at the Council, a ready host at innumerable functions and festivities. We were told that recently in the Gallic tradition he had taken to himself a new mistress whom he had installed in a flat in the old city. The doorbell had rung, and the mayor unwisely answered it himself. It was Madame, who seizing the former Premier by the ear, dragged him home with the injuction that he was far too old for that kind of nonsense. We all drank to him, save for Dame Joan.

In Strasbourg I developed the taste for Alsace wines, which are to this day strangely unappreciated in England and hence are still excellent value. The Sylvaner is the plainest of the quintet: we drank it copiously from small earthenware jugs in *Weinstuben* and *restaurants de quartier*, a cheerful accompaniment to local dishes such as onion tart and quiche Lorraine; the Pinot blanc is no great improvement upon it. We drank that in May during the asparagus season. I sat next to Madame Pflimlin on one such occasion (bunches of yellow/white asparagus served with seven different sauces). With great tact she told me that there were only three things the English did better than the French: asparagus, strawberries and men's trousers. I did not disagree. The three best local wines are the Pinot gris (Tokay), the Gewürztraminer and the Riesling – which has little in common with the German variety. The Gewürz is an excellent apéritif, and is wonderful when drunk chilled on a summer's evening in an open-air café gazing fixedly in the direction of the blue line of the Vosges. The Pinot gris and the Riesling, of a good year and grower, would be served at lunch or dinner at the Crocodile, the best restaurant in the town (along with la Maison des Tanneurs) to which the more fortunate would be asked once during the session. So good was the food, and so large the helpings, that I found I could only manage one meal a day, the money saved being spent on a final visit to the *charcuterie* to buy small delights to take home.

I did not live entirely for pleasure. I prepared my maiden speech with care, although I have forgotten the theme. I began by reminding the Assembly of the dictum of Henry V, the Holy Roman Emperor, that he spoke French to his wife, Italian to his mistress and German to his horse. I shocked the interpreters, but my audience, which consisted of a scattering of octogenarian Belgian station-masters, remained unmoved, having succumbed to the effects of a six-course lunch at the Crocodile.

The Assembly did its work, such as it was, through a multiplicity of multi-national committees which divided on party lines. The British Tories kept themselves to themselves, resisting the embrace of the 'Christians'; likewise the Gaullists, who were generally against everybody and everything. The Left was thus much less fragmented, and the socialists of whatever nationality tended to dominate the work of the Assembly. There was much jockeying for office which added to the fun. Duncan Sandys and I broke ranks to vote for a nice old German socialist with an 'Old Bill' moustache, Georg Karl Ackerman, for the presidency of the Assembly. My favour was returned a year or so later when the socialist group supported me in my successful attempt to become the chairman of the WEU (Western European Union) Defence Committee in Paris.

Strasbourg was at its best in May and September. In January we would stand shivering in the sleet, waiting for taxis and even buses (I don't think I have been on a bus anywhere since the early seventies) to take us the two miles or so north to the Palais de l'Europe. Once inside, we divided our time between fleeting visits to the hemicycle to listen to the debate, and the café, where we would scramble for the English-language newspapers, drink small cups of bitter black coffee and gossip the hours away. Cars would be sent to pick up those of us fortunate enough to have been invited to some official lunch in Strasbourg; as for the rest of us, we would eat a modest lunch in the café. I would sometimes, when overcome by cafard, go to the pictures in the old town. I remember going to see *L'Histoire d'O*, the film of the pornographic novel; the lights went up at the interval (to cries of '*esquimaux gervais, chocolats, bons-bons*'), and I counted fifty Parliamentarians of every nationality huddled in their dirty raincoats. My chief memory of the January sessions is of congenial dinners in tiny restaurants; la Bourse aux Vins opposite the Sofitel was a particular favourite of mine; it was run by a formidable madame whose pretty daughter waited at table. Indeed, so popular was la Bourse that it was eventually bought up by a jealous Sofitel, who were wise enough to keep Madame firmly behind her *caisse*.

In May, Strasbourg, although it was popularly reckoned to suffer the worst climate in France and the poorest communications (points that were never put to Ernie Bevin or made by Pierre Pflimlin), was very much at its best. The sun shone brilliantly and the city and country were *en fête*. When the Assembly continued over a weekend the hospitality included the inevitable asparagus feasts, journeys by official cars into south Germany as far as Baden-Baden with short walks in the Black Forest, and coach rides to the Kaiserhof, Kaiser Bill's castle in the Vosges, thirty or so kilometres south of the city. This would be followed by lunch en masse at an *auberge*, and then by a curious spectacle in which live serpents were tossed in the direction of two secretary birds who prompty stamped on their heads and swallowed them to much Gallic applause. Perhaps the most pleasant outing of all was lunch *al fresco* with friends by the banks of some canal or riverside inn, where we would eat *matelote à la crème* (a dish made from freshwater fish) with buttery noodles and petit pois and drink much Pinot gris.

In October we would climb into a fleet of hired charabancs and follow *les routes des vins*, stopping frequently to sample the vintage to the sound of mayoral greetings and oompapa bands, sustained by roast-pork sandwiches and the gift of bottles to be shipped home on the return charter flight. Such festive days can be exhausting; we would return at seven o'clock in the evening, in my case at least to retire to Room 8 at l'Hôtel Gutenberg, where I would toss uneasily among the buzzing of the bees, striving to overcome the effects of over-indulgence.

Two events which took place at Strasbourg stand out: Dom Mintoff's visit and the opening of the newly built Palais de l'Europe by President Giscard. Mintoff, the Prime Minister of Malta, held the rotating chairmanship of the Council of Ministers at the time. He brought fraternal greetings to the Assembly and read out a bad-tempered, self-serving speech which was given the bird by the Assembly, not one socialist attempting to come to his aid.

The opening of the new Palais in 1976, built at vast expense to replace our prefabrication, was a very grand ceremony indeed (although not as grand as the opening of the Odeon, Swiss Cottage by Merle Oberon and Alexander Korda in the summer of 1939). The new Palais does in fact resemble the Odeon with each of its many floors painted a different colour and a hemicycle fit for Demosthenes, several restaurants, beauty salons and unisex hairdressers. France did not begrudge a single franc of its enormous cost, for Europe has yet to decide upon its capital city, Strasbourg, Luxembourg and Brussels still competing for the prize. Giscard himself did the honours, cutting the ribbon, kissing the *maire* on both cheeks, standing in line to receive the salutations of a thousand deputies.

If I was idle in Strasbourg, I was busy in Paris. The Western European Union had been set up in 1954 following the signing of the Brussels Treaty. The sessions of its Assembly were held in a brutal modernist building in the avenue Wilson (Woodrow not Harold), near the Trocadero in the 8th *arrondissement*. The building was brutal, but not as brutal as the modern tapestries with which its hemicycle was decorated. The Brussels Treaty committed the Western European allies to a common defence, and the Assembly, which consisted of

Parliamentarians drawn from the seven countries, Britain, France, the Federal Republic of Germany, Italy, Belgium, Holland and Luxembourg, met for a week at a time in December and June. As with the Council of Europe, the Assembly was subdivided into committees, each with its elected rapporteur and chairman. I determined to make myself the chairman of the Defence Committee, the first step being appointment as its rapporteur, responsible together with the Clerk of the committee Stuart Whyte for the writing and publication of twice-yearly reports of defence subjects (e.g. the first use of battlefield nuclear weapons; European arms procurement), which were debated and passed first by the committee, then by the Assembly as a whole. The final document would be solemnly sent to the foreign ministers of the seven and never heard of again.

It was a pleasure to return to Paris twenty or more years after Prue and I had tripped the light fantastic in 1951 while students at the Sorbonne. The face of the city had changed. Charles de Gaulle had become an airport. The familiar green buses had lost their open rear platforms and the city had been blighted by skyscrapers at La Defense and Montparnasse. The taxis had become sleeker, less box-like. Some even had women drivers, the front passenger seat occupied by an Alsatian dog. Only the smarter bistros had retained their brown paint and marble tops. But the Metro had kept its old characteristic smell (cheap scent, sweat and garlic), and apart from the modernized Neuilly-Vincennes system seemed not to have changed at all. Below ground, it was still *la belle époque*. The first-class compartments were bright red, the *portillons* automatic, and the staff as surly as they had been twenty years previously. The down-and-outs still slept on the platform benches out of the bitter cold of a December Paris night. One thing however had quite definitely changed: the klaxons against a background of which Gene Kelly had danced in *An American in Paris* had fallen silent, victims of the rigours of the Fifth Republic.

If there was a difference it was that I could afford to take taxis, an undreamed of luxury twenty years before. Paris was more expensive than Strasbourg, and I took care to spend my seventy-four pounds carefully. Hotels were not as cheap as the Gutenberg: I stayed a night or two at the Hôtel d'Alsace on the left bank but the room in which Oscar Wilde had so famously complained of the wallpaper ('either it or I will have to go') was booked up indefinitely by visiting Americans. Eventually, I moved to the vicinity of the Trocadero, staying often at the Windsor in the rue Delibes, and even at the Hôtel Lauristan in the rue Lauristan, although I was ignorant of the street's reputation as the home of the Milice, the French Gestapo, who had a house of torture there. The Germans had operated a similar establishment in the avenue Foch. With friends I would lunch most days at a *restaurant de quartier* on avenue Georges Mandel eating the dish of the day (a properly pink gigot) and drinking a half-bottle of Chenas. As a reward for writing a report, and getting it passed by the Assembly against the inevitable opposition of the Gaullists, the officers of the Defence Committee (the chairman when I joined was Edmund Nessler, a Gaullist deputy) would be invited to lunch at one of the great restaurants of Paris, like le Taillevent. It was always a set lunch, but very good of its kind. The Sancerre, clearly the house wine, was very much better than any of the Loire wines that I had had previously. Not unnaturally, French restaurants do tend to keep the best to themselves.

The military aspects of the Cold War and a love of wine competed for my attention in the six years I remained a member of the Western European Union. As the committee's rapporteur, I was responsible for more reports than ever before, travelling, with Stuart Whyte in tow, to take evidence to Turkey where I laid a wreath at the tomb of Kemal Atatürk. I was told by our ambassador to refer to him in my little speech as 'a great European'. I did so, but his tomb, which is near Ankara, is very un-European indeed; its style a cross between Hittite and Hollywood. In fact, there was scarcely an allied country we did not visit. We hired a retired German general, de Mazière, to redraw the battle-lines in central Europe, held a European arms procurement congress in Paris, went on exercises with the Italian Army in Sardinia, and paid several visits to Washington.

In 1974 I ran into Frank Laws-Johnson at Charles de Gaulle airport. In 1950, he had been my bank manager at Barclays in the rue Quatre Septembre, responsible for giving me my parental subvention of thirty pounds a month. He had done more besides; he had introduced me to his daughter Veronica, who was following the same course as I was at the Sorbonne. We became firm friends, as did Prue and she. Frank promptly invited me to stay with him and his wife Vera at their flat in Neuilly, and I did so three times a year for the next four years. In his sixties, Frank was remarkably fit and a championship-standard player of royal tennis. More to the point he was a wine buff, having bought up in the fifties the bankrupt stock of wine belonging to the Chapon Fin, a great restaurant in Bordeaux. Thus he acquired several thousand bottles, many of which littered his already cluttered apartment. Under my bed lay several cases of champagne.

Vera and Frank would give a dinner party on the occasion of my visits. I list the wines served at one such dinner for six guests not to boast, but to marvel. The food deliberately took second place; Vera cooking a chicken with rice, pâté, and a plate of excellent cheeses. We began with champagne, Mercier '61, then Meursault '44, Calon Segur '24, a magnum of Cheval Blanc '47 (described by

Hugh Johnson as 'the finest claret ever bottled') and a Montrose '22. I was drinking far above my station. Frank claimed that he had not spent more than a pound on any bottle in his cellar. The French guests were generally amazed; unless they are in the wine or restaurant trade, the French do not drink as well as the British might expect. They have existed on supermarket wine for years. My compatriots were dazzled by Frank's offerings, but one Scot somewhat less so. I forget his name but he claimed to be the last district officer in the British Empire – of the Solomon Islands – and he was on his way home to Fife. Tall, taciturn and gingery, looking rather like the actor Gordon Jackson, he broke his silence by suddenly saying to me across the table 'I have sent people to prison for adultery'. I said how lucky I was not to be a Melanesian.

When the debates in the avenue Wilson were more boring than usual (and no one was duller than Joseph Luns, the Secretary General of Nato; although he invariably divided his speech into English, French and German, he was totally incomprehensible in all three languages), I made my excuses and left. Once I retraced my footsteps to my old digs at 22 rue de Château Landon in the 10th, a working-class *arrondissement*, the apartment overlooking the railway lines leading to the Gare de l'Est. Sadly, the steam locomotives of my youth which had groaned upon the rail à la Housman twenty years ago as I had slept uneasily in my tiny bed had been replaced by diesel traction. Jean Gabin had given way to Gerard Depardieu. I walked back to the Métro Gare de l'Est, and returned, stop by stop, to the Trocadero.

On another occasion, I took a bus to the boulevard Saint-Germain and walked up past l'Ecole de Médecin on to the boulevard Saint-Michel. The cake shop where I entertained Elizabeth Copeman to tea in November 1950, thereby meeting Prue when they were both living in the rue de Moscou, was still serving rich teas. I walked along la rue des Ecoles, looking for la rue de la Place and Chez Henri, the tiny restaurant where Prue, Veronica, David Stern, John Grisewood and I would eat lunch almost every day. We ate steaks with relish; they were undoubtedly horse; also *radis au beurre*, *filet d'hareng* and the lovely oily potato salad that only the French can achieve. Sadly, the street had been redeveloped and Chez Henri was replaced by a hideous block of flats. I sought the Institut Britannique where we had spent long hours reading the continental *Daily Mail* and playing liar dice, but it also had been turned into flats. I strolled down past the Panthéon, across the Boul Mich to the Luxembourg Gardens, with its complement of elderly men wearing berets (symbol of Vichy?), past the Théâtre de l'Odeon and back to Saint Germain. Here, at least, nothing much had changed: the 100,000 Chemises, where I had bought my shirts, the pavement cafés with their heated terraces, the crowds of students; there were fewer duffle-coats perhaps, and hair was worn longer. The cinemas which Prue and I had patronized more assiduously than the lecture halls were in place, one of which was still showing *Citizen Kane, version originale*. Wearied by so much nostalgia, I took a taxi to the British Embassy and drank champagne with the Hendersons. I could not have done so twenty years before with the Duff-Coopers.

It is difficult to resist the flattery of ambassadors. The Council of Europe had a British ambassador all to itself, resident in Strasbourg, good for a delegation party three times a year. But he was in a different league from the splendours of the Paris embassy. I lunched and dined there with 'Nikko' Henderson who was later to be posted to Washington. In Paris, he and his Greek wife were in the Cooper class. The guests at one lunch in 1977 included Baron Philip de Rothschild (we drank Lafite), Katharine Graham, the owner of the *Washington Post* (she asked me what it was like to have a woman leader; I said it was like being at home all day), and a nice Italian admiral who as a young man had been the gunnery officer in the battleship *Vittorio Veneto* at the battle of Cape Matapan ('you had radar; we did not'). The conversation turned to the Windsors, living half-embalmed in a great house in the west end of the city. I asked how was Mrs Simpson. 'You mean the Duchess of Windsor,' said Lady Henderson severely. She then told of a recent dinner-party she had attended chez Windsor. The chef had been among the finest in Paris. After dinner, the party withdrew to the drawing-room where the Duke took up his embroidery, carefully sewed the legend 'I love you' upon it, then stood up and solemnly presented it to the Duchess. 'Very un-English' was Lady Henderson's disapproving Attic comment.

Lord Gladwyn was a Liberal delegate to the Western European Union. Once when I was speaking from the rostrum a clerk passed me a note which read 'Lunch with me, Gladwyn'. I was happy to do so. We drove, via the British Embassy, where Gladwyn had served with such distinction some years previously, to his club in the Marais, so smart, rumour had it, that only Giscard's relations were among its members. While drinking an apéritif we were approached by a nervous waiter who inquired whether a table had been booked. Gladwyn, who was as formidable as he is distinguished, looked him in the eye and said '*Je suis l'ancien ambassadeur anglais en France*'. The waiter withdrew. Upon our second apéritif I noticed a more senior figure plucking up courage to speak to my host. '*Une table, c'est impossible* . . . you have not paid your subscription since . . .' Gladwyn raised himself to his full height and replied '*Je suis l'ancien ambassadeur de la Reine Britannique en France.*' The steward capitulated and we were shown promptly to a table. The lunch, which was as good as

131

Gladwyn's sang-froid had been admirable, must have been very expensive indeed. I have long admired Gladwyn, a fine old Whig with strongly held pro-European views. As chairman of the Government Hospitality Committee, he was for many years responsible for the wine served at official lunches and dinners. Not surprisingly, he was an old friend of the Frank Laws-Johnsons.

The twin hazards of political life abroad are boredom and the remorseless hospitality. The composition of the Tory delegation rarely changed; the 'colleagues' could stay on for as long as they wished, providing they did not make a nuisance of themselves by borrowing money and failing to pay it back. Many grew old in the restaurants of Paris and Strasbourg. The Labour party shuffled its pack more frequently, and I spent time with the more congenial newcomers like Dick Mabon and John Roper, both of whom were later to join the Social Democrats. Our friendship would not have gone unnoticed by the sillier old things on our side.

In time, Simon Wingfield Digby surrendered the leadership of the British delegation to Sir John Rodgers whose remarkable conviviality – at every party and reception he was first in and last out – set the tone for the Tories in Strasbourg. After some years and much intrigue he was succeeded as leader by the less-pleasant Sir Frederic Bennett MP for Torquay ('I have four houses and the gold plate is in London'), a rich banker married to a sweet wife, who insisted on driving to Strasbourg three times a year in his enormous Roller, where its shining paintwork was inevitably scratched by the local *mauvais garçons*. Paul Channon was on the delegation for a time and seriously considered standing for the presidency of the Council of Europe. Reggie Maudling had apparently told him that Margaret Thatcher had said she had no time for that multi-millionaire, and Paul, in consequence, felt that he had no future back home. Happily we managed to argue him out of so insubstantial an ambition. And Margaret did find time to put him briefy in her cabinet.

It would be churlish to complain about the remorseless hospitality that accompanied such trips abroad. It is very pleasing to be met at airports by the ambassadorial Rolls and driven to one's modest hotel behind a fluttering Union flag. But *vins d'honneur* and mayoral receptions call for a lot of standing around recruiting oneself with champagne, while grabbing tit-bits from passing waitresses. And foreigners, even the very best sort, to say nothing of one's colleagues, can be en masse both inaudible and wearying. I enjoyed formal lunches, and *dîners intimes*; I soon abandoned large receptions larded with speeches, all of which needed translating into at least two languages.

MPs when travelling abroad, whether officially or off-duty, can call upon the British embassy for succour and support. I did so during a Council of Europe committee visit to Vienna, inviting myself to stay with the ambassador and his wife. The embassy is a huge nineteenth-century building on the Ring; we dined in some splendour in the company of a group of Austrian aristos, including the man who had rescued the horses of the Spanish Riding School from the advancing Russians. Most embarrassingly, my wallet was pinched along with most of my money. I suspected the valet (shades of Cicero), but was reluctant to complain to the ambassador. I did so to the Foreign Office on my return, but heard no more of it. The episode served to discourage me from inviting myself to stay with ambassadors again.

In Lisbon, I had a happier experience. In the summer of 1976, I was asked to stay with the Ures – John Ure was then the first secretary at the embassy – in their flat over looking the Tagus. My hosts told of the day President Caetano was overthrown and a Portugese frigate sailed up the river, and its main armament trained on the jubilant crowds celebrating the coup in Black Horse Square. Just as the ship seemed ready to open fire with what would have been catastrophic effect, she turned about and sailed down the river towards the open sea. It transpired that the captain had given orders to open fire, but his officers and crew had refused to do so.

By 1979, I had had enough of service abroad. It certainly killed any desire to stand for the European Parliament. Seven years of fogbound airports, uncomprehending constituents and peripheral concerns cured my itchy feet. The action, as I was ruefully to discover, takes place at home. I gained vastly in knowledge of defence, and in self-confidence, and the money saved by a regime of lunchtime omelettes (in the absence of an invitation to lunch at someone else's expense) helped with the school fees. But I stayed abroad too long. While I scoured the kiosks for the *Herald Tribune*, Margaret Thatcher defeated Ted Heath in the Peasants' Revolt of 1975, the Conservative party took on a Cromwellian tinge, and my contemporaries won preferment. I would have done better to stay put and congratulate shadow ministers on the quality of their speeches. My sojourn abroad was foolish, but it was fun.

16 The Rise of Petticoat Government

The Aldershot constituency is 'the Home of the British Army', and there are road signs to that effect posted all around the town. Should one drive to attention? The army town had been rebuilt in the sixties with the help of John Poulson (it has had to be largely rebuilt since), and somewhere among the tatty barracks, grounded Dakotas and vehicle car parks is a plaque commemorating the opening of the new buildings by 'James Ramsden', who had been a junior War Office minister in Harold Macmillan's government, the same Ramsden whom I had so upset by my *Spectator* article entitled 'The Watch on the Weser', in which I had listed the order of battle of Nato's forces on the Central Front. The brick gates to the original Victorian barracks were retained, through which several million men must have marched, including my mother's three brothers, Campbell, Sidney and Oscar, in two world wars. The Prince Consort's Library is an attractive late-Victorian survivor, but the wooden 'Summer Palace' where Victoria and Albert used to stay when they reviewed the army in the great days of Aldershot did not escape the planners' zeal.

That the sovereign should be a frequent visitor to Aldershot is hardly surprising, but what is astonishing is that there should be the tomb of a Napoleon and his empress in nearby Farnborough. Louis Napoleon died in Chislehurst in 1872 and I persuaded the local authority to mount a celebratory lunch (and service in the abbey) to mark the centenary. The Empress Eugénie had lived in Farnborough until the early years of this century. The tomb, which also includes the body of the Prince Imperial, killed fighting with the British in the Zulu War (Queen Victoria once remarked that he looked like a hairdresser but that has not prevented a nearby pub being called after him), is a smaller version of L'Hôtel des Invalides in Paris, and its roof can be glimpsed from Farnborough station rising proudly above the trees. With Republican rectitude, the French ambassador refused to attend the ceremonies, but the Bonaparte family, including the Pretender, arrived in force; small, sinister men in double-breasted black suits, with taller, blonde wives, the men looking like so many mafiosi.

As I have said, the Queen was a frequent visitor. Her most memorable visit occurred in 1974 when the Old Contemptibles were finally wound down. There was a service at the garrison church, and tea in the gymnasium. Perhaps a hundred veterans, their wives, and many widows attended, the veterans in their nineties, survivors of the original seven thousand (out of twenty-five thousand) who had borne the brunt of the great German offensive through Belgium and Flanders in the late summer and autumn of 1914. Haldane's old regular army had earned the Kaiser's contempt. The padre compared their feat of arms to that of Drake and the defeat of the Spanish Armada. The Queen sat alone between the choir stalls, and after a short service received for safe keeping banners from a dozen representatives of the Old Contemptibles. When at the end of the service the congregation rose and sang 'Land of Hope and Glory' no eye was dry. The ceremony stirred those deeply held patriotic feelings the British now hide beneath layers of protective paint; the veterans frail but proud, the last of a generation capable of sacrifice and endurance beyond our capabilities whose strength and discipline was drawn from the long and stable years of Victorian England. We wept for our past, and for our future.

There was an element of comedy. The Queen, sitting splendidly alone before the altar, was accosted by the verger who insisted on rattling a collection bag under her nose, despite the convention that the sovereign does not carry money on her person. As he persisted, the Queen began to rummage desperately in her handbag, tossing out predictable flotsam. After what seemed an age, she evidently found something, pushed it firmly into the verger's bag, and we all breathed again.

The same year, 1974, was the year of the two elections. The first took place on 28 February. I remember Ted Heath coming to the '22; the atmosphere was not ecstatic, but resolute. Most of 'the colleagues' seemed confident enough, encouraged by the very evident signs of apprehension shown by the Labour party. 'Who Governs?' seemed a good enough slogan at the time, and the Prime Minister's speech was a blend of firmness and moderation; 'this must not be a union-bashing election' was his message. The House had that end-of-term atmosphere I remembered from 1964, and I could not escape a twinge of anxiety although my majority in Aldershot was fourteen times larger than it had been in Rochester and Chatham.

Many of the old things were not standing at the election: Fitzroy Maclean, whom I admired and had got to know well, Simon Wingfield Digby with whom I had drunk *les vins d'Alsace*, John Peel, whose wife had given to all the delegation wives in Strasbourg the gift of a rubber-tipped saucepan-scourer, much to their bewilderment, Sir Robert Cary, and Sir Geoffrey Lloyd, an exquisite homosexual who had inherited the Birmingham 'machine' from the Chamberlain family and had once been Stanley Baldwin's PPS. I noted in my diary the imminent arrival of some very able people who had been adopted for safe Tory seats; they included Nigel Lawson, John MacGregor (who had succeeded me as chairman of the Bow Group in 1967), Douglas Hurd and Leon Brittan. 'The competition,' I wrote anxiously 'will be stiffer.'

There was to be one other famous casualty: Enoch Powell. His disenchantment with the Heath government was total; he had opposed entry into Europe and set his face against an incomes policy. Heath and he also loathed one another. An incident in the Chamber which took place at the end of the Parliament passed almost unnoticed. Anthony Barber, the Chancellor of the Exchequer, got into difficulties over whether or not the effect of the rise in oil prices was inflationary or deflationary, and Denis Healey, Nicholas Ridley and Enoch, who was sitting next to me on the government benches below the gangway, rose in turn to interrupt. Barber was clearly in some difficulty. Then Enoch again half-rose to his feet and with a sweep of his arms cried loudly 'imbecility, imbecility' (his Black Country intonation was very obvious) in the general direction of the government front bench. I caught sight of Spencer le Marchant, a very large Tory whip who was in normal circumstances renowned for his conviviality, bearing down upon Enoch, presumably to sort him out. Hurriedly, Enoch's neighbours grasped at his coat and hissed at him to sit down. Happily, he did so just in time. It was to be Enoch's last appearance in the House as a Conservative; his withdrawal from his seat at Wolverhampton was announced the next day and his opinion, expressed publicly during the election, that the nation should vote Labour, might well have tipped the balance against the party. If so, Enoch's revenge on Ted Heath (and the Tory party) was complete.

My fifth election took place in high winds and driving rain, the candidate and his small band of brave supporters standing shivering at street corners or sitting, unwarmed by oratory, in freezing school halls. It passed without incident. An election in a safe seat is fought within a self-contained world into which news of the outside filters as if into a city besieged. It did appear for a time as if the Tories were winning, but the polls flattered only to deceive. We polled more votes than Labour nationally, but won fewer seats. My majority dropped to just over ten thousand or 17 per cent of the vote. The Labour vote – their candidate came third – was, at fifteen thousand, the highest figure reached in any of my Aldershot elections. My result was fractionally better than Guildford (David Howell), and very much better than in neighbouring Farnham where the Liberals ran Maurice Macmillan quite close.

Living in Farnham as we did, we were quickly made aware of a whispering campaign waged against Maurice by the Liberals; it was well known that he was a reformed alcoholic who now never touched a drink. Nevertheless, stories as to his being seen 'weaving' in and out of the shops in Downing Street, Farnham, or being spotted drunk and incapable in some Surrey village, all of which were flagrantly untrue, did the rounds of our friends and acquaintances in the town. Such canards were gleefully spread by his political opponents. The potency of the Liberal challenge in the first of the two 1974 elections was revealed by the fact that Michael McNair-Wilson only held on to Newbury by a thousand votes (intimations of the 1993 by-election in that seat), while Mark Woodnutt who was defending the Isle of Wight with a seventeen thousand majority lost it to the Liberals by seven thousand votes. Woodnutt's reputation was, however, tarnished by his financial dealings. Despite the unscrupulous nature of much (not all) Liberal campaigning, the party did best against sitting Conservatives who had made themselves personally vulnerable by either neglect or nefariousness.

What does a candidate achieve? He rarely wins votes, although he can campaign on the basis of a reputation already won. His real function is to rally his troops. At elections there is a renewal of the honeymoon period between a candidate and his supporters (Chips Channon once wrote that fighting an election was like having a hectic love affair). He is no longer 'the Member' but their candidate, chosen once again by them. In the electoral battle, he forges new friendships and renews old ones. In theory, at least, they should be enough to last out a Parliament; the accumulation of credit in the bank on which he can readily draw when he needs to. In the seventies, I accumulated quite a sum, most of which I had to draw upon during Mrs Thatcher's eighties.

The tedium of the campaign was sadly interrupted by the death of my mother. She had had a kidney removed during the war, when we lived at the Royal Naval Hospital, Barrow Gurney, and her remaining one now began to fail. She was admitted to SS John and Elizabeth's hospital in St John's Wood where she had been a frequent visitor. She had in recent years lived a miserable life, racked by continual ill-health. I drove to London but mother was in a coma and failed to recognize me. I left sadly for home, convinced that she was dying. I was filled with the terror of death; the terror of dissolution. Charles Snow writes somewhere that to the dying the most appalling thing must be the prospect of disintegration and a fearful sense of loneliness. After dinner I sat in the Castle Street drawing-room and listened to Melissa, who was seven, laughing while she took her bath. I thought of Mother as she would have been seventy years ago in the cottage at Wistanstow, bathing in a tin tub before the kitchen fire, as happy and high-spirited. Both Mother and Melissa might have been the same person; the one the product of the other, the child given the gift of life by her dying grandmother. Trite perhaps, but apt, and a little comforting. We achieve a kind of immortality through those whom we have helped to create.

The next morning Mother had rallied a little and was conscious. We all four drove up from Farnham to see her on a grey, February day, the houses en route along the A3 and across London displaying their election colours. She was very weak but recognized us. Heather held the three-year-old Joshua up in her arms for Mother to see.

But the damage was done, and she would not last much longer. She told the ward sister that she wanted to be buried in Golders Green, a typically unsentimental, even astringent remark. She died on the Thursday before polling day and was cremated at a shabby little ceremony at Golders Green. How she would have hated it. In March, I drove my father and Nicholas to Shropshire, where Mother's ashes were buried next to her niece Daisy's grave in Wistanstow churchyard. Father's brother and sister-in-law, Michael and Doris, Uncle Campbell, and his widowed sister-in-law, Aunt Annie, John and Joyce, Campbell and Margaret, Nicholas and I, made up the mourners. It was a deathly cold day, with driving rain and snow. In the evening we entertained our Shropshire relations to an undistinguished 'supper' at the Lion at Leintwardine. Cold pork pie and undressed salad. So my mother, born in 1898 in a labourer's cottage 'up the Common', at Wistanstow, nurse, midwife and doctor's wife, and such fun as I remember her before she was struck down so early by failing health, completed her life's journey. May she lie peacefully under Wenlock Edge.

The defeated Tories reassembled at Westminster in a state of shock. A second election was inevitable, and the likelihood of a second Labour victory à la 1964/66 so strong as to weaken Tory morale severely. Dissatisfaction with Ted Heath, which had been kept within bounds in the years of his premiership, grew apace. He had never been a popular figure. His intense shyness which manifested itself in a reluctance to engage in small talk is perhaps best illustrated by this story which gained wide currency in the early seventies. Mrs Sara Morrison, the wife of Tory MP Charlie Morrison, was made a vice-chairman of the party with the brief, so said the wags, 'to turn Ted into a human being'. They both attended the agents' annual dinner which is traditionally held on the eve of the party conference at Blackpool, Bournemouth or Brighton. Sarah noticed that conversation between the Prime Minister and the wife of the chief agent had dried up, so she wrote on her napkin 'For God's sake say something', folded it carefully and passed it up through the diners to the top table. Ted received it, opened it up, glanced at the message and wrote 'I have' before passing it back.

To his intimates Ted Heath was both warm and friendly, but his intimates did not include the great majority of Tory back-benchers, some of whom, at least, still carried scars inflicted by Ted when he was the party's Chief Whip at the time of Suez. He was a highly competent Prime Minister (Reggie Maudling told the '22 in my hearing that Ted was the most effective of the three Tory Prime Ministers under whom he had served) with none of the dictatorial qualities which Mrs Thatcher was to show when in office. But he had made enemies. The anti-European wing of the party, small but vociferous, never forgave him for bringing about Britain's entry into the Community. The traditional right-wing, the 'Suez rebels' and the Smith Lobby over Rhodesia, condemned Ted, as they had Harold Macmillan previously, as 'pink': a left-wing Tory only too eager to sell the whites in Africa 'down the river'. And the 'new' Right which combined a Powellite nationalism (John Biffen) with a doctrinaire adherence to free trade (Nicholas Ridley) was rebuffed by Ted's U-turn in the face of rising unemployment. Selsdon Man had died in infancy. All the Tory leaders of my experience have had their share of enemies; disloyalty the Tory party's secret weapon, not loyalty as Lord Kilmuir once proclaimed. But the idealism over Europe with which Ted Heath sought to suffuse the Tory party was never quite enough; in contrast, Mrs Thatcher's noisy populism was far more to the taste of simpler Conservatives.

After the long summer recess which I spent in part in Alderney with Heather and our two children, Tory MPs were summoned to the ballroom of the Europa Hotel in Grosvenor Square in September 1974 in anticipation of a second election. Edward du Cann presided over the gathering with his usual aplomb, while the ghost of Lord (Henry) Brooke at whose feet I had sat at the Hampstead Young Conservatives in the late forties, sat unblinking on the platform. He had become terribly thin. Willie Whitelaw apologized handsomely for a leak from our manifesto and was as handsomely forgiven. Ted Heath made a curious speech, calling for national unity. Morale among those of 'the colleagues' to whom I managed to speak seemed low. We were haunted by the memories of the 1966 election when Harold Wilson, widely regarded as the Baldwin of the age, had rebounded back to office with a large majority. Keith Joseph, a charming Jew with a nice talent for self-destruction, had seemingly just been 'converted' to Conservatism, having been in the past a collectivist. At least, he had said as much in a speech which struck a chord among many Conservatives. Perhaps defeat had rendered us a touch hysterical? The phoney political war between March and July (only three major votes in the Commons, the Tories being unwilling to precipitate an election), had served to weaken still further Ted's hold on the party. Were we to lose the election his position as leader of the party would be untenable.

If one general election a year is more than enough, two is a monstrous imposition. The reward for re-election is the warm refuge that is the Palace of Westminster; three weeks of public exposure equalling at least four years of comparative comfort. Six weeks, or more, of public exposure in one year merits a seat in the House of Lords. Once again I went through the motions. I walked up and down shopping parades shaking hands, hung around the schools furtively like a child molester, waiting for mums to collect their young, and made infrequent speeches in British Legion halls. I have never had the temperament for fighting elections; the sight of an orange Liberal bill in the window of a house that surely sported blue six months previously plunges me into depression. In the event I need not have worried. My share of the vote fell by 1 per cent and my majority rose by the same amount.

I suppose we did as a party rather better than we feared. A 10 per cent drop in the voter turnout kept the Labour party's overall majority down to three; 1974 mark 2 was not to be another 1945. Once the dust had settled, the Tory party reassembled at Westminster in an even worse mood than when we left it. David Walder who sat on the executive of the '22 told me that it was unanimously of the view that Ted should go. But he seemed in no hurry to do so. It was bruited about that Willie – the heir apparent? – was telling his friends ('in total confidence') that Ted was not behaving like a gentleman. He should have resigned.

Some amusement was caused by the sight of stout Tories scrambling over garden walls. The TV cameras had been alerted by Conservative Central Office (who had in turn been tipped off by the wife of one of the conspirators) that the officers and executive of the '22 were to meet secretly at the Milk Street offices of one of du Cann's doomed city enterprises. When rumbled they fled in all directions, some into the hands of the press. Du Cann himself was believed to have leapt boldly through his garden window, and, unscathed, climbed the wall to freedom. Was it the first of his nine lives?

Alan and Jane Clark invited me to a party at their Albany flat. I had been rereading Chips Channon's diaries and, spotting Julian Amery (who looks and sounds as if he had stepped straight out of them), congratulated him on a mention. We talked about Field Marshal Wavell and the fact that Channon had fallen in love with him, a passion only dented by Wavell's habit of wearing

Chips' suits. Amery told me that Wavell had dined with Nancy Cunard who asked the somewhat taciturn soldier what he thought about love. He replied to the effect that love is like a cigar: superb when it is lit for the first time, never quite as good on being relit. Amery said that Chips was an elegant homosexual who took immense pains with his social life. 'He seemed always to be living on top of his form.' Alan was as attentive as one might expect from an ambitious right-winger with time to make up. He had a clear interest in a change at the top. Jane, who is much younger, could have passed as Alan's daughter.

We Tories could talk about nothing but Ted Heath. Should he go? Who would run against him? I dined in the House with Norman Fowler, David Walder and Jim Prior. Midway through the cabinet pudding, Heath appeared and greeted Prior warmly, 'Good to see you'; there was lots of shoulder shaking, but by no word, glance or gesture did he acknowledge the existence of the rest of us. As he left, Jim, who had been his PPS, said to us despairingly 'What on earth can I do with him?'

On Thursday 31 October, the 1922 Committee met for the first time in the new Parliament. Edward du Cann greased the meeting in his customary manner and announced that eighteen members had sent in their names to speak in what had been billed as an inquisition into the state of the party. The inquisition (inquest?) was opened by Kenneth Lewis, the Member for Rutland. Lewis, a prosperous travel agent and a cheerful eccentric of no great weight in the party, spoke rather well and concluded reluctantly that Ted should go. The applause was quite generous. The '22, responding heartily to 'Walder's Law' (that the first three people to speak on any subject at the '22 are mad), then fielded what amounted to its first eleven. Robin Maxwell-Hyslop (widely regarded as a nasty bit of work), Norman Tebbit (about whom Ted Heath was later to say that on no account would he have ever given him a job), Ken Warren (an engaging schoolboy) and Sir John Rodgers (inaudible but repetitive in either English or French) all went in to bat for the same side. A touch of comedy was provided by Hugh Fraser, one of the steadily diminishing number of toffs in the party, who muddied the waters by calling for the party's electorate (MPs) to be widened to include various party worthies from the National Union. At this there were loud cries of 'No'. Fraser then paid Lewis a series of extravagant compliments spoilt only by the fact that Lewis became Harris, an error that was greeted with much hilarity. Fraser, who looked as if he might have ridden with Montrose, clearly had no time for travel agents. Reggie Maudling said that as he had failed either to 'emerge' or be elected, his views on the leadership might not amount to much, but he backed Ted. The debate, which lasted an hour or so, was also contributed to by Anthony Meyer who defended Ted Heath, as did John Loveridge. It was concluded by the two Freddies, Burden and Bennett; regardless of what they had to say, which was not a great deal, it would be hard to say which of the two was the more unpleasant.

After an hour or so of debate, we adjourned and went and sat in the Smoking Room. Michael Alison, churchy and right-wing, stopped me and said that what had happened upstairs in Committee Room 14 'Must mean the sack'. I said nothing but sat with John Biffen, Peter Tapsell, Nigel Lawson and Norman Lamont, none of whom was a Heath loyalist. It seemed that the tactics now were to re-elect the old officers and executive of the '22 and for the reconstituted committee to 'request' formally that Heath offer himself for re-election.

I was no longer a supporter of Ted Heath. Some of my reasons were less creditable than others. I was piqued by the dinner-table snub and disappointed that my talents, such as they were, had not been recognized during the period of his leadership. I was weary of having continually to defend him in private to my constituents, the less charitable of whom made frequent allusions to his sexuality. 'Why hasn't he a wife?' was the complaint of the stupid and the ill disposed. My response, which was to emphasize his sporting prowess, his music and his achievement in taking us into Europe, was inevitably countered by references to his unattractive manner on the box, the three-day week, and his bachelor status. The voters of Aldershot evidently much preferred dull wives to no wives at all.

More creditably, I had come to the conclusion that Ted Heath had not the quality that Napoleon demanded of his marshals: he was not lucky. We had lost three of the four general elections the party had fought under his leadership. The first in 1966 could be forgiven, but the adverse effect of the twin defeats of 1974 on the party's rank and file, and on its MPs, would be difficult to exaggerate. It is the vanity of Conservatives to believe themselves to be 'the natural party of Government'; to find themselves once again in opposition to Harold Wilson, a man for whom most of them felt an unjustified contempt, was bitter indeed. Heath seemed to disregard the small change of politics; he wasted no time in gossip (which is, like humbug, one of the essential lubricants of public life), and he would be unlikely to know the name of one's wife. He was crippled by shyness.

It was time for a change, but to whom? In November and December 1974, the names most often mentioned included Edward du Cann (could we really have been serious?), Keith Joseph (until he made a fool of himself in a speech in Birmingham when he blamed the working class for their daft kiddies), Willie Whitelaw (but would he stand against Ted? – it appeared not) and Mrs

Margaret Thatcher, about whom the usual view was that she was a clever woman but with far too narrow a focus. 'We would all be obliged to take refuge in our clubs,' I was told by Ian Gilmour. That was no comfort as I had no club, having resigned from the Garrick to save money on my return to the House four years before. The old things, when asked about Margaret, usually mumbled something about the party not putting up with petticoat government.

The re-election of the officers and the executive of the '22 all went according to plan. Du Cann was even given an ovation by the full committee. The '22 was thus the focus of an incipient revolt; its officers and executive parading up and down the committee corridors like so many revolutionary Portuguese 'colonels' with roses stuck up the muzzles of their rifles. The request to Ted to attend and address the committee was fixed for Thursday 14 November. I wrote in my diary: 'Ted was dignified, even courageous. He reminded the committee that his predecessors had endured similar unpopularity. He said he would consider the means whereby a leader might be re-elected (Alec Douglas-Home had resigned in 1965, leaving the field open to contenders), but he made no secret of the fact that he, himself, would stand.' It was also reported that a committee had been set up to consider an election and all its ramifications. Its members were to include Heath, Peter Carrington and du Cann. As the committee had a pro-Ted majority, the antis feared that their flank had been turned. Ted's speech was quite humble in parts, and he went on to say that he would be calling more widely upon back-benchers for occasional front-bench performances. He was applauded, somewhat coolly, for all of seven seconds. He then left the room and the usual fourth-raters took the floor for an inconclusive and ill-tempered debate. If it is necessary for politicians to succeed first to disguise their ignorance, and then to make a virtue out of their limitations, it is remarkable how few Tories have in my time managed to do so. But a career in politics is open to men of huge talent, and those with none.

Tory MPs, returning to the House after a Christmas break to sit dolefully upon the opposition benches, could talk of little else save for the forthcoming leadership contest. Keith Joseph ('if we must be led by a Jew, let it be by a romantic Jew', David Walder) withdrew his challenge to Ted Heath. Joseph was clever enough to know his limitations; riddled with self-doubt, he would have been a hopeless party leader. Edward du Cann was considered by those who mattered in the party as not being 'sixteen annas to the rupee', Robert Carr ('the nicest man in London') was not thought up to the job. Willie Whitelaw refused to run, showing as much loyalty to Heath as he was later, as the non-playing captain of the wets, to show to Margaret Thatcher when she was

Premier. He, too, always 'played the game'. Thus the field was left open to Margaret Thatcher, aided and abetted by Airey Neave who had reasons of his own for disliking Ted; together they began to collect the votes of the disgruntled and the disenchanted to add to the old and 'new' right wing of the party.

Neave had scored a 'home run' from Colditz and was regarded as a war hero (he was not the only one in the House: Tony Barber, Francis Pym and Fitzroy Maclean were among several others), but he had little political influence. He had suffered a minor heart attack as a junior minister and had been obliged to relinquish his office. Heath was reported to have said to Neave that his coronary had put an end to his career. Neave took exception to Heath's bluntness and devoted his talent for intrigue and capacity for detail to bringing Ted down. Had he not been murdered in the Commons car park by the Irish National Liberation Front he would have served Margaret in Ireland.

What was known about Margaret? She was a complex, improbable and paradoxical figure; a grocer's daughter with an accent not entirely her own. She was clearly an outsider in what was still an insiders' party. She was bumptious. Peter Rawlinson, who had been Harold Macmillan's Attorney General wrote in *A Price too High* of his first meeting in 1959 with Mrs Thatcher. They had attended a meeting held for Tory MPs who were barristers, sitting at the feet of the then Attorney, the redoubtable Reginald Manningham-Buller. Mrs Thatcher was – wrote Rawlinson – pretty, well-coiffed but disturbingly tight-lipped. She spoke with a vehemence rather too exaggerated for the subject and had the irritating habit of putting the emphasis on the wrong word. She was, according to the author, duly swatted by Reggie Bullying-Manner. Those were the days.

That early snapshot seems to me to have caught a good deal of Margaret. Rawlinson describes another incident which is worth retelling: after retiring from the bar, Rawlinson offered to do voluntary public work. This message was promptly returned by the Cabinet Secretary, Robert Armstrong: 'He can expect no preferment from me.' Rawlinson, who was already in the Lords, was not in search of preferment.

Of the many books that have been written about Margaret Thatcher (her own work *Margaret Thatcher, the Downing Street Years* is more of a manifesto than a memoir), Hugo Young's *One of Us* is the best. I will claim credit for his title. Cecil Parkinson told me in 1980 that whenever Michael Heseltine's name was mentioned in Margaret's presence she would mutter 'he is not one of us'. I promptly used it in one of my newspaper articles. It stuck. Hugo Young makes many good points about Margaret, not least that all the major influences in the development of Margaret Roberts were men, in particular her father Alderman Alfred Roberts of Grantham.

In the eighties, at her apogee, I visited Grantham to write a piece for the *Telegraph*. The town once voted 'the most boring in England' is one long main street with a handsome church and close with Georgian houses. Alderman Roberts' famous shop, Number 1 The Parade, was in the twenties and thirties on the old A1, but by 1985 Grantham had been by-passed and the shop turned into a restaurant. At least the back room (the parlour?) was the restaurant, the shop had been lovingly recreated as a typical thirties shop with pots of Roberts' jam for sale. The scales on which the young Margaret had learnt how to cope with the nation's housekeeping, were given pride of place. It was, in effect, a shrine.

Margaret's mother played little part in her life as did her unknown elder sister, Muriel, who was to marry a farmer. Her father, a formidable Independent in local politics, was the decisive influence. His robe-clad portrait hangs in what was the town hall. He taught her the Victorian virtues. I sought in vain for any evidence of his daughter's fame, but apart from the shop/restaurant, then called The Premier, there was none. There was a statue of Isaac Newton but no Margaret Thatcher Street. There was, however, a junky souvenir shop next to the station on the old LNER main line which sold mugs on which there was stuck a transfer of a sugary small girl under which was the legend 'I was a proper little madam'. Was it Baby Jane Hudson or Margaret Hilda Roberts? Who knows? I took one home as a souvenir.

When Margaret Roberts married Denis Thatcher she cut all ties with her early life. She broke, as Hugo Young claims, 'with her town, her class and her religion'. Denis Thatcher, who became perhaps unfairly something of a figure of fun, was a prosperous member of the commercial middle class, a member of the Church of England (Margaret was brought up as a Methodist) whose political views reflected not so much the Anglican church as 'middle England'. He was rich enough for his wife never to be in any sense dependent upon her parliamentary salary. Mrs Thatcher also owed something to Edward Heath. The Tory party had voted for a carpenter's son as its leader in 1965; in 1975, once again in opposition, it voted for a grocer's daughter. In 1970, Ted Heath put Mrs Thatcher in his cabinet as Secretary of State for Education; she was the obligatory woman. Geoffrey Howe told me that Ted's cabinet had consisted of several circles; Mrs Thatcher sat like Uranus in the outermost ring, her opinions rarely, if ever, canvassed. She was a silent supporter of the Heath government who, after Ted's defeat but not before, was only too happy to rock a sunken boat.

In the 1975 Leadership election I voted for Mrs Thatcher, but I was no 'Thatcherite' for there was then no such thing. Many Tories from the centre and left of the party voted for her. She won, and won comfortably, for no better reason than that she was not Ted Heath. Willie Whitelaw would have enjoyed an even larger majority. Margaret saw her chance and took it. She was new, she was a woman and she was unsullied by defeat. Later I was to call her election 'the Peasants' Revolt', and the name caught on. It was a revolt in the sense that the party's establishment, by and large, stayed with Heath; it was a backbenchers's revolt led by the officers and executive of the 1922 Committee. Mrs Thatcher herself used the term 'fellow revolutionaries' to describe her supporters in the civil war that was to convulse the Tory party for the next fifteen years.

After she had been elected, the parliamentary party was once again summoned to the ballroom of the Europa Hotel, this time to witness her coronation. Ted Heath, who had gone to Spain to lick his wounds, sent a reluctant telegram of congratulation. Quintin Hogg and Willie Whitelaw both made speeches. Mrs Thatcher, looking radiant, told the party to pull up its socks. 'We have work to do', was her message. As the party left the hotel, I fell in step with Geoffrey Howe. He had tears in his eyes. 'I would draw my sword for her,' he told me. He was to do as much, and to great effect, in November 1990.

17 Opposition Forces

While the Tory party was in opposition in the late seventies, I had two strings to my bow: defence and broadcasting, or television to be more accurate. I gave up my chairmanship of the WEU's Defence Committee at the end of 1977, but succeeded at long last in being elected one of the three vice-chairmen of the party's back-bench Defence Committee. Margaret chose 'the Young Winston' for the front bench as deputy to Ian Gilmour, the defence shadow. When the news broke, Otto Pick told me with typical Slav gloom that Churchill's appointment marked the end of my hopes for political advancement. I refused to believe him but he was right.

Ian Gilmour was none too happy with Margaret's choice ('I do not object so much to what Winston says but I do dislike his tone and volume'). Mrs Thatcher picked Winston, who is a small chip off a very large block, on the strength of name and name alone. Winston performed adequately, but gave off noise rather than intelligence. The Fred Mulley defence team disliked him intensely, as he was invariably offensive to them. But Winston, who has something of his grandfather's temperament but none of his flair, soon quarrelled with Margaret over Rhodesia and was abandoned by her. He remains to this day on the back-benches, a sad Nicholas Winterton-like figure but with more style and better manners than the Member for Macclesfield.

My vice-chairmanship meant that I was in theory available to speak from the opposition front-bench, which I did on one occasion warning the House of the dangers of indiscriminate arms sales. My speech did not go down too well with 'the colleagues', most of whom would sell arms to Satan on the grounds that were we not to do so then the French would. The government seemed to approve of it (while continuing to sell arms to all comers). I was on firmer ground on broadcasting. I was elected chairman of the party's Media Committee at the time of the publication of the Annan Committee's report on the future of broadcasting. This meant that I became, for all intents and purposes, Willie Whitelaw's deputy (broadcasting came under the Home Office) but my front-bench role was never made official, although I spoke from there on several occasions.

I was once, however, approached by Mrs Thatcher's private office with a request that I write a speech for delivery by her to an Institute of Journalists' dinner. I did so, including in the draft a selection of my better jokes. I was told later that she failed to raise a single laugh. I did not know at the time how lacking she is in humour, but even so the fault was mine; women are not at their happiest reeling off a series of set-piece jokes, however topical.

I have a short memory for jokes but I believe that one of my offerings to Margaret was this one about Ronnie Knox. Knox, the distinguished Catholic theologian (he was responsible for Harold Macmillan's near-conversion to Rome) used to visit Normandy on what might be called a busman's holiday. The services in the parish church were then conducted in Latin and presented no difficulty. When asked how he coped with the thick patois at confession, he replied, 'I wait for a minute or two and then interrupt, saying gravely, '*Vous avez, avez-vous?*'

Reggie Maudling was a major casualty of the late seventies. After Margaret's seizure of power she brought him into the shadow cabinet as spokesman on Foreign Affairs. It was not long before he fell victim to her crusading zeal in the 'fight against communism'. Nato's policy at the time was based on 'defence and *détente*' and Margaret, who believed in the first more than she did the second, could not have been entirely happy with either Gilmour at defence or Maudling at Foreign Affairs. After several semi-public rows between them she sacked Reggie, replacing him with John Davies in November 1976. At lunch one day Maudling told me that he had found her quite impossible to deal with, offensive, narrow in focus, a prisoner in her private office of *francs-tireurs* such as the ex-Marxist turned far right-winger Alfred Sherman. 'God help us,' sighed Reggie wearily, helping himself to a second portion of plum duff.

I reminded Reggie of the occasion when he had been physically attacked by Bernadette Devlin while sitting on the government front-brench. 'Any married man should have known what was coming,' said Reggie. It so happened I had been sitting behind him at the time. Reggie crouched behind his arms, like a boxer caught on the ropes: Alec Douglas-Home, with patrician disregard, looked the other way; Francis Pym, the Chief Whip, stood up and flapped at the enraged Devlin with his handkerchief. The day was saved by the Labour Chief Whip, Bob Mellish, who put Bernadette in an arm-lock and frog-marched her out of the Chamber. 'I suppose he was more used to that sort of thing,' said Reggie.

But Mrs Thatcher was not Maudling's sole problem. Reggie was a wise politician but not a wise businessman. It was a tragedy for him that, while in opposition in the sixties, he failed to resist the temptation of committing himself to two dubious business ventures which collapsed before he could properly extricate himself. Of the two the more serious was the Real Estate Fund of America of which he was president between 1968 and 1969, which led to three years of litigation in New York. But it was Maudling's entanglement in John Poulson's commercial empire and the latter's bankruptcy which focused upon him the sensational attention of the mass media, including a hostile television programme which compelled him to sue (successfully) for libel.

The trouble started in 1966 with his joining one of Poulson's companies for which he helped to obtain a contract for designing that great white elephant of a hospital at Gozo, Malta; it lasted until July 1977 when the House of Commons received the report of a select committee set up to investigate his conduct and that of two other MPs, one Labour, Albert Roberts, the other (John Cordle) Conservative.

On the publication of the report, John Cordle promptly applied for the Chiltern Hundreds and thankfully disappeared from view. Older hands had never forgiven him his comment on adultery at the time of the Profumo affair ('must the Queen meet this adulterer?'), believing, as we all do, that pots should not call kettles black, particularly in public. Cordle's unlamented departure made it possible for a rescue operation to be mounted for Reggie Maudling. The debate was as harrowing an affair as I can remember. Foot moved the motion to accept the select committee's report ('if there is one thing worse than a lynch mob, it is a sanctimonious lynch mob') in a good speech. Maudling had clearly been unwise, certainly greedy, but not dishonest. Even so, the far Left coupled with the republican Labour MP Willie Hamilton, called for the expulsion of Roberts and Maudling. I remember well how terribly Reggie suffered from nerves; on several occasions he almost dried up, his mouth and facial muscles twitching uncontrollably. But he defended himself bravely and at the end of his speech threw down his notes and quit the chamber, believing that it was necessary for him to do so. But he was invited back and took his place to listen to a most powerful speech in his favour from Ted Heath who proclaimed Reggie to be an honourable man. I waited until ten o'clock and then voted twice: once to take note of the report and once against expulsion for which eleven MPs voted.

Cancer claimed Reggie Maudling two years later in February 1979 at the age of sixty-one. Whether the disease was triggered by the trauma, who can tell? It has certainly become a fashionable medical theory that psychological or physical trauma serves to suppress the body's immune system, thus opening the door to cancer. Maudling was one of the four very distinguished young conservatives who entered the House in 1950, Edward Heath, Enoch Powell and Iain Macleod the others. Of the four, Reggie had the least dynamic personal ambition but the steadiest and calmest political judgement and the most generous and warmly political viewpoint. Heath was the most able of the quartet, Macleod the most charismatic. Powell, driven by demons, proved to be his own worst enemy.

Among the Conservative MPs who retired from the Commons in 1979, thereby missing the Thatcher years, were David James, Robert (Robin) Cooke and Jasper More. My friend David Walder died suddenly in 1978, having suffered a heart attack in a restaurant. He was dining with Tony Buck, who took him from one hospital to another in search of resuscitation. When at last they found a hospital willing and able to cope, it was too late. I was told of his death when I went to pick up my letters from the Members Post Office. The party rallied to his bereaved family. His son Rupert's education at Eton was paid for by a group of Tory MPs, the most generous contributor being Albert Costain, the MP for Folkestone. David's wife, Elspeth, spent a decade or more working for Hansard in the Palace of Westminster. Sadly she died of cancer in 1991.

I wrote earlier that I did not think David would have thrived politically under Margaret. His sceptical intelligence would not have welcomed the new ideology that Margaret brought in her train; nor would he have had much time for the adventurers who, by capturing her ear, quickly comprised her court. Outsiders like Alfred Sherman and Robert Crozier; insiders like Ronald Miller and Gordon Reece. For Margaret had swiftly made room for her 'six good men and true' (to whom she referred so frequently in *The Downing Street Years*, the BBC television series that followed the publication of her book in the autumn of 1993); for example, she sacked Michael Wolff from Central Office ('he was too close to Ted') and resurrected an acidulous back-bencher, Angus Maude, who had suffered from years of well-merited neglect. Maude, who had played no little part in the intrigues that led up to her election as party leader, was made deputy chairman of the party.

David would have derived no advantage from this changing of the guard. Like most politicians I have a large acquaintance; but, in my case, few close friends. David had become one of them, and I was sorely to miss his friendship, his humour and (with regard to my anonymous article in the *Observer* in 1980) his good advice.

A Member of Parliament, once he leaves the Commons for whatever reason, is not much missed. The waters just close over his head. A colleague can be away sick from the House for months, even years, and his return will be barely noticed; by the same token he can pick up the threads of his political life where he left them; he will be treated by friends and enemies as if he had never been away. Few if any MPs of whatever party leave anything tangible behind them: a ministerial career, unless it is especially glittering, soon goes unremarked; a back-bencher, who can become quite famous, if only for fifteen minutes, is quickly forgotten. Who now remembers Mrs Bessie Braddock, who ran Liverpool's Labour machine for so many years? Or Sidney Silverman, the Labour MP for Nelson and Colne, the Dennis Skinner of his day? Or Desmond Donnelly, who with Woodrow Wyatt held the 1964/66 Labour Government to ransom? Donnelly killed himself in the bedroom of a Heathrow hotel, a dismal last stop on the road to eternity.

One Tory back-bencher who did make a mark on the Palace of Westminster was Robin Cooke. He was invited by Michael Heseltine, as Environment Secretary in 1979, to become a special adviser on the Palace, and he was just the man for the job. Cooke was an early environmentalist with a strong aesthetic sense. Michael and I had known Robin at Oxford where we thought him both supercilious and unattractive. An Old Harrovian at Christ Church he was, when we came up, a pillar of the Oxford Tories. As president of OUCA, and editor of a magazine called *Oxford Tory*, he was one of our leading opponents. He was one of the floppy fair-haired, brown-trousered brigade and there was no love lost between us. But his rather grand and patronizing manner was somewhat undermined by my knowledge, which I was happy to share with all and sundry, that my father and his had been medical students together in Bristol. 'Old Bob Cooke' had apparently been something of a rough diamond, who had combined a career of cutting up Bristolians with dabbling in property and had, in consequence, made a lot of money, enough to cover Robin with a thick coat of Harrovian gloss. Despite his son's Oxford air and graces and his frequent rudeness, there was nothing smart about his dear old dad.

Robin rose like a rocket through the politics of Bristol. In 1955, he stood against Anthony Wedgwood Benn in Bristol South East, reducing his majority by 6,000. At a by-election two years later, when he was still only twenty-six, he was returned as Conservative MP for Bristol West, the smarter part of the city, stretching as it does from the zoo to the top of Park Street and including the dizzy heights of Clifton. He was thus the first of our Oxford rivals to arrive at Westminster (in 1957 Michael was still doing his National Service in the Welsh Guards and I was struggling as a trainee account executive in an advertising agency called Lintas). We were not a little jealous of his success.

I do not think Robin was much loved in Bristol. He was a confident personality about whom a colleague was quoted without attribution as saying 'He wore bold shirts and smelt of bath salts'. He could be disdainful of his political opponents both within and without the party, and to use an old phrase, 'he took a lot of knowing'. If one persevered, his friendship could be rewarding. What was so unusual about his career was that it only blossomed once he abandoned Bristol (or, perhaps more likely, the Bristol Tories abandoned him in favour of the young William Waldegrave) and accepted Michael Heseltine's invitation to tart up the Palace. Robin set about this task with a will. Plasterboard was stripped from the ceilings of the Speaker's House, an array of dusty pictures discovered in cellars were cleaned and properly hung; a picture of Pugin was found still in its original frame; in particular the Harcourt Room was decorated with a charming collection of coloured working drawings of the Great Exhibition, while reproductions of original William Morris wallpapers and carpets covered many of the Palace's thousand rooms. As the outside stonework of Barry's masterpiece was slowly cleaned, its interior sprang to new life, thanks entirely to Robin's taste and initiative. He was given his knighthood in token of his services; one of the rare examples of a political 'K' being awarded for something other than silent service.

In 1980 Heather and I spent some days in Dorset (I was writing a piece on Hardy's Dorset for the Saturday edition of the *Financial Times* and we were entertained to lunch by Jennifer and Robin Cooke at Athelhampton, the beautiful medieval house that Robin's father had given the couple as a wedding present, and which would be badly damaged by fire in 1991. We followed close on the heels of *Dr Who*, for Robin let the house and grounds out to film-makers of all kinds. In 1986, I ran across him in the Library corridor; he was walking with two sticks. Flippantly, I enquired whether his incapacity was due to the attentions of a jealous husband. He replied to the effect that he was dying of motor neurone disease. After Robin's death at the age of fifty-six in 1987, Jennifer Cooke later married Edward du Cann, only to die of cancer in 1995.

David James, who retired from Parliament as Member for Dorset North in 1979, was dotty. His reputation for eccentricity dated from 1964 when as Tory MP for Brighton, Kemptown, he lost his seat to Labour by seven votes. When, a few days after Alec Douglas-Home's defeat (and my own at Rochester), I went to Conservative Central Office to interview the then chairman of the party John Hare, I murmured some words of sympathy. We had, after all, just lost a general election after thirteen years in office. 'It's all that silly bugger David James's fault,' cried Hare. 'The fool spent most of the three-week election campaign in Scotland looking for the Loch Ness Monster.' Indeed, he had, and the tabloid press had been full of it. The papers claimed that every so often a cable would arrive from some godforsaken Scottish village addressed to the Kemptown Tory agent 'Have almost found the Monster. Hope all goes well with the campaign.' I reminded the chairman of these communications. Hare became very animated, that is for a Conservative. 'Seven fuckin' votes, a marginal seat lost,' he shouted, 'and we're lumbered with Harold Wilson.'

James, or Guthrie-James as he later became, managed for some inexplicable reason to get himself adopted for Dorset North, returning to the House in 1970. I expressed some surprise at this one evening to Sir Harwood Harrison, an old buffer who had been knocked down by a taxi while coming to the House. 'Quite mad,' he said, 'but he had a good war.' It appears that he had tried twice to escape from a German prisoner-of-camp: on the first occasion he adopted the identity of a Bulgarian naval officer, Lieutenant Buggeroff. This improbable disguise served him well for a time, but he was eventually picked up by the Gestapo. On his second attempt he was a Swedish sailor and he did manage to stow away and made the passage to Sweden lying prone under a ship's boiler. Had he succeeded in finding Nessie he would undoubtedly have been returned for Brighton, and the course of history would have been very different. David James died in 1986 aged sixty-six.

Jasper More, the last of the Tory party's 'library squires' also gave up in 1979. He sat for Ludlow, and my Shropshire ancestors must have touched their caps to him and many other generations of Mores who had represented south Shropshire since the Commonwealth. Echoing the words of Solon, 'Call no man happy until he dies', More disclaimed all worldly ambitions beyond those of being happily married, of living in his ancestral home and of representing his county in Parliament. Although he is described in his *Times* obituary as 'an eccentric', he was certainly not dotty in the sense that so many Tory MPs are. He was a delightful man with the best manners of anyone (except perhaps Harold Macmillan) that I have ever known. One example will suffice: I spoke to a dinner in Ludlow in the eighties after Jasper had been replaced as the local Member by a Birkenhead builder called Eric Cockeram. 'Cockers' was absent; he was doing business in South Africa, but at my place-setting was a letter addressed to me from Jasper, welcoming me to Ludlow.

In 1978, when Jasper More was still in Parliament, I was invited to speak at a Young Conservative weekend conference held at the Long Mynd Hotel overlooking Brockhurst, Church Stretton. As I was to perform on the Sunday morning, Jasper invited Heather and me to stay the weekend with him at Linley Hall, near Bishop's Castle, a part of Shropshire that fairly merits the description 'the back of beyond'. In his book *A Tale of Two Houses* Jasper told the story of how the Mores, who had fallen on hard times, managed to regain and then restore Linley, the only Palladian house in Shropshire, the other, his mother's family's house, being at Westport in the remote West of Ireland.

We drove hard through a November day, losing our way around Wentnor, arriving a little later for dinner. More was descended from what Namier described in his survey of English politics in the eighteenth century as one of the four great Shropshire families. His wife, Clare, was a Hope-Edwardes, a charming if formidable woman whose social antenna, as sensitive an instrument as one might expect when deployed by female members of the English upper class, twitched alarmingly but discreetly as we sat down to dine on Spey salmon and petit Chablis (purchased from David Mitchell, yet another colleague). I was a Tory MP: I had been educated at Shrewsbury; I had been to Oxford. Could I pass for white? I had relations living locally: 'What were their names?' she enquired. I said 'Morris, Jones and Evans; I doubt if you know them.' The conversation then changed to the correct pronunciation of Shropshire place-names, for example 'Ratchup' for Ratlinghope, and 'Delbury' for Diddlebury. Emma, Clare's companion (there was splendour but no servants), claimed to have met Mary Webb – she remembered her goitre – and Jasper, not to be outdone, recalled meeting A. E. Housman while at Cambridge.

After dinner, Jasper disappeared only to emerge wearing the cap and uniform jacket of a guard of the Bishop's Castle Railway, a private railway which ran for twelve miles between Craven Arms and Bishop's Castle from 1863 to 1935. The local gentry had been among the original shareholders, but the line never made any money, operating under the receiver for the best part of seventy years. The trains were infrequent and so slow that passengers could leap from their mid-nineteenth-century carriages, pick mushrooms and run to catch up with the train. Jasper gave me a third-class parliamentary ticket from Eaton to Bishop's Castle that I still have somewhere.

Linley Hall was full to the brim with treasures: a prayerbook signed by Charles I, a lead ingot, found in the grounds, stamped with the name of its owner 'Hadrian', pictures by Reynolds, and a portrait of Jasper by Halliday, holding the whip; and a picture of the house painted by John Napper. In the seventies, More had been a government whip, his task, among others, to write a daily record of events in the Commons to be delivered each evening to Buckingham Palace for the sovereign to read while dressing for dinner, a task which, had it ever come my way, I think I would have done rather well. Heather and I were given a small suite of rooms; I can remember getting up early the next morning to see the sun rise over the rim of the Long Mynd, the ten-mile long mountain that dominated the view to the east. It was the most beautiful winter's morning, the trees still partly in scarlet and yellow leaf, and the scene worthy of

Arcadia. How I wanted to live in Shropshire! Later, I commented to Clare More on the silence. She agreed, it is 'broken only by the honking of the Canada geese'.

After making my speech on 'the English disease' (Tories in opposition always go in for self-flagellation), we drove to Cheyney Longville some ten miles away to have lunch with my Aunt Annie. Her husband, my mother's brother Oscar Morris, who had been a gamekeeper at The Grove estate at Craven Arms before becoming a postman, had died recently after many years crippled by arthritis. In my first incarnation at Rochester I had tried unsuccessfully to persuade the Post Office to agree to fix a small engine to the rear wheel of his pushbike. The cottage was meanly red-brick, although shaded by an enormous walnut tree. We had a lunch of roast beef (overdone), floury potatoes and runner beans, good and hearty. Whereas Linley had had eight lavatories (Jasper had said as much the night before), Annie's cottage had one, and that was in the garden. It carried the legend 'Don't sit here all day dreaming of that seventy-five thousand pounds'. I hope that Heather, who was, you will recall, the niece of Littlewoods Pools founder Sir John Moores, took the hint.

When we were leaving Annie told us that the landlord had just agreed to put in an inside loo and bathroom, but that the rent would go up to eight pounds a week. Such were, and probably still are, the social contrasts of rural England. Jasper More died in 1987 at the age of eighty. He was almost the last of his kind, the library squire whose political career was not driven by a desire for fame or fortune, but undertaken solely as an extension of his sense of social obligation. He is still remembered with great affection in Shropshire, proving a very hard act to follow as Ludlow's MP.

His widow Clare died in March 1994. In the late eighties I was invited to lunch with her at Linley. Over the cutlets she said 'Doorbell rang the other day; went down to open it and there on the gravel was Norman St John Stevas and his friend; they were both wearin' identical apple-green blazers. "Ah," I said, "the House of Lords' Archery Club, I presume?" ' Clare then told me Norman was interested in buying Linley Hall. 'Has he any money?' she inquired. I said I had no idea; I presumed he lived on his wits like the rest of us. Anyway, that was the end of Norman's foray into south Shropshire.

18 Fights and Flights

The end of the seventies coincided with the fall of the Wilson/Callaghan government, marking the end of a miserable decade that had disappointed so many of the expectations raised during the sixties. The taste of freedom had turned sour. Harold Wilson's reputation, which as I write is on the point of revival, was then dismally low. His resignation in 1976 was attributed to many reasons, none of which were to his credit. Had he really just had enough and called it a day? Were there not more sinister reasons? He had surrounded himself with a court of sycophants, his twice-yearly honours lists contained the names of the financially disreputable, his cronies went to jail, and, through the failure of his policies and political longevity, he was reviled by the press.

Perhaps no Prime Minister should serve more than one term in office? Harold Macmillan's good years lasted from 1958 to 1962, the practical length of one Parliament; Wilson, had he not won in 1974, could have claimed a successful term of five years. Ted Heath barely survived a 'term'. Mrs Thatcher should have bowed out gracefully after ten years, as Peter Carrington suggested to her on his visit to Chequers in 1988, a visit that was no doubt prompted by Lord Whitelaw's retirement from the cabinet. Margaret's refusal to act upon Carrington's disinterested advice led directly to her defenestration in November 1990. But that is another story. It does seem that press and public, the one acting upon the other in a way that is hard to disentangle, lose patience with the policies and become bored with the personalities of our leaders. John Major seems particularly vulnerable to this process. Do editors respond to public opinion or do they form it? Much must depend upon events, such as the extraordinary Falklands War that doubled Mrs Thatcher's shelf-life. In less remarkable times, politicians are quickly sucked dry like so many lemons. Whether this is due to the insatiable appetite for trivia and novelty of the popular press or the intractable nature of our political problems is open to question. Whatever their rhetoric, our different leaders have all been attempting to do the same thing; the management of the nation's decline, an act that stands in need of constant dissimulation.

The combination of James Callaghan and Michael Foot (with a little help from David Steel) managed to keep us Tories at bay for more than three years. Callaghan dominated Prime Minister's questions. Michael Foot provided the passionate, late-night oratory necessary to defend the indefensible; together, they were a formidable parliamentary partnership.

In 1976, I sat directly behind our front-bench for the debate to nationalize the shipbuilding and aviation industries. There was much uncertainty as to who would win. The two Michaels, Heseltine and Foot, wound up before an excited House, the members of which had dined well. I voted and returned to my place. As the result was about to be announced the four tellers jostled one another in an attempt to take the winning position on the right-hand side. It was a tie, and we all cheered hugely. According to custom the Speaker gave his vote to the government. While we voted for the second time, the tension grew markedly, for another tied vote would mean the Speaker voting for us, and the defeat of the government. But to our horror and disbelief Labour won by one vote, seemingly plucked out of thin air. The word passed like wildfire through the opposition benches that Tom Pendry, a Labour MP, had been obliged by Michael Cocks, the government Chief Whip, to break his pair. It was only later that we learnt that this had not been the case. An elderly Labour MP had been discovered fast asleep in the Library and hustled out to vote.

We howled with rage and yelled 'cheat'. Labour MPs below the gangway burst into song – 'The Red Flag' – for the first time since 1945. Michael Heseltine, beside himself with anger, seized the Mace, and brandishing it advanced upon the government front-bench. It was not clear whether he intended to offer them this symbol of Parliament as a prettily ironic gesture or was about to do someone an injury, but Jim Prior deftly disarmed him, and replaced the Mace, the wrong way round.

At this all hell broke lose. Both sides started to push and shove and I moved with others to put myself between Michael and the cohorts of the Left. Tom Swain, a Derbyshire miner who was never at his best late at night, struck Anthony Nelson, one of our sixteen-year-old merchant bankers, a glancing blow. Geoffrey Rippon, as purple as a bishop, lashed out at the songsters with his rolled-up order paper. The serjeant-at-arms resorted to what was primly reported in the press as 'nautical language' in an attempt to damp down the fires. I ran into Michael Heseltine a moment later in the Members' Lobby; he was quivering with passion. His peers all thought he was daft, but as he told me later, the party activists were much taken by his gesture. He had been stopped in Piccadilly and shaken by the hand more than once.

There was a strange postscript. The next day Willie Whitelaw got into my taxi outside the Savoy. He was furious with Michael as he felt that the episode of the Mace had distracted attention from the government's apparent duplicity. (It was swiftly established that Pendry had not broken his pair.) Willie had clearly lunched well, as indeed had I. As we passed a mounted policeman at the gates of St Stephen's entrance he said, 'I do so approve of our mounted policemen carrying swords.' After I pointed out that in fact they all carried sticks, he seemed greatly put out.

The defeat of the Callaghan government on a vote of confidence debate in the spring of 1979 ushered in the general election. How then did the Tories regard Margaret? My party activists in Aldershot had favoured Ted Heath at the time of the election for party leader, and were shocked by my support for Margaret. This was not uncommon, some constituency parties going as far as holding votes of their own, the results of which they passed on pointedly to 'the Member'. Fifteen years later, the position was reversed with the bulk of the activists in Aldershot and elsewhere supporting Margaret.

In the four years since the coup Mrs Thatcher had established herself among Tories as the party's leader. She enjoyed a high public profile, not least in the tabloid press which she had cultivated assiduously, in particular Larry Lamb, the editor of Rupert Murdoch's *Sun*. He was later to be knighted for services rendered. She had adopted a habit which I found distressing, namely having her photograph taken in the turrets of tanks or the cockpits of fighter aircraft, appearing as Bellona, the Roman Goddess of War. I said as much in a leader page piece in the *Telegraph*, only to be pursued as an 'anti-Thatcherite' in that great family paper's correspondence columns. Tass added considerably to her reputation by dubbing her the 'Iron Lady', and she was certainly a very noisy anti-communist. In the House, she spoke poorly, reading rapidly from a prepared script while at Prime Minister's questions she often came off second best.

There had been several slim volumes published about her life and views by right-wing Tories like Russell Lewis, a pleasant Welshman who seemed to have abandoned a political career in favour of life at the *Daily Mail*, and ambitious back-benchers like George Gardiner whose doggy devotion to her was eventually to be rewarded by a knighthood. She had been the subject of a thousand admiring newspaper profiles. Her gritty voice and unblinking eye had been made familiar by television. She was on her way to achieving cult status.

What alarmed the more thoughtful Conservatives was not simply her views, which could be frightening enough – 'I put myself forward . . . because I am a true Tory and believe they (*sic*) can make this country better than anyone else. And because I saw the Tory party going much too much to the left. There did not seem to be anyone else who had the thoughts and ideas I had, and it seemed to be absolutely vital for the country that I stood' – but the zealotry with which she espoused them.

Disquiet in the party was partially hidden behind a superficial loyalty and a cheerful anticipation that the election, after the agonies of the 'winter of discontent' was in the bag. It centred, too, not only on Margaret's person (tales of her imperiousness in the shadow cabinet had filtered down), but on her Court, for no sooner had she been elected leader of the party than she was targeted by the grinders of axes, the bulk of whom had little or no connection with the Conservative party, all peddling old right-wing nostrums of a sort that had failed to find a patron elsewhere. Those of us on the left of the party anxiously looked to people like Peter Carrington and Willie Whitelaw to provide a guiding hand: Edward Heath, who had not unreasonably taken umbrage at what he saw as a concerted effort by Margaret and Co. to rewrite the party's history at his expense, was regarded as unlikely to be able to bring any influence upon her. There would be no room for Ted in Margaret's new order.

My seventh election campaign (my fourth in Aldershot) was one of the most pleasant I can remember. A June election, with the result not in doubt, it was an opportunity to spend the mornings being driven by officers of field rank to remote villages like Rotherwick and Mattingley, where we would take coffee with generals' widows in pretty tile-hung houses filled with the tick of French carriage clocks, cabinets containing choice pieces of Worcester, and walls covered with original Naples pictures, the accumulated *bijouterie* of several generations. The General would stare moodily from within his silver-framed photograph on the grand piano, pondering no doubt how best *reculer pour mieux sauter*. Lunch would be taken in some country pub, patronized by the braying classes. Beer, cheese and the tang of Branston pickle is a madeleine which invariably brings back to me the tart taste of soliciting for votes.

After lunch, we would turn the Land-Rover, decorated with flatteringly youthful portraits of the candidate, towards the avenues of Farnborough, named after the forgotten courtiers of the Second Empire. By about four o'clock I had had enough of being nice to strangers ('We've not seen you since the last election'), and would return home to Farnham where, if the local Liberals were to be believed, the Tory candidate was being revived with cups of bitter, black coffee. I would put my feet up in our cottage opposite the William Cobbett pub, watch the six o'clock news, eat a modest supper, and then drive to a British Legion hall for a modestly attended public meeting. Three weeks of fresh air, sun and unaccustomed exercise served to recharge my batteries which had become drained by too much foreign travel, *choucroute garni*, and votes of censure. My majority went up and Mrs Thatcher went from a knees-up at Conservative Central Office to 10 Downing Street clutching a piece of paper thrust into her hot hand by Ronald Miller (he, too, was to be knighted for services rendered) on which were written those famous words of St Francis of Assisi:

> Where there is discord may we bring harmony.
> Where there is error may we bring truth.
> Where there is doubt may we bring faith.
> Where there is despair may we bring hope.

Hindsight suggests it would be difficult to imagine a more inappropriate text.

The 1979 general election was also remarkable for what was perhaps the most famous piece of party political propaganda, the Saatchi brothers' 'Labour isn't Working' poster showing a dole queue. It was good of its kind (unemployment figures were to soar under the Conservatives) although not quite as brilliant as Joseph Goebbels' decree that after every roll-call the assembled stormtroopers would all yell out 'here' when the name of the 'hero' Horst Wessel (murdered in a street fight with communists) was deliberately added.

On the Saturday after polling day (Downing Street had not telephoned which came as no surprise) Heather and I drove to Cranley Onslow's house in Sussex whence we set out in Cranley's large Renault to drive to Strasbourg via the Dover ferry. Cranley's telephone had not rung either. 'She's done nothing for me,' was Cranley's stoical remark. She would, however, two years later when he was appointed Minister of State at the Foreign and Commonwealth office with Francis Pym as Foreign Secretary. Cranley, who was then in his late fifties, is a member of the collateral branch of the Earls of Onslow, married to June, the daughter of the Earl of Kinnoull. He was thus an estate owner in a party of estate agents.

We drove swiftly along deserted toll roads, stopping for a night at Laon in French Flanders, a hilltop city with a curious lattice-masted cathedral. After Laon, we drove to Reims, where we lunched on baguettes and champagne in the cathedral square, and then to Verdun. I had just finished reading Alistair Horne's book on the battle – the most terrible of the Great War – and we wanted to see l'Ossuaire. This building, surely the ugliest in the world, is a huge stone-built mausoleum, long and low like a strange crouching beast, crowned with a short, stubby tower. Inside there have been tossed more than a hundred thousand skeletons, French and German. There are small, dust-covered windows of thick glass. We peered inside the charnel house at the uncountable, nameless dead. I know the march towards European unity has been checked by selfishness and cynicism, but we wanted to remind ourselves of the unimaginable horrors of European civil wars, the avoidance of which was the original intention of the founders of the European Community.

Cranley, who was to play a considerable part during the Thatcher years both as a minister and later as chairman of the back-bench 1922 Committee, seemed as tired of the antics of the Council of Europe as I was, and over a good dinner in Strasbourg we decided to call it a day. I did not expect ministerial office although Cranley evidently did, so I opted for membership of the North Atlantic Assembly, which was in the whips' gift. Michael Jopling, the government Chief Whip, raised no objection to my service abroad. Presumably, he had no other plans for me.

The NAA was yet another unelected assembly of Parliamentarians, but with a big difference: the Americans took part. We were thus reinforced by Congressmen and Senators who, together with their large staffs, would set up 'control rooms' in grand hotels in congenial cities across the world. At Reid's Hotel, Madeira, the 'controls' included unlimited supplies of Jack Daniels' sippin' whiskey to raise morale, boxes of kaolin as the second line of defence against the local cuisine, cases of coke, and boxes of toilet paper. The Yanks travelled in style. The US Air Force was placed at the disposal of the delegation: silver aircraft with 'The United States of America' on their flanks, within which were armchairs, bourbon and elegant stewardesses.

I have only to list the sites chosen as meeting places for the North Atlantic Assembly to show how congenial they were. We met in Venice in June, on Madeira in May, and in Munich in October. The senators included Joe Biden whose presidential hopes were later to be dashed when he was discovered to have 'borrowed' Neil Kinnock's perorations (I would have thought there were worse sins), Ted Kennedy, who the years had turned into a burly Irish barman, Sam Nunn, who knew more about the minutiae of defence than anyone else and a delightful elderly senator from Minnesota called Charles 'Chuck' Mathias, who certainly looked the part. He was courtly without being Southern. The president of the Assembly was Congressman Jack Brooks from a district in the south of Texas, who might have sprung from the pages of Robert Caro's first volume of the life of Lyndon Baines Johnson. He was folksy, astute and intolerably long-winded. An American on the staff of the Assembly secretly compiled a tape from the electronic record of our proceedings which he called 'The Best of Jack Brooks'. It included this observation delivered *sotto voce* on the platform after a difficult plenary session: 'The members of the Assembly? Smooth talking, silk-suited, quadri-lingual sons of bitches . . .' Try 'quadri-lingual' in a south Texas accent! Senator John Tower of Texas was another freeloader; he was a small, dapper, fierce bantam-cock of a man, whose wenching and boozing were to prove a stumbling block when he sought the Senate's consent before taking up the appointment as Secretary for Defense. Although he promised to mend his ways, and to do so promptly, the Senators were unimpressed. The Americans were colourful, to say the least. I remember Spencer Oliver of the Young Nato Parliamentarians showing me round the well-stocked office of a Democrat Senator in the Capitol Building. There must have been a dozen or more women of various ages. 'The plain ones,' said Spencer, 'are the Senator's relations.'

Another excuse for going on my travels again (besides the Americans) was an entirely new British delegation. A colleague of the North Atlantic Assembly was the then Labour MP for Woolwich, John Cartwright. We suggested the NAA set up a special committee to study the problem of cruise, Pershing and the Soviet ss20s and the Bureau of the Assembly agreed. John and I were appointed the committee's joint rapporteurs; with the help of three NAA staff members, Simon Lunn, Job Dittberner and Jeff Seabright, we spent four years studying Nato's response to the deployment by the Soviets of their medium-range ss20 nuclear missiles. Nato responded to the threat by deploying cruise missiles at Greenham Common and Pershing missiles in Germany. The now-forgotten issue was a matter of great controversy at the time and we, or rather the Nato Assembly, persuaded Brassey's, then owned by Robert Maxwell, to publish our report in hard-cover. It must still be gathering dust on many library shelves.

However, even I eventually grew tired of the endless travelling; expeditions that began (and, what was worse, ended) at Heathrow, the *anus mundi* where travellers have been known to age ten years in the course of a day's delay, debilitated by the aggravation, the vile food and the endless passageways. Then the dragging in from airport to city centre, the bleak comforts of an 'international' hotel, and the remorseless official hospitality that shook the last drop of adrenaline from a fast-emptying bottle, the tyranny of a three-day programme and the boredom induced by constant companions.

I did learn one lesson from my travels abroad, a lesson that owes something to the Iron Duke's dictum that is known to all soldiers, but of a wider significance: never be without a way out, a line of retreat, an escape route which can be taken when boredom and discomfort threaten. An invitation to a rustic dinner on a forested hilltop in Hungary is all well and good provided you do not have to wait until the last drunken Dutchman rejoins the bus. Hire a car, or ring for a cab; take a leaf out of Oscar's book and invent a Bunbury whose precarious health can summon you home to Shropshire from Bonn (or Birmingham) at a moment's notice; take a hard look at the delegation's list of diversions and strike out at least half; stick close to your friends and never travel without several good novels.

In 1984 I called it a day and abandoned the North Atlantic Assembly, but not before I had finally upset my apple-cart by an injudicious and anonymous article attacking Mrs Thatcher and all her works in the *Observer*. I had long sought fame; I was about to achieve it.

19 Rebellion

In February 1980, wearied by Mrs Thatcher's enthusiasm, and disillusioned by her economic policies, I wrote an unsigned article in the *Observer* which the paper's subs entitled 'Why Tories must halt the charge of Margaret's Light Brigade'. It was a pithy attack on Margaret and all her works. My confession of authorship, albeit a reluctant one, brought me instant fame, or notoriety, after fifteen years on the back-benches. The public row was short but intense with the right-wing 'populars' in hot pursuit. The fallout, particularly among my supporters in Aldershot, was very great. My *Observer* article was seen by party loyalists as traitorous and deceitful; by the political Left as heroic and well aimed; and by my friends as one of the better examples of how to shoot oneself in the foot.

My error was not so much the views expressed in the piece, indeed they were widely shared, even among Tories, but to have written it anonymously. As Hugh Stephenson wrote later in his book *Mrs Thatcher's First Year*, 'The impact of the article was somewhat reduced when Julian Critchley was forced to reveal that he was the author, for the substance of what he said was overtaken by the feeling that an anonymous article was an underhand art form. There was no doubt, however, that he was expressing the views of a substantial part of the Tory party in Parliament.'

Why then did I write it? And, having decided to put pen to paper, why did I not sign it? I had spent most of the previous August at my cousin's house in Nether Stowey, Somerset, tramping the Quantock Hills and pondering my future. I had clearly come to a turning point. I had not gone into politics as an extension of my sense of social obligation like so many other Tories (I was not grand enough); I was, and always have been, a careerist. I would have welcomed office, particularly in the defence field, in which I had long specialized, and had not totally acquiesced in the promotion of my juniors. But I had received no telephone call from Downing Street in the wake of our triumph in June, and it seemed highly unlikely that an invitation would ever be forthcoming. I was not one of nature's Thatcherites, and was too long in the tooth to be made a

Parliamentary Secretary. An appointment to minister level was even less likely. The door had irrevocably closed.

Solitary holidays have much to be said for them as a means of recharging one's batteries but they do tend towards gloom. I supposed I could soldier on giving loyal and largely silent support to a government, the radical fervour of which I would increasingly come to dislike, in the hope of a knighthood as a consolation prize; or I could play the part of a *franc-tireur*, a free spirit ranging the back-benches using my voice and my pen to strike an individual note. The passive Tory back-bencher is usually buttressed by city directorships or by a lawyer's practice, and I needed at least to double my parliamentary salary. Journalism seemed the only practical source of any additional monies. My first wife was in receipt of a nominal one-third of my income, and I had two more children from my second marriage. Heather and I had been obliged to sell our house in Castle Street in 1976, and move to a smaller, unsatisfactory cottage near the Maltings in Bridge Square, Farnham, where we were deafened either by the middle class in search of culture or by drunken local yobs at the nearby William Cobbett. We were chronically short of money. However, no sooner had we moved downmarket than I was appointed public affairs adviser to the advertising agency SSCB-Lintas, for whom I had worked in the mid-fifties. The £3,000 a year I received from the agency for more than twelve years (index linked) would have kept us on the better side of the Farnham tracks. We used the money instead to send Melissa to Farnborough Hill Convent and Joshua to the Royal Grammar School, Guildford (half the price and twice the academic record of nearby Charterhouse).

At Nether Stowey, I decided to be my own man. The role might be fun but it certainly would be hazardous, for there would always be the danger of defenestration at the hands of the Aldershot party activists who, if forced to put a premium on party loyalty, would be more generous than I might be. And I would be breaking to the left in Conservative party terms, something which is always hard to do. Party activists are nostalgic souls, always ready to go 'back to basics', lovers of Hovis commercials and hankering after 'solutions' such as deportation ('repatriation') for blacks, British 'independence' from Europe (but not, curiously, from America); suckers for any political snake-oil salesman who cares to enliven the party's annual conference with a robust appeal to atavism as did Peter Lilley in his attack on single mothers in October 1993. Sitting on a rock overlooking the gloomy mudflats of the Bristol Channel, I concluded that this major minor figure in the Tory party would set out to become a minor major one. As an ambition it seemed modest enough. I walked back to the car and drove back to the village, determined to flex my muscles.

I did not have long to wait before doing so. In the autumn of 1979 I put myself at the head of those Tory back-benchers who took strong objection to the proposed cuts in the external services of the BBC, which are funded by a grant of aid through the Foreign and Commonwealth Office's vote. The external services were, in a very real sense, the voice of Britain and played a valuable and credible part in explaining and defending our foreign policy. They suffered from Mrs Thatcher's disdain on two predictable grounds: they came under the Foreign Office, which she despised, and they were operated by the BBC, an organization which she was inclined to think ought to be a state-run authority, broadcasting in the interest of the government of the day. I tabled an early-day motion against the cuts, and it was not long before it attracted the signatures of nearly a hundred Tory back-benchers. The press, delighting in the first split in Conservative ranks since Mrs Thatcher's accession, played it up for more than it was worth.

My campaign was conducted in such a way as to offend the government Chief Whip, Michael Jopling. Dissident back-benchers are supposed to take the whips into their confidence and to keep them informed as to intention; a curious arrangement to which I was not a party, giving as it does a sizeable advantage to the government. Instead I announced my intention of fighting the proposed cuts on *The World This Weekend* to which the unhappy Jopling was listening while sipping sherry at his mother-in-law's house. I am afraid my declaration of war came between him and the Roast Beef of Old England.

During the week that followed (the haroosh in the press continued) we arranged to meet, and when we did so, passed a *mauvais quart d'heure*. I told him I thought the cuts were parsimonious and that I would contest them with all the weapons at my disposal. 'What are they?' he asked politely. 'The media,' I replied. It was the first time I had ever spoken at length to Michael Jopling, who had been a surprise choice as government Chief Whip. In Ted Heath's Government he had been a junior Minister of Agriculture. It was a pity to have fallen out with 'Joppers', a large, good natured man, a friend of Willie White-law's, and a moderate Tory. In those days he drove motorbikes with his very pretty leather-clad wife perched winningly on the pillion. Later, he followed in my footsteps to Paris and Strasbourg where he tripped the light fantastic along with the best of them.

I had thought that at least I had impressed my personality upon him but I was soon to be disillusioned. It so happened that Michael Jopling went up to Peter Tapsell in the Aye Lobby the same evening, and placing his hand upon his shoulder said 'Julian, you and I must continue our conversation'. Tapsell was very angry indeed, and upbraided the unhappy Jopling, but I was hugely entertained. Tapsell and I have been receiving each other's letters and messages for years, for there is a physical resemblance, but so hilarious a misunderstanding soon became common knowledge, and Jopling and I did not meet again until I had acknowledged the authorship of my *Observer* article, an occasion when he believed himself to have regained the advantage. As for the 'battle' of the external services, the government quietly dropped its proposed cuts, perhaps Mrs Thatcher's first U-turn. Fifteen-love.

I seem to have been unlucky with my 'Chiefs': first Redmayne, and then Pym. I should make it clear that my relationship today with Richard Ryder is quite excellent: I have become a party loyalist, we both follow boxing, and infirmity has seen to it that I am a very infrequent attender.

My successful campaign against the cuts in the BBC's external services which culminated in an adjournment debate on a Friday afternoon, when three of us gave Peter Blaker, the Foreign Office minister, an uncomfortable ride was an opening salvo; I reloaded my gun and waited for another target to present itself. I hadn't long to wait.

The early months of Mrs Thatcher's first government were set to martial music; brass over which her shrill soprano (soon to become contralto at the behest of her image-makers) could be heard urging friend and foe to go over the top. There is still a quality to that gritty voice which, when combined with a fierce and unrelenting glare and the repetition of the obvious, amounts to the infliction of pain. Her supporters seemed to relish her exhortations; those of us who had doubts cringed as she continued remorselessly to trample our susceptibilities. If Mrs Thatcher was born and bred for politics she was not born to rule, as Hugo Young observes. In *One of Us* he writes. 'She possessed no trace of the effortless superiority of the Balliol men, Macmillan and Heath, who went before her. For her, each step up the ladder was a struggle against the odds posed by her gender and her lack of fraternity with her male colleagues . . .'

I am not sure her gender was a handicap; if it was she promptly turned it to her advantage. From the start her leadership style broke with the past. Mrs Thatcher had little time for cabinet government or for 'the consensus', a term which rapidly, and quite unfairly, was given an unfavourable connotation ('Do you think you would ever have heard of Christianity if the Apostles had gone out and said "I believe in consensus"?' she once demanded). Was she really comparing like with like? She was more than capable of taking her colleagues' breath away. By leading from the front she set a smart pace; her mastery of detail gave her an advantage in argument, an advantage which she reinforced by the deliberate use of her sex. She could be downright rude to her cabinet colleagues in a way that no man would have been allowed to get away with. She had a taste for favourites, and not just from within the cabinet. Like most dominant figures, nothing much 'grew' beneath her; from time to time she encouraged heirs apparent, usually young men of good looks many years younger than herself. Cecil Parkinson was one; another good example is John Moore, a pleasantly insipid if handsome right-winger. Moore, promoted to the cabinet and dogged by ill health, disappeared without trace towards the end of the eighties.

It did not take long for the cabinet, in particular, to realize just how different Mrs Thatcher was from her immediate predecessors. The genie had escaped the bottle and swallowed the cork. Her behaviour at the Dublin summit in January 1980 when she publicly scolded both Giscard and Helmut Schmidt and demanded 'our money' back from the Community shocked the pro-Europeans in our party and cheered mightily the rump of the antis. Whatever the merits of a demand for a reduced subscription to a club which we had joined late in the day and after three sets of negotiations culminating in a successful referendum campaign, the effect of her scolding upon those she was obliged to persuade (Schmidt feigned sleep during an after-dinner monologue by Mrs T), as well upon the spectators, seemed as futile as it was displeasing. There was a great row which took place largely behind the scenes in which Establishment figures threw up their hands. Finally, it was left to the Foreign Office team of Peter Carrington and Ian Gilmour to reach agreement; their story, recounted on the BBC fourteen years later, made compulsive viewing. 'We could not have been made less welcome [at Chequers] had we been the bailiffs,' said Gilmour. It was an inauspicious beginning to Mrs Thatcher's unhappy relationship with the European Community, her hostility to which was eventually to play a decisive part in her downfall in 1990.

I was angry and determined to write an article which would express the anxieties of many of my friends. I was tempted to emulate the series of pieces which appeared in *The Times* in the mid-sixties under the signature of 'A Conservative'. These 'turnovers', appearing on consecutive days, were an attack on the Conservative policies of the fifties and sixties and, in particular, on the policies of Harold Macmillan. Their appearance caused a stir, and some innocent fun, as the newspapers and others speculated as to the identity of the author. The pieces were a brilliantly argued demolition of the basis of post-war Conservatism, 'the politics of consensus', and in the search for a name to put to them most people did not look beyond that of Enoch Powell. But Mr Powell denied authorship and the fuss died down. The articles were the first shots in the fusillade of dissent which, ten years later, Sir Keith Joseph in particular articulated without disguise. And Mrs Thatcher was Keith Joseph's candidate to challenge Ted Heath.

I suggested the idea to John Cole who was then the *Observer*'s political correspondent. He told me that the paper would take one piece, unsigned, if that was what I wished. Unwisely, I did not take the advice of my friends. I did ask Sir Nigel Fisher, who was sympathetic to my point of view, and his advice was to publish anonymously lest I offend my constituency party. Sadly, David Walder had just died; his opinion would most certainly have been sought. As secrecy was of the essence I was reluctant to canvass further views. I wrote the piece and sent it to the *Observer*. It appeared on Sunday 17 February 1980.

Why the Tories must halt the charge of Margaret's Light Brigade, by A Tory

Lord Chalfont recounted last week the view of a Tory MP who had compared the progress of the government with that of the Crimean War, 'but with this difference: Florence Nightingale is leading the Charge of the Light Brigade and Lord Cardigan is attending to the sick and wounded'.

As a judgement it is unkind, disloyal, pertinent and funny. It is also indicative of the growing disquiet, felt both within the cabinet and on the back-benches with the pace and direction of Mrs Thatcher's Light Brigade.

It is a matter both of policy and personality. Mrs Thatcher is didactic, tart and obstinate. Her economic policies are 'Thatcherite' rather than Conservative for her treasury team have placed the Public Sector Borrowing Requirement upon a pedestal . . .

We are suffering from A-level economics. In consequence of this new ideology, economics have been elevated above politics in an almost Marxist fashion, and it cannot be long before the Conservative party pays the price. As the cannonade increases so must the casualties . . .

We have been no more successful abroad. We were defeated at the Battle of Dublin where, without adequate preparation, and with the wrong tone of voice, the Prime Minister took on her allies and lost. Perhaps she should have behaved a little more like Helen of Troy and a little less like Hector . . .

There is anxiety within the cabinet at the Prime Minister's taste for charging uphill (as one cabinet minister put it 'the Prime Minister flies by the seat of her pants'), but the moderates stand at the periphery, engaged upon their separate tasks, unable so far to combine effectively to bring about a change in economic policy . . .

The piece, which was twelve hundred words long, continued in much the same vein, ending with the statement that there were many Tory MPs left 'who had no wish to be consumed by the sacred flame'.

Thirteen years later I must attempt some modest textual criticism. The phrase 'didactic, tart and obstinate' (which was made much of by a shocked tabloid press) belonged to Willie Whitelaw. 'A-level economics' (which attracted almost as much hostile attention from the newspapers) was Kenneth Baker's, who was at that time a frustrated back-bencher, privately scathing of Mrs Thatcher and all her works. The Helen of Troy/Hector joke was mine. The 'tone of voice' belonged to Ian Gilmour. The cabinet minister who was worried about Mrs Thatcher's knickers was Michael Heseltine. It was the first openly expressed adverse criticism of Mrs Thatcher and her government by one of her MPs: the first shot in a battle which was to rage unremittingly for the next ten years until her downfall in November 1990, echoes of which reverberate to this day, *vide* John Major's crack at the beginning of his 1993 Blackpool party conference speech of 'memoirs to the left of him, memoirs to the right of him, volleyed and thundered'.

At first there was no apparent reaction to the piece. The article was not mentioned in Monday's newspapers, and although one or two people asked whether I was responsible for it little or nothing was said. On the following Saturday I returned from a Conservative Group for Europe conference at Brandon Hall in Warwickshire having made one of my better speeches. (Incidentally, prominent among its organizers was Beryl Goldsmith, who was to come stoutly to my aid when the row broke; more recently, as Norman Tebbit's secretary, her views on Europe may well have changed radically, but I was grateful to her at the time.)

All was still until the mid-afternoon of the following Sunday when I was rung by the diary editor of the *Daily Mail*. He wanted to know whether I was the 'Julian' whom Sir John Junor, the editor of the *Sunday Express* knighted by Margaret in January 1980, had referred to as the author of the anonymous attack upon the Prime Minister. I said I was not. No doubt the *Mail* had already spoken to the other two Julians: Julian Amery, the Brighton imperialist, and Julian Ridsdale, the less-prominent Member for Harwich.

I had scarcely recovered from that bombshell when the telephone rang again. This time it was Commander Mike Chappell, a constituent of uncertain temper who lived in Darby Green. His widow Esther was later to become the president of the Aldershot Tories and a firm friend. He demanded to know whether I was the 'guilty party' of John Junor's column. I admitted to being so. Whereas I could bring myself to lie to the newspapers, I was not prepared to do so when challenged by friends.

I was in a very tight spot. I rang Antony Buck, a friend in the House and a Queen's Counsel whom I would have done better to consult before putting pen to paper. He advised me to come clean: to ring back the *Daily Mail* diary and admit authorship. This I did. The diary editor received this information with some glee. I also telephoned the president of the local Tories, General Tom Foulkes, and the chairman, Jack Bedser, and gave them what must have been unwelcome news. I was then in the unenviable position of having to wait for the storm to break, a sense of foreboding not helped by the knowledge that I had foolishly made a difficult situation far worse.

The explosion, when it came, reverberated around my head. It is impossible to calculate accurately the response of the press to any given situation; an outrageous word or deed can pass almost without comment, depending to some extent upon pressure of events on available space; in my case the papers seemed bereft of any other news. The *Mail* was scathing in its diary report. Many years later Sir David English (another of Margaret's knights), the paper's editor, told me that I should have bluffed the whole thing out. Enoch must have been lucky with his Mike Chappells.

My telephone never stopped ringing. I hurried to London to defend myself on ITN's midday news. My only course was to stick to my guns, but to admit that it would have been wiser to have signed. My description of Mrs Thatcher as 'didactic, tart and obstinate' seemed to have shocked hardened commentators on the political scene. Today such a description would pass without comment: so many books, so many autobiographies, so many first-hand accounts of life with Margaret, to say nothing of Mrs Thatcher's own appearance on the BBC's *The Downing Street Years*, would now make my modest if second-hand comment totally innocuous. But in politics timing is all.

The story continued into the Tuesday with the rest of the press chiming in. The most abusive volley came later, predictably enough from the *Sunday Express*. John Junor, that unamiable old Scot, beat me about the head with his claymore, calling on my constituency party to disown me and describing me as fit only to be 'the second pianist in a whorehouse'. I thought his comment would have made a good title for my book *Westminster Blues* but W. H. Smith objected.

There was a postscript some years later. My wife and I were staying the weekend with the Howes at the Foreign Secretary's grace-and-favour house, Chevening. Junor was invited to Sunday lunch along with the Menuhins. I sat alone in the marble entrance hall, strumming the grand piano, waiting for the old swine's arrival. Sadly, he did not make the connection; but a little research showed that he had used the same term of abuse on at least twelve other of his victims. It was not the first time, or the last, that the *Sunday Express*, usually in its 'Crossbencher' column, which years ago was required reading, has tried to come between me and my supporters. It has yet to succeed.

My reception in the House ranged from mute hostility to glee as ancient enemies warmed their hands at the fires of my discomfort while my friends, regretting perhaps that I had made a fool of myself, stood me drinks. It was not long before I was once again summoned to attend upon a more confident Michael Jopling. This time he knew who I was. 'It's very off side', he kept saying. He said he had known who the author was by the end of the week, but he would not say how. 'We have our methods of finding out.' He went on to say it would be a long time before the party would forgive me, if ever. In effect, he rang down the curtain.

I learnt later that the whips' office, at Downing Street's prompting, had set out to discover who the offender might be. They drew up a shortlist on which my name appeared together with those of Peter Tapsell, John Watson and John Selwyn Gummer. It would not have been too difficult to draw up such a list. The author was likely to have been a dissident back-bencher with no love for the government's monetarist policy, and a writer with a turn of phrase (such as Ken Baker's 'A-level economics'). I was told much later by Morrison Halcrow, who was then the *Telegraph*'s deputy editor, that it was the view of Jock Bruce-Gardyne, at that time a loyal back-bencher, that it could only be Critchley 'as it was so well written'; a view expressed at a *Telegraph* editorial meeting.

I was, of course, quite aware of these acts of detection. Jopling's source might have been Lord Barnetson, who was at the time the chairman of the *Observer* and an admirer of Mrs Thatcher. I did receive a letter signed 'Tory Minister' written upon blue House of Commons writing paper which claimed that I had been shopped by Adam Raphael, who was an *Observer* lobby correspondent, though I doubt that were the case. Later, Adam was responsible for the *Observer* paying me an annual retainer as I continued to write for the paper, deputizing for Alan Watkins, in particular, for many years. Barnetson was the more likely source, but it is more probable that the whips arrived at their conclusion by process of elimination. I was not challenged as to authorship: they might well have done so in the case of the other names appearing on their shortlist.

For a fortnight I was snowed under with letters. One-third were literate and favourable, most of the rest abusive or twaddle. The abusive ones were easily spotted – green ink, cheap stationery and an ill-educated hand: providing they did not bear an Aldershot postmark, most were burnt unread. But there were some disturbing ones from the more educated end of the constituency. My officers publicly defended my right to criticize government policy while deploring my anonymity, a device which enabled them to hold the line against those who would have tried to censure me. The most hostile branch was Crondall, the smartest village in east Hampshire (it then contained two admirals), where I was told I would not be welcome. The branch chairman sent a letter of support to the Prime Minister; his vice-chairman immediately sent another in which he came to my defence. Both letters were made public in the village. At the end of a hectic fortnight the editor of the *Aldershot News* wrote a leader column in which he wondered what on earth all the fuss was about. I was grateful to him.

It is very unpleasant indeed to be hounded by the press. Tabloid journalists would bang on our front door (they got short shrift), photographers hung around outside for a day or two, and we were menaced by the telephone. The haroosh that inevitably follows a revelation of some sort or other – a vengeful, money-grubbing mistress, an angry father, even party activists who 'go public' on some speech or opinion expressed by an MP – is something which is experienced by a minority of unlucky MPs. Nicholas Ridley's unhappy lunch with the editor of the *Spectator* when he spoke his mind about the Germans; David Mellor's semi-comic calvary (although not for him); Cecil Parkinson's pillorying by sheets broad and narrow; even Lord Lambton's long-forgotten escapades, to say nothing of the antics of 'Jolly Jack' Profumo and many other more recent nine-day wonders have long led me to believe that the only safe pleasure for a politician is a bag of boiled sweets.

But I must return to the consequences of my anonymous article. At the end of February the opposition called a censure debate on the government's economic policies and I was called. I made what I think was a good speech, and the House filled up as I spoke (always a good sign). I repeated much of what I had written for the *Observer*. Roy Hattersley sent me a note saying it was brave and elegant, and so did Robert Atkins from our side. It was reported in every paper with the *Financial Times* being especially complimentary: 'The most articulate of the Tory "wets".' I had felt pretty sick with apprehension for most of the day, and as soon as my ordeal was over left the Chamber for a drink and a sandwich. I ran straight into Mrs Thatcher who grasped me by the wrist and said how sorry she was to have missed my speech, and that 'everything would be all right'. Did she mean my umbraged constituents, or her economic policies? I could not tell. It was a kind gesture in the circumstances.

This was not the end of the affair. Unfortunately for me the timing of my escapade could not have been worse for the first Wednesday in March is traditionally the date for the Aldershot Conservatives' largest private meeting, the Annual Women's Conference, held over lunchtime on the well-sprung dance-floor of the Aldershot Officers' Club where Joan Hunter-Dunn had once danced the night away. It was an occasion when we were visited briefly by a cabinet minister. This year I had invited Angus Maude, a devoted Thatcherite who had been rescued by her from a long life spent on the back-benches and whose task in her cabinet was to worry about the presentation of government policy. In retrospect, he seems to have been an odd choice on my behalf. He told the press he would not be coming after all.

I had also invited Sir Paul Bryan, a senior back-bencher and a director of Granada Television, to speak after lunch on the problems of the media (I was at the time the chairman of the party's Media Committee). He said he would turn up, not wishing to embarrass the local party, a point which Maude disregarded. But Bryan made it a condition that I should not sit on the platform beside him. I had little choice but to agree to his condition. In Maude's stead I managed to persude Stephen Murray of the IBA to come and speak in the morning. So Maude was conspicuously absent, Bryan was boring, and Murray far over the heads of the Ladies of Aldershot.

Maude's snub rekindled the interest of the press, who turned up in large numbers to what is usually a private and pedestrian meeting. They must have been pretty bored but at the end of the afternoon their patience was rewarded. I was obliged to read out a statement apologizing for my original article and for not signing it, and reaffirming my support for the government. I thought discretion to be the better part of valour. I managed also to include a paragraph stressing my right to speak out against policies of which I disapproved. The next morning's *Times* wrote of the errant Member eating humble pie. It was for me the worst part of the whole affair. 'General Tom', the Association's president, was very decent about the brouhaha; 'Critchley was put up to it' was his very military view. Jack Bedser, my chairman, said he did not care what I wrote as long as I signed it.

There was a silver lining. John Biffen, learning of my plight at Maude's withdrawal, published a statement in which he said he would be happy to speak for me 'anywhere, anytime'. It was a magnificent gesture of friendship from a cabinet minister who had long admired Mrs Thatcher and was no 'wet'. It was typical of him. As for Angus Maude, all I could do was to remind him gently in the Smoking Room of the occasion in the sixties when he had been sacked from the shadow cabinet by Ted Heath for writing an attack on party policy in the pages of the *Spectator*. He smirked but said nowt. Ironically, when he died in the autumn of 1993, the *Mail* rang me and asked me to write a signed obituary of him. I did so with alacrity. Sometime, somewhere, somebody has the last word.

In summary the whole exercise was a foolish mistake. I would have done far better to have signed the piece. But Norman Lamont said the episode 'had been the making of me'. Apparently I had moved from relative obscurity to relative infamy. It put an end to any faint hope I might have had of gaining office, which came as something of a relief. It had damaged my standing among the Aldershot Tories, although making me something of a hero to the left-wing. A stranger stopped me in New Palace Yard and said how much she admired my courage. But I had not really been brave, for my generalship, such as it was, owed more to General Nivelle than to Marshal Foch.

There is a Spanish proverb which asserts that 'The blow that does not break you, makes you'. I took care to mend my fences in the constituency and my readoption as candidate took place without a hitch three years later. But I also felt freer than ever before to speak out against both the style and substance of Mrs Thatcher's policies. After fifteen years in the House I was, at last, my own man.

20 Going Potty

I have never been asked to lunch or dine at Downing Street – a glance at the Court columns of the smarter newspapers will reveal a regular series of 'entertainments' provided for visiting dignitaries to which MPs and others are invited, but I have yet to break bread. I was asked to drinks by Harold Macmillan in 1960, before the renovation of the building. I remember it as a narrow, dark, panelled Georgian house of the sort smart publishers have bought in Bloomsbury and subsequently ruined. I drank gin and tonic and listened to the Prime Minister talk about the Somme.

In Margaret's day at Number 10, the house was much lighter, seemed bigger, and was furnished in the style of New York's Waldorf Astoria. I took advantage in 1981 of what amounted to an 'open' yearly invitation in June to drinks there on the evening of the royal garden party. There was a notice carried by the weekly 'whip' asking for the names of those MPs who wished to attend.

Royal Garden Parties (more than one is held each summer) are a happy hunting ground for mayors, the chief executives of county and district councils, and their ladies. The Palace becomes a sort of Whipsnade Park for the deserving who attend in their thousands. On the day, the mayoral couple first arrive at the Palace of Westminster by car in time for lunch as guest of the local MP. (In Rushmoor, an amalgam of Aldershot and Farnborough, the mayor was invariably driven from one function to the next in an old, 'liberated' Mercedes-Benz, believed by many to have once belonged to Hermann Goering). After a large and cheerful meal my guests would drive in chains down the Mall to the Palace, the windscreens of their limos emblazoned with coloured laissez-passer. Over the years, I went to the garden party with both my wives and all three of my daughters, me squeezed into morning dress, wives suitably behatted and begloved, daughters done up to the nines and quite unrecognizable.

The performance was always the same. Seven thousand people, Ks, Cs, and MBEs, black military attachés in uniforms designed by Ivor Novello, and squadrons of wheelchairs occupied by the disabled – they were deployed like Darius' Persian hordes across the large, secret gardens and the lake; the mass of infantry, sometimes wheeling alarmingly as the Queen or another royal was spotted mingling elsewhere in the throng. The only sensible thing to do was to sit outside the refreshment tent drinking Earl Grey and eating tiny chocolate-covered Lyons' swiss rolls wrapped in blue and silver paper, while waving cheerfully in the direction of anyone we knew.

Drinks at Number 10 were jolly enough. Mrs Thatcher would stand at the door, shaking her guests by the hand. She knew our wives by name, no easy task in the Conservative party. The party consisted of Tory MPs, their neglected wives and forgotten families, and as there would be no ten o'clock vote on that day we would make up fours or sixes for dinner, either in the Harcourt Room or, on one occasion, with Judy and Tony Buck and their daughter at Claridge's. But after my *Observer* article I had no wish to thrust myself forward as an unwelcome guest, and Mrs Thatcher certainly did not ask me to a function at Number 10, so the Downing Street party became a thing of the past. John Major has never asked me either, although I have yet to be unkind about him. Perhaps Michael Heseltine will one day break my duck?

The Falklands War of 1982 saw Mrs Thatcher at her brilliant best. The challenge to British interests was unequivocal, and a riposte on our part vital if the credibility of our defence policy, and that of Nato, was to be sustained against a potential Soviet threat. Acquiescence to Galtieri would have sent a wrong signal to a more dangerous enemy.

At one level it did not much matter who ruled a group of barren and barely inhabited islands deep in the South Atlantic; in a rational world some sort of lease-back arrangement with joint sovereignty would have made sense, but since when has politics, national or international, ever been a rational activity? At another level it mattered very much indeed. Had Britain accepted the Argentinian occupation of the Malvinas, our reputation as a good ally would have been seriously weakened and our national self-respect totally undermined. Had we done nothing the government would not have survived. If there was no negotiated settlement (for which we were obliged to search), force had to be met with force.

A year before the invasion of the Falklands in April 1982, Nicholas Ridley, who was then a junior Foreign Office minister, had tried to negotiate a lease-back arrangement with the Argentinians: he had made a statement in the House which had been rubbished by both sides; the Tory Right joining with the Labour front-bench in ridiculing his efforts. No attempt had been made by the whips to smooth his path. Sir Bernard Braine, a spokesman for the Falklands interest, was pink with rage. Sir John Biggs-Davison could barely contain himself. The traditional right wing of the Tory party was outraged. Ridley, who was exhausted having flown back from the the South Atlantic and driven straight to the House, did his laid-back best, but the compromise was clearly doomed. It was therefore all the more surprising that the government should have persisted with its proposed cuts in the Royal Navy, announced in 1981, which had already brought the admirals to the point of mutiny. Had they been carried out as planned, the expedition to recapture the islands could not have been mounted.

The service chiefs are among the world's most shameless lobbyists. The First Sea Lord, Admiral Sir Henry Leach, invited me to a discreet lunch at Admiralty House where we were served a dull meal (mince, tinned peas and mashed potatoes) by two jolly Jack tars. I was let in rather furtively and was surprised that the 'First' (as he was known) had not made it a condition of my acceptance that I first hire an able seaman's uniform. Leach seemed to have little time for his Secretary of State, John Nott. Neither had I, although he had once asked me for the name of my tailor. I had been invited because I was one of the three vice-chairmen of the party's back-bench Defence Committee. I told him that we were all worried about the extent of the proposed cuts and that the officers of the committee were due to visit the Prime Minister in Downing Street to tell her so tomorrow. The Admiral seemed pleased, and wished us luck. 'I admire her greatly,' he said, 'but she will listen to John Nott.'

The appointment was for eleven o'clock the next morning. Tony Buck was as nervous as a kitten; as chairman (and one-time navy minister), it would be his task to warn Mrs Thatcher of the consequences of her parsimony. Victor Goodhew, MP for St Albans, was his strong, silent self. Winston Churchill, however, did not seem to be affected by nerves; indeed, upon our arrival at Number 10, he spoke out loudly about his grandfather, and by doing so put Mrs Thatcher briefly in her place (she always insisted on calling the Great Man 'Winston', much to the fury of the Churchill family).

Impatiently, and with a fixed and dangerous smile, she heard Young Winston out. We were then seated on a circle of chairs. Tony Buck, having cleared his throat, shuffled his notes. The Prime Minister was gracious, but combative. Her head cocked slightly to one side, she fixed Buck with her unblinking stare. She was also, as we had been warned, not a good listener, frequently interrupting the hesitant Buck and launching into tedious monologues. At one stage she noticed that my attention was wandering. 'Why are you looking around the room, Julian?' she demanded. It was the voice of the headmistress. I said I was admiring the furniture and decoration, which did include some rather special nineteenth-century Staffordshire figures of Wellington and Peel on the mantelshelf. She was not appeased. I should have asked her, of course, whether she intended to withdraw HMS *Endurance* from the South Atlantic, and if she thought it wise to do so, but I did not. It did not seem worthwhile. In fact, she continued to defend her decision to withdraw the ship at Prime Minister's questions (despite Peter Carrington's privately expressed objections) up to the week before the Argentine invasion on 2 April.

On the Thursday before the Argentines struck I went to Cambridge for a Königswinter Conference. Such meetings are held twice a year in England and in Germany to cement Anglo-German friendship and are attended by a coven of politicians, diplomats and academics. We met in King's College. On the first evening we dined and were lectured on the Cold War; by the Friday, rumours of conflict in the South Atlantic were followed by news of the Argentine invasion. The Cold War was forgotten, and the delegates huddled round the television watching the Argentinian armoured personnel carriers drive into Port Stanley. 'We are with you,' hissed two German friends as we crossed the darkening quadrangle to dine in hall.

It was warm; the wind had dropped and there was the first hint of spring in the air. The daffodils were *en fête* in the Master's Garden (one should not write about Cambridge without paying tribute to the underrated novels of C. P. Snow). Late on the Friday afternoon I had gone for a walk and spotted in a nearby antique shop a small Staffordshire pottery jug by David Wilson, decorated in the classical manner. I bought it for £40, the first piece of Staffordshire pottery in a collection which I was to sell at Christie's for £23,000 ten years later. It was my 'Falklands' jug, the start of a collection that was to be paid for out of the proceeds of my journalism.

In college, the excitement and incredulity grew as news of the invasion monopolized the news bulletins. Peter Carrington looked both grave and embarrassed, as well he might. There were shots of Admiral Leach en route to Downing Street; he carried with him, we were later to learn, the outline plans for the Task Force. There was no sign of Mrs Thatcher. General Galtieri appeared on a balcony in Buenos Aires to break the news to a crowd of many thousands. The screen seemed filled with exultant blue and white Argentinian flags. As soldiers, the Argentinians were something of an unknown quantity, although it was the view of a retired German general that as the 'Argies' were half Italian and half Spanish, only the Spanish half would fight. A message was delivered from the government whips' office summoning Tory MPs back to a Saturday sitting of the Commons the next day, a unique occasion in my experience.

We left Cambridge after an early breakfast. I drove Ray Witney and two other Tory MPs to London, arriving at the Palace of Westminster promptly at eleven o'clock. The principal speakers from the government benches were John Nott (who was given the bird) and Margaret Thatcher, who was listened to by our side in frigid silence. There was little she could say, and what she did she said badly. Ray Witney made a brave speech in which he urged negotiation, but the mood was ugly and the sentiments gung-ho. At three o'clock the debate concluded on a motion to adjourn, but almost the entire Tory party then tramped upstairs to Committee Room 14 where a combined meeting of the back-bench Foreign and Defence Committees was to be held to which the Foreign Secretary had been summoned.

As an officer of the Defence Committee, I had a place on the platform. 'If the buggers want my resignation, they can have it,' said Carrington as he took his seat on the right of the chairman. The '22, however constituted, so often a theatre of the absurd, can swiftly become a theatre of cruelty. On that Saturday afternoon, the large committee-room was packed almost to the rafters, the anticipatory noise quite deafening. The Tory party, which for much of the time is torpid, had come alive, lashing its collective tail like an angry disturbed alligator. All the 'old fools' were there: Freddy Burden, Michael Brotherton, Freddy Bennett *et al.*; the 'catering corps' in what constitutes the regiment that is the Tory party.

The Martyrdom of Lord Carrington was one of three such meetings at which the Conservative party wrought its anger upon individuals who, for a variety of reasons, had been summoned to appear before the 1922 Committee. After his ordeal, Peter Carrington promptly resigned and was replaced by Francis Pym. The 'buggers' had got their way. In 1986, Leon Brittan was forced to resign as Secretary of State for Trade and Industry in the aftermath of the Westland Affair, following a meeting of the '22 in which anti-semitism played a large part. He carried Margaret's can. One of the silly old things, John Stokes, later to be knighted, called publicly for Brittan to be replaced by 'a red-faced Englishman'. We had more than our share of them. And George Howard, the chairman of governors at the BBC, together with the DG Alasdair Milne, were almost swept away on a tide of bad temper and worse manners. George Howard, Willie Whitelaw's fat friend, put up a stout defence of the BBC, the independence of which has never been properly understood by the simpler Tory, who continues to this day to assert (despite all the evidence to the contrary) that we have the best newspapers in the world and the worst broadcasting. Alistair Milne kept his head down and, wisely perhaps, left it all to George who played to the hilt the role of a Whig grandee with a pack of Tory shopkeepers baying at his park gates.

But to return to the Falklands. The war became a vast sporting event watched nightly by the nation. The slow progress of the Task Force southwards, the continual search for a negotiated settlement (which, had it been achieved, would have been almost impossible to sell to the 1922 Committee), the unspoken realization that Mrs Thatcher's future and that of her government were dependent upon the recapture of the islands, the sinking of the *Belgrano* and of HMS *Sheffield* and the lethality of the Exocet missile: all these factors and more amounted to the longest period of sustained political excitement I can remember. Popular economic discontents were largely forgotten, buried beneath a rediscovered patriotism as typified by the scenes of the ships of the Task Force setting sail from Portsmouth. It was the very best sort of war: fought at a distance against a second-class enemy and with no fear of retaliation on the homeland. And our servicemen were all regulars. It was a bit like the Boer War but without the Boers; in keeping with those times, as the warships cast anchor at Portsmouth, the Royal Marine band struck up 'The Soldiers of the Queen'.

In retrospect, the Falklands War was, like Waterloo, 'a damn' close-run thing', although we did not know it at the time. The Junta made the mistake of stationing the best Argentinian regular units on the Chilean border, leaving the Malvinas to be defended by a largely conscripted force. The excursion of the *Belgrano* towards the southern flank of the Task Force was to have been matched by an air strike from the carrier *25 May* to the north, but as there was no wind (almost unknown in the South Atlantic), the aircraft could not take off. Furthermore, five bombs dropped by land-based aircraft which struck British ships failed to explode owing to their faulty fuses. As the war progressed, it might be said that even Mrs Thatcher held her breath.

It would be churlish to take credit away from the Prime Minister. She was, quite simply, at her best. Her single-mindedness was better suited to conflict, and although her demand that we 'rejoice, rejoice' at an early success grated on the ears of many, her willingness to take decisions (not always the case in peacetime), endeared her to her naval and military commanders. The sinking of the *Belgrano* was, in my view, justifiable; although the Government's later reluctance to tell the whole truth about the incident was politically damaging. The service of thanksgiving at St Paul's and the victory parade through the City of London gave unnecessary offence: Denis Thatcher's oblique attack on the Archbishop's perfectly proper sermon was a rebuke at second hand; while the presence of the Prime Minister rather than the Queen on the dais with the Lord Mayor raised many an eyebrow, not least among senior officers in Aldershot.

Victory in the Falklands restored the fortunes of the government, and with it the Prime Minister's waning popularity. The voter who had been short of bread no longer lacked for circuses. It was very heady stuff, rather like winning the World Cup away from home. It was clear that a general election could not be long delayed, and that when it came the Tories would have little difficulty in winning. The beginning of Mrs Thatcher's 'imperial period' dates from the summer of 1982.

Her political pre-eminence happily coincided with a healthy demand for my journalism. Whereas I had in the past written largely about defence, I was now asked to write about almost anything I chose – as long as it had a joke or two about Mrs Thatcher. I have, perhaps, the gift of irony, and a Tory MP who was willing to poke fun at her imperiousness and self-righteousness was a gift to many editors, not least in the so-called Tory press. In the eighties, I became a well-paid gadfly.

I also wrote three books, all of which became 'best-sellers', a largely mean-ingless marketing term. The first was *Westminster Blues* (published by Elm Tree), the second *Heseltine, the Unauthorized Biography* (André Deutsch), the third *The Palace of Varieties* (John Murray). All three sold five thousand or so in hardback, and ten or more in paperback. They were all better and more widely reviewed than they were financially successful, the most profitable event for me being the decision of the *Express* to serialize *Heseltine*. I made more money from the spin-offs from the publication of all three than I did from the publishers. Unless you are an Archer, a Dobbs or a Townsend, there is much more money to be made from journalism than from writing books. My anonymous *Observer* article brought me to the attention of Russell Twisk's *Listener* for whom I wrote regularly for several years: frequent 'Centrepieces' and an annual trudge around the Liberal, Social Democrat, Labour and, most enjoyably, Tory party conferences.

My *Heseltine*, which could not in any sense be described as an academic biography, pleased neither Michael nor Anne (wives of subjects of biographies are always the harder to please), but left me in the happy position of being regarded by the media as the expert on Michael, despite the fact that we have seen little of each other for twenty-five years. The Westland affair and Michael's bid for the leadership of the party four years later brought me into a reasonably profitable prominence. But I did maintain, and still do, that the book was a sympathetic portrait of a man I admire; sympathetic without being fulsome or flattering. I was certainly prepared to put my career on the line on his behalf in November 1990.

A few days after the publication of *Heseltine* in 1987 I had a telephone call from Kelvin Mackenzie, the editor of the *Sun*. Would I care to write a piece of

800 words on a political theme and bring it round to him in Fleet Street with a view to my writing a weekly column to be paid at the rate of £400 a go?

I came to the conclusion that it would be both priggish and unprofessional to refuse. I hate the cheap British press and all that it has come to stand for: its cruelty; its invasiveness and its political crassness; I vowed I would not stoop, and that what money I earned (tabloid 'contracts' are notoriously short-lived) would be spent on valuable pieces of Staffordshire pottery to be cherished or sold as circumstances permitted.

Writing for the popular press is not as easy as one might think. I composed my eight hundred words and set off for the *Sun*'s offices. I was kept waiting for fifteen minutes or so, clutching my copy in my hot hand. Mackenzie had been playing squash; he arrived with a towel wrapped round his neck and continued to play strokes with an imaginary racquet. I told him I had taken care not to write 'down'. 'Write down?' he exclaimed. 'Write up, write up with the *Sun*.' It seemed as good a slogan as any other. 'We want you to give us class on Fridays,' he said. I said I would strive to do so. He took the envelope and placed it on his desk, unopened. 'Loved your *Heseltine*. When I read that Michael Heseltine "could not see a parapet without ducking below it" I knew you was our man.' I suppose I made four or five thousand pounds out of the 'soaraway *Sun*', money that I distributed among the smarter pottery dealers of London in return for Lakin and Poole, Enoch Wood and Tittensor. I learnt later from the *Sun*'s lobby correspondent that I had been thought 'very professional' but had been dropped eventually for making jokes about Margaret. It served me right.

I am an uncertain nymph, or should it be shepherd? My passions, such as they are, are transitory; my cold eye alighting briefly on the beloved only to glance elsewhere. I am talking not of my private passions but my public ones; as for the former I am no John Osborne – I have been married twice but my lips are more or less sealed. I remember the view of marriage held by the Prince of Salina in *The Leopard*; 'a year of flames and thirty of ashes', a dictum which in my case can certainly be multiplied by two.

But to revert to my public passions. My father and his brother were both compulsive collectors: my father of Oscar Wilde and the French Second Empire; my uncle, of netsuke and Persian carpets. They were forever dropping into antique shops. I have collected stamps, railway locomotive numbers, modern paintings (Rosoman, Napper, Gill and several Haitian primitives), and, for a short time, churches. Around 1979–80 I became an ecclesiologist, prompted by John Betjeman's love of churches I was forever stopping before out of the way parish churches, scrutinizing the list of rectors for Keble men, inhaling that unique mixture of damp hymnbooks, Mansion polish and dead flowers; the veritable odour of sanctity, hoping to find that rarest of architectural features the Saxon triple chancel arch (there was one in the Isle of Thanet but it was 'restored' by the Victorians). But I was soon myself again, and instead of putting pennies into offertory boxes I was putting pounds into the hands of pottery dealers.

After the aforementioned David Wilson cream jug (*circa* 1812) that I picked up in Cambridge, the slope was slippery and made more so by the success of my pen. After I wrote in a *Times* profile that 'Mrs Thatcher could not see an institution without hitting it with her handbag' I treated myself to a silver and blue sporting lustre jug; after I called the Prime Minister 'the Great She Elephant' (a compliment in Swaziland where it is a title reserved for the likes of the Queen Mum), I purchased a Lakin and Poole figure of Ganymede, the cup-bearer of the gods. But I also began in a more humble way, nose pressed to the windows of antique fairs and markets, my eye caught by the cheerful vulgarity of mid-nineteenth-century equestrian figures of Victoria's children or of Mazeppa, tied willingly to her circus horse.

I made friends with dealers. Most of them do the bulk of their business within the trade, their more expensive items – some having been acquired at house sales or provincial auction-rooms – ending up either in the Brompton Road, or Church Street, Kensington or, surprisingly, in Stow-on-the-Wold where Cotswold-loving Americans in search of a glimpse of a minor royal pause for lunch. Prices are lowest in small country towns, and what a joy it can be to pay a visit to a strange, small market town, and lunch at an unreconstructed Georgian hotel on a rack of spring lamb and half a bottle of unlikely Burgundy (Chambolle Musigny Les Amoureux?), before spending an afternoon rummaging in antique shops. The chances of finding anything very good are remote, although I did pick up a Prattware jug of Nelson while on a pilgrimage to Grantham.

I like busts best. Pottery busts of the great and the good come in three sizes: the small, three to four inches high; the middling, which are the most coveted, eight to ten inches and the large, up to twenty-two inches, for which one needs either a library or a pillar and a marble hall. The best of them were made by either Richard Riley or Enoch Wood; not all are readily identifiable – no name, no maker's number – which adds to the fun and the frustration. I had a Peel, a Prattware Napoleon and a Prince of Wales (Prinney) on whom the radical Staffordshire potters had lavished their disapproval. The Prince is jowly and flushed, like us Tories, having lived unwisely and too well. I decided not to sell a large bust of Minerva who graces my Shropshire study or a small bust of the brave Old Duke of York, who reminds me of Lord Pym.

As I have written, the Staffordshire potters were radicals to a man. The busts, the jugs and the chimney ornaments, the so-called 'flat backs' commemorate the Whigs and not the Tories, although Peel, once he had repealed the Corn Laws, was treated generously enough. The great Napoleon begins as a villain but by the 1830s and 40s has become a hero. The Reform Bill, the Corn Laws and the Chartist movement feature most prominently. A figure I once sought was Duncombe, a radical MP who not only presented the Chartist petition to Parliament but was also chosen as the best-dressed Member, one of the few honours to come my way.

But the early potters did not let their prejudices come between them and their profits. For every Orator Hunt there must have been a thousand young Victorias, while the unlucky Queen Caroline, whose cause was taken up by the Whigs so as to tease George IV, is commemorated by plate, plaque and jug. The Staffordshire potters played throughout the nineteenth century a part which is played today by the *Sun* and the *Mirror*. They, too, held the front page, substituting the name of the latest murderer, trickster or sporting star on ready-made moulds, selling within hours of his execution the figure of Dr Rush or William Palmer, or of Jenny Lind or Amelia Bloomer. The carefully mixed brew of sex, sport and royalty existed long before Murdoch and Maxwell. The potters modelled in clay the nineteenth-century equivalents of David Mellor and the dreadful Miss Sanchez, Tony and Benvenida Buck, Fergie, Di, Parkinson and Keays, and Hartley Booth, their likenesses taken from theatrical handbills or from copies of the *Illustrated London News*.

Having scampered through the foothills of the antiques world, I did once visit the Grosvenor House Antiques Show. A hundred padded stalls were set out in the great ballroom, each with an exquisite young man perpetually washing his hands. Gone were the tens and hundreds, and there was nothing as vulgar as a price ticket to be seen. The prices, if one dared to ask, were in the thousands. I was boxing out of my class. I was also English. The fair seemed full of the better sort of German, by East Prussia out of Frankfurt, while the Americans all looked like George Bush. I ran into my one-time sister-in-law, Sarah Baron, who was once married to my putative brother-in-law Alastair McAlpine, a prominent member of Queen Margaret's Court. Paula divorced me a fortnight or so before her half-sister's marriage to him. Sarah told me of an American couple who flew their interior decorator from Houston to the Grosvenor House to help them choose between three sofas. In the end, they bought two of the three. Even though it was the last day of the sale, and some dealers were willing to accept a 20 per cent reduction in price, it was all far too expensive for me. I took a cab to the Victoria and Albert Museum where there is displayed a marvellous collection of Staffordshire, all beautifully displayed in those long and near-deserted galleries (the best collection is to be found at the City Museum and Art Gallery at Hanley, Stoke-on-Trent, where it is looked after by its curator, Mrs Pat Halfpenny). For a moment I was tempted to become the Raffles of Mrs Thatcher's Conservative party.

The politician's pocket can more legally be lined by his pen: one has only to think of Roy Jenkins (I have recently re-read his *Dilke* and found it fascinating), Roy Hattersley, Gerald Kaufman and George Walden. Alan Clark's diaries were the political publishing success of 1993; far racier and more readable than Margaret Thatcher's ghost-written 'manifesto'. Matthew Parris, who was allowed to languish on the Tory back-benches for so long, has made a much greater success of a career as a political journalist. His homosexuality was a factor in his failure to win promotion from the back-benches; not the fact of it, which was known, but his decision to 'come out'. He was told by Michael Jopling, then Chief Whip, that he should be more discreet; 'I do not believe in God,' said Joppers, 'but I don't go around saying so.'

Quite so. Tory Chief Whips are strong but usually silent men, not known for their dicta. In this context the only story worth repeating is a boast of Martin Redmayne, Harold Macmillan's and Alec Home's Chief Whip. I was told that immediately after our defeat in the 1964 general election he summoned the newly elected to Committee Room 10 to put them in the picture. They were, predictably enough, few in number. He concluded by saying in his best military tones (he had been a brigadier, but so had most Tories of his generation), 'Pay no attention to rumours. For instance, there is a rumour that I may not stay on as Chief Whip; it is quite untrue.' Within a fortnight he had been appointed opposition spokesman on transport.

Politicians, like actors and parsons, are essentially performers; we are as good as our last speech. This applies to ministers as well as back-benchers. Ministers, however, rarely have to rely upon themselves for their scripts, which are written for them by clever Wykehamists in their private offices. The less competent cannot even stick to their text. Back-benchers on the other hand generally write their own material, although there is a tendency for MPs to make use of the talents of their graduate researchers to provide a first draft. Ministers, who speak from the front-bench, have the considerable advantage of being permitted to rest their notes on the dispatch box; back-benchers stand uneasily poised between rows of benches, their shins hard up against the bench in front, the edge of their seat catching them painfully behind the knee, a constriction that discourages the extravagant use of gesture. Nevertheless, a good speech in the House remains the quickest route to promotion. Outside the Chamber there are two alternatives: the unpaid performance, usually to a party audience, and the paid performance, almost invariably to a group of businessmen. The latter is self-evidently to be preferred.

The King of the so-called 'rubber chicken circuit' was undoubtedly Michael Heseltine. After he walked out on Mrs Thatcher in January 1986, having failed to persuade her to permit a full cabinet discussion of his proposals for the future of Westland, Michael embarked on a nationwide campaign of unpaid party speaking, usually at women's lunches held in British Legion halls or Conservative clubs. It was the equivalent of Gladstone's Midlothian campaign. These are the traditional venues for an event the origins of which are probably post-war. I suspect that Lord Woolton must have had something to do with it. There is no account in Chips Channon's diaries of its author submitting himself to so unfashionable a custom before Hitler's war. He was far more likely to take luncheon with the Cunards, Nancy and Emerald, than to travel to Colchester to address the ladies of Essex. I have spoken at many Tory lunch and supper clubs, a wearying experience in which two glasses of cheap wine of the sort for which not even Oz Clark could find a good word (or Jilly Goolden, several), reconstituted tomato soup, the grains of which cling to the edge of the bowl with the tenacity of first wives, a leg of chicken with tinned potatoes followed by a tinned peach and cheap ice-cream, are no compensation whatsoever. Oswald Mosley wrote in his memoirs that a speaker, whatever the function, should not rely on alcohol but on his own adrenaline. Would that I could.

The marriage of food and oratory is not made in heaven. The MP is frequently judged by the quality of the guest he can manage to attract to the constituency annual dinner. This is essentially a fund-raising and social occasion on which people will spend a surprising amount of money on both the ticket and the inevitable raffle. In Aldershot I managed over the years to persuade such party 'stars' as John Major ('Your Member is a good egg' – it was the time of Edwina Currie's brush with salmonella), Jim Prior, Enoch Powell (incredibly tedious), Virginia Bottomley, Keith Joseph (tortured), Ted Heath (magisterial) and many others whose names and speeches I have mercifully forgotten. I was never in a position to ask a favour of Margaret, much to the annoyance of some of my supporters. In return, I would accept an invitation to speak at one of their second-division functions, like a women's lunch. It is in this way that politicians take in each other's washing.

I do remember with some pleasure speaking in Hendon at the annual dinner in John Gorst's constituency. The atmosphere was Jewish, the beef was salt and the company more fun than usual. Throughout the dinner a gloomy old man, lost in an erotic reverie, played thirties popular music on a portable electric organ. Mrs Gorst, who was sitting on my right, turned out to be the ballerina who had danced the lead with the Festival Ballet on the occasion in Oxford when I had been hired as an extra: together we opened the dancing, 'stately Buck Milligan' and the sugar-plum fairy.

Fame, or the reputation of being an amusing after-dinner speaker, can bring invitations to give a paid performance. After Kenneth Clarke's first budget in November 1993, I read in *The Times* that Lord Lawson ('Fat Nige' to his less respectful colleagues), had been paid a fee of £10,000 to comment on the budget at a City dinner. I was never in his league but I did receive a fee of £3,000 at the height of the Lawson boom to travel to Weston Park on the Shropshire/Staffordshire border to give an after-dinner talk to twenty-five Japanese businessmen. The dinner was good, the businessmen drunk and exhausted (they had arrived by chopper from a factory tour) and I duly went through my routine, raising not a single laugh. But I had the last one; I calculated while on my feet that each one of my unconscious audience was being clocked up at the rate of £120 a head.

My residual stutter had eventually disappeared, and my timing, thanks to much practice, hugely improved. I was less successful in Stratford-up on-Avon. 'Celebrity Speakers' (not to be confused with 'Prime Performers'), an agency run by Bernard Braden and Barbara Kelly, asked me to drive to a hotel in the town and deliver an after-dinner speech to a sales conference organized by a Midlands engineering firm. The fee was £1,500. I asked my son Joshua to drive me, and after a hard week we travelled on a Friday evening through the winter dusk from Oxford to Stratford along that notoriously slow and crowded road that has now been relieved by the opening of the M40. The pre-dinner drinks began at seven amid much Brummagem cheer. The dinner began at nine, by which time I was already whacked, and the 'conference' as merry as Warwickshire crickets. At eleven thirty I was finally called to speak by the firm's boss who was not sitting on my table. The gloss had already left the occasion, and I could hear some of my neighbours gloomily running a sweepstake as to how bloody long the speaker would stay on his feet. I decided to make use of my officer-like qualities, and to speak not for twenty minutes but for ten minutes. I did so, and won a few laughs from an exhausted audience, the bulk of which must have been wishing it was tucked up in bed. Joshua and I then drove back through the night to Farnham along uncluttered roads – I certainly could not have slept well in the hotel. The next morning I had a telephone call from

Braden. Mr Richard Ireland, a director of the firm and a self-important common little man with a Sparkbrook accent, had in consequence of my ten minutes cut my fee in half. 'Did I mind?' I must have hesitated. 'We'll make it up to you,' urged Bernie. He never did. Still, £750 was a lot more than I usually got for speaking to the party faithful and recently converted.

What can be fun are the occasions when publishers arrange for their authors to speak at so-called literary lunches. Pretty girls, usually Sloanes, escort their authors from studio to studio and take them on long journeys to speak at provincial lunches. In Manchester I sat next to Freddie Forsyth whose shot cuff could not disguise a Rolex carved, no doubt, from a solid block of gold. I did not ask him the time. Antonia Fraser spoke about the life and loves of Henry VIII, while Lionel Blue told his audience of literate Mancunians the story of the Catholic American tourist who stays the night in Dracula's castle. At midnight there is a blast of wind, a clap of thunder, and a foul fiend stands in the open window. The terrified woman holds up her crucifix; the apparition replies (in a Jewish accent) 'Lady, is this your unlucky day . . .'

There is no chance of one's fee being cut in half, as there isn't one, after lunch the four rival authors sit at tables signing books as if their lives depended on it. I have done several such lunches, and a dinner at the Randolph in Oxford, and hope to perform at one or two more. In Ludlow I struggled up the hill on my crutches for a signing of *Borderlands – Shropshire and the Welsh Marches*, a coffee-table book with photographs by Dave Paterson. I signed fifty copies and sold, much to my surprise, two of my paperbacks, *Hung Parliament* and *Floating Voter* to a parson. 'I see Enoch Powell thinks them salacious,' was his cheerful comment. The publishers' Sloanes are always eager to persuade their authors to submit to interviews of one kind or another, usually conducted by fierce feminists lacking in humour. My advice would be to avoid Julie Birchill, Kate Muir and Lynn Reid-Banks.

21 Farewells

The 1983 general election was remarkable not only for the size of Mrs Thatcher's majority, which was 140, but also for the departure from the Commons of three Tory MPs, each of whom was memorable in his own peculiar way. Billy Rees-Davies who was finally ditched by his constituency party in West Thanet, Derek Walker-Smith, who abandoned Hertfordshire for the House of Lords, and 'Jock' Bruce-Gardyne who failed to win readoption in his constituency, but was made a life peer later in the year.

Of the three by far the most colourful was Billy Rees-Davies, known as 'the one-armed bandit', having lost an arm while fighting in Africa with the Welsh Guards. David Walder always asserted he had lost it in bed. His disability gave him a list to starboard, and his habit of wearing a dark cloak lined with red silk which he would throw awkwardly around his shoulders while standing in the Members' Lobby gave rise to his alternative nickname 'Dracula'. He was a barrister always in contention with the authorities of his profession; he was twice suspended from the Bar. On one other occasion he failed to appear at the Kent Assizes as he was speaking to a Tory luncheon club in his constituency at the point when he should have been making the final speech on behalf of his client. This gave rise to hilarity in the whips' office and beyond as Billy was believed to be as rare a bird in Thanet as he was in Westminster. *The Times'* obituarist, a master of the raised eyebrow, described his private life as 'animated' and claimed that in the House he was 'more rakish than effective'. Towards the end he drank heavily and was barred from driving. He sat for Thanet for thirty years before the constituency worms finally turned, which proves, in his case at least, the immense latitude that can be allowed the Member by his party activists who must have been aware of his goings-on, stories appearing frequently in both the national and local press (or was it just apathy?). Victor Ludorum while a boy at Eton, Billy in the real world rarely played the game.

Sir Derek Walker-Smith, later Lord Broxbourne, was also a lawyer but a very respectable one indeed. When I used to dine regularly in the Members' Dining

Room in the late eighties he would frequently come down the corridor from the Lords in search of more congenial, or perhaps just younger companions. Although splendidly pompous and never at a loss for a Latin tag, he was great fun; a benign old buffer who practised a lapel-clutching form of oratory hand-crafted for impressing judge and jury. He was for a time chairman of the 1922 Committee, and Minister of Health in Harold Macmillan's government. However, he could never manage to persuade the Tory party to share his opposition to the Common Market. In the sixties, Derek Walker-Smith, together with Sir Robin Turton (gaunt and tongue-tied in comparison), and the young Peter Walker (before he thought twice about it) were the three mus-keteers, receiving the cheers of several party conferences but never their votes. Bill (Nametape) Cash, Sir Teddy Taylor and 'Mother' Teresa Gorman, who today rage against Britain's role in Europe, are in a different league. What was remarkable about Derek Walker-Smith was his distinction in three different political fields: as the senior Tory back-bencher, as a minister, although not in the cabinet, and as a loose party cannon aimed at the heart of Europe. He was also the last Tory MP who invariably wore a black lawyer's jacket and striped trousers. He was as plummy and 'pre-war' as Julian Amery.

In January 1990, I waited in line in the Members' Cafeteria to buy a cup of tea. Standing in front of me was a tall, emaciated man wearing a woolly hat. He took it off and exposed an ivory-coloured bald head. He greeted me by name. I did not immediately recognize him and my bewilderment must have shown. 'Its Jock,' he said, 'Jock Bruce-Gardyne. I've got cancer.'

Jock Bruce-Gardyne, a handsome man in his prime, was another 'original'. A clever right-winger with a contempt for the rituals of constituency life, he was forever either losing seats or failing to get himself readopted after the Boundary Commission had divided his seat three ways. He was a Treasury minister in Mrs Thatcher's early years who wrote pithy, monetarist leader columns for the *Telegraph*. He was fond of telling a story against himself. An Angus farmer, once a constituent of his, found himself in Knutsford, Jock's second Cheshire seat. The farmer enquired tentatively the size of Bruce-Gardyne's new majority. On being told 20,000, he said, 'Ooch, that will nay be enough for our Jock.'

Jock was an ideologue but with a sense of humour, and very accident prone. Some cad at the *Financial Times* published a private 'thank you' letter to Sam Brittan in which Bruce-Gardyne, then a minister, poured scorn on the triumphalism and trumpery that followed the Falklands War. Embarrassment was total, and the fallout probably made it impossible for him to be reselected as a candidate for the 1983 election. It was to Mrs Thatcher's credit that she promptly sent him to the Lords. I did not know Jock very well, but I admired him. He met 'the last enemy' in 1990 with jaunty courage.

I had a good 1983 election. My name did not appear in the newspapers, and I spent the best part of four weeks being bounced from one end of my constituency to the other, accosting perfect strangers. My telephone remained silent, my postbag dwindled to almost nothing and the soles of my shoes grew holes. I spoke, but only infrequently, and when I did I was careful not to suggest, as did Kenny Everett at that frightful rally in Birmingham, that we bomb the Russians into submission.

I was once more a foot-soldier in the great campaign. I would return home late at night, dizzy with fatigue, and slump before the telly to watch my elders and betters. Norman Tebbit, proof of the proposition that North Sea oil did everything for Mrs Thatcher's cabinet save refine it, Michael Foot leaning on his white stick and Roy Jenkins, who upon his walkabouts gave his well-known impression of a good man fallen among thieves.

I have grown increasingly to dislike party politics; all those people and all that noise. The grim determination of those who should know better not to face the issues or to answer questions. In 1983 we witnessed Michael Foot's tortured equivocations when asked to face up to the implications of the unhappy compromise that was Labour's defence policy, and Mrs Thatcher's breathless refusal to discuss the inevitable rise in the levels of future public spending, falling back on the irrelevancy that the plans had been costed 'for the next three years'. There was so much rhubarb and so much rubbish. The failure of the Labour party even to consider using the techniques of presentation and projection (they were not to do so until 1987) which contrasted with the glib efficiency with which we built upon our popularity. Maggie rules OK? Who could forget the sheer awfulness of our specially commissioned theme song ('Maggie Thatcher'), and the projection by Conservative Central Office of one woman as the presidential candidate. Indeed, had it really been a presidential election I would have voted for Roy Jenkins. Kenny Everett and his Young Conservative rally would have seen to that. It was a relief to switch off the TV and get back on the streets.

My fifth election in Aldershot was virtually a two-horse race. The Labour candidate lost his deposit and I was chased to the tape by an energetic Young Liberal wielding a municipal drainpipe. But nationally the result was never in doubt. Victory in the Falklands had transmuted what many had previously seen as Mrs Thatcher's obstinacy into resolution. I can remember one incident from the campaign. In Mattingley at a farm owned by Miles Hudson, the president of the Aldershot Tories, I was invited to enter a long hut packed to the eaves with battery hens. Their heads poking through the bars, they faced one another in their thousands across an aisle for all the world as if they were Members of Parliament. The air was filled with dust, and the chamber reverberated to the noise of protest, petulance and pique; all that was needed was Mr Speaker Thomas with wattle and spurs. I shut the door swiftly upon such horrid symbolism.

Is all the campaigning worthwhile? It is without doubt an exhausting business, unaccustomed physical activity combined with the psychological strain of leadership, of projecting oneself from either platform or pavement. My *Observer* article had long been forgotten and I was busily accumulating credit in the bank. It is hard work being nice to people for four weeks; I marvel at the stamina of the great: the sight of Michael Foot, not far off seventy, humping his own bags in the wake of his defeat and Mrs Thatcher inexhaustibly feeding off her own zealotry. I do not think my activity made any difference to my vote (55 per cent), I could not have been seen by more than 800 of my 80,000 electorate. But it was a necessary ritual.

The mid-eighties saw the beginning and the end of the short life of the Social Democrats. I would not have let Dr David Owen take me up the mountain to show me the kingdoms of the world but Roy Jenkins would have been a more congenial guide. I might have succumbed and joined his party. At the time there was much to be said for doing so. I had admired Roy Jenkins ever since his campaign in favour of Britain's entry into the Common Market in the early sixties; he seemed a most attractive political figure: articulate, literary (he reviewed books for the *Observer*) and excessively moderate. If only the remainder of the Labour party had been like him. But one might as well have wished that the Conservative and Unionist party had modelled itself on Iain Macleod. I watched the better end of the Labour party hive off in favour of the Social Democrats, and enjoyed vicariously the pleasures and excitments of setting up a new, and apparently more sensible, political party. What fun it might have been to re-emerge in new colours, to be set to work building the New Jerusalem (in contrast with Nigel Lawson's Treasury, then known as 'Jerusalem the Golden'), and to escape from the rigours of Mrs Thatcher's Protectorate.

As part of my political journalism I went for three years to the annual Social Democrat Conference, visiting Manchester, Buxton and Torquay in turn – towns which made a welcome change from the much patronized Blackpool and Brighton. How very different was the atmosphere at all three venues. There was plenty of nut cutlet but very little rhubarb. The Social Democrats had brought their pretty wives to the Chinese restaurants of Manchester, after which they drove in their Volvos to the University of Salford, hitherto famous for its collection of the paintings of L. S. Lowry. The conference was a decorous affair, everyone being short of tongue and long of temper, making Salford quite unlike Matthew Arnold's Dover Beach 'where ignorant armies clash by night', which can all too easily typify Labour and Conservative seaside activities elsewhere.

At Tory conferences we are bored by the mayor, take the Almighty into our confidence and are presided over by some aimable old buffer whose cheerful incompetence is invariably rewarded with a knighthood. It was not like that in Salford. There was no sign of the Revd Nicholas Stacey (or of God) although Paul Masson had flown in bringing fraternal greetings from the Napa valley. It was all a little smug; an atmosphere of brown rice, Cabernet Sauvignon and the Ham and High. In debate, points were made rationally, rhetoric cut to the bone and humbug largely absent. That was not at all what I was used to.

The delegates at all three conferences reminded me of a saying of Verlaine's: '*Pas de couleur; rien que la nuance.*' They were all so genteel. The Tory party conference has become over the years a working-class festival, full of those who rallied to Mrs Thatcher's populist standard and have stayed on to make John Major's life a misery. Each year, under Mrs T at least, a prominent Tory was tossed from the platform into the crowd, a necessary sacrifice for the party's good. Such a fate did not befall the only Tory apostate at Salford, Mr Christopher Brocklebank Fowler.

Buxton, a dark-stone town set amid wild moors, was an ideal setting for David Owen to play Heathcliff to Shirley Williams' Cathy. The conference showed the Social Democrats at their most austere. On the other hand, Roy shone at Torquay. It was quite balmy. Roy Jenkins told me that Torquay used to be called 'the Naples of the South West' in the publicity material put out by the old Great Western Railway. The train journey was enlivened by Sir Robin Day, whose cheerful gossip, delivered at the top of his voice, silenced an open carriage. In 1985 I was the guest of the BBC's Radio Four; three days of high thinking and low living, to be paid for by a 'conference special' broadcast.

The Social Democrats held their conference at the Palace Hotel in surroundings of comfort, even luxury. The sun shone brilliantly and the terraced gardens fell away to tennis courts and even cricket nets in which some flannelled fools wiled away the sunlit hours with Willow and Leather. The more earnest sat in an indoor tennis court, the roofs and flanks of which had been lined with a shiny material of the sort woven for whores' drawers, listening to Dr Owen break the mould; the more sybaritic sipped a sweetish white wine while strolling in the grounds, their twin anxieties being what to order for dinner that evening and the uncouthness of their Liberal partners. The well-cut suits, the two-toned shoes and the well-modulated voices reminded me of what the Tory party must once have been like. Those three Social Democrat conferences in the mid-eighties were not at all what I had become used to. Where were the *garagistes*, the estate agents and the speculative builders who had made the Tory party their own?

It was all very worthy and just a tiny bit dull. The Social Democrats had no history and were all the happier for it. It was probably true that there were occasions when the Gang of Three became irritated by Dr David Owen, but three years was not long enough for a good hate. In what the Social Democrats used to call 'the old parties' hatred keeps bubbling up, a factor that can be relied upon to make their party conferences more interesting. I made this point to a youngish Social Democrat who was insisting on making his own salad-dressing in a glass. 'If we hate anyone,' he mused, 'I suppose it is the Liberals.'

Why then did I not join the Social Democrats? I remember sitting long in Brussels cafés with John Cartwright, the Labour MP who had 'gone over', toying with the idea of conversion followed (as it inevitably would have been) by a public and totally immersed baptism. John was co-rapporteur with me for the North Atlantic Assembly's report on cruise and Pershing. He was amiable, clever and persuasive. He was also to survive until the 1992 election. I was rung up by importunate journalists eager to learn if and when I would quit the ranks of Mrs Thatcher's Roundheads for Roy's more congenial Cavaliers. I kept my counsel for I was not convinced. Any inclination I might have had to abandon ship was knocked firmly on the head by Ian Gilmour, the most cerebral and witty of the 'wets'. 'It is not Margaret Thatcher's party,' he argued, 'it is as much ours as hers'; indeed her populist liberalism was quite foreign to the Tory tradition. Was not Mrs Thatcher's rule 'the longest hijack in history?', he asked using against me a crack I had once made in a newspaper article. And anyway, concluded Ian 'the Social Democrats can't last, they are not interest-based'. He was right.

Of course there was another reason for staying put. I had held Aldershot with 55 per cent of the vote, but the electors had not been voting for me, they were simply 'voting the ticket'. Were I to stand in Aldershot as a Social Democrat against a newly selected Tory candidate I would be almost bound to lose. In my mid-fifties with two wives and four children to support, and no capital apart from our house, I had no wish to go on my travels again. As an anti-Thatcher Tory eager to put pen to paper there was a ready market for my 'disloyalties'. (Peter Riddell told me I was hated by the more passionate of her supporters); as a run-of-the-mill Social Democrat I would have probably disappeared without trace, as did Christopher Brocklebank Fowler. I dipped my toe in the water, but it was nowhere near warm enough.

Francis Pym was dropped by Mrs Thatcher immediately after the election. No longer Foreign Secretary he became a brooding presence on the government's back-benches and the focus for revolt when a group of the disaffected raised the banner of Conservative Centre Forward in 1985. Sadly, despite his many attributes Pym lacked leadership qualities and was totally without political excitement. He was nowhere near as clever as Gilmour, but he was an ex-Foreign Secretary and government Chief Whip. Gloomy by nature and small in stature, the Falklands War had cast him in a defeatist role for which he had seemed unfairly suited. Nevertheless, he was the best leader à la Rab Butler we'd got. We held several meetings in Pym's large room in the bowels of the Palace of Westminster. We strove for secrecy but we did not get the better of Tristan Garel-Jones, the deputy Chief Whip. In search of recruits, Ian asked Tristan his opinion of an obscure, newly elected MP, a query that alerted the deputy to the fact that something was up.

We were joined by Peter Tapsell, a clever man and impressive performer who had languished upon the back-benches, and by several others including Nicholas Bonsor. There were twenty of us. Pym was anxious not to create 'a party within a party', although once we went public it would be impossible to escape the charge. We were as decent and undecided as the July conspirators in Hitler's Germany. Like Claus von Stauffenberg, Pym had only one arm and one eye.

It was to take more than a handful of the disaffected to get rid of Mrs Thatcher in 1985. She had defeated Galtieri and won a second general election. As important, the economy was at the beginning of the Lawson boom, and the Prime Minister's public reputation was at its peak. Labour had been discredited by schism and defeat, and the bulk of the quality press (except the *Guardian* and the *Observer*) were strong supporters of the regime. From Margaret's point of view, the rot was not to set in until 1989 when the economy faltered and the Stalking Horse, Sir Anthony Meyer made his brave bid for the leadership.

Meanwhile we conspirators argued fitfully over what to call ourselves; 'Conservative Centre Forward' with its echoes of Tommy Lawton, gave a vague impression of sepia footballers clad in knee-length shorts, but try as we might no one came up with a better title. 'Tory Reform' might have been preferable. We decided to break the news by inviting Peter Jenkins, then the political correspondent of the *Sunday Times*, to a private lunch at the Basil Street Hotel, and he duly splashed the group's inception all over the front page of the paper. On the Saturday evening Pym spoke to the Oxford University Tories in the Union, a speech which although owing little to Danton was shown on all the television news bulletins.

Before travelling to Oxford, Pym, a former Chief Whip, called upon the present Chief Whip John Wakeham to tell him as a matter of courtesy that revolt, albeit genteel, was in the air. How I wish I had been a fly on the wall. Francis Pym, Ted Heath's Chief Whip, had been a competent political operator, his principal achievement being the piloting through the Commons of the Bill in favour of Britain's entry into Europe. But in John Wakeham, once the president of the Surrey Young Farmers, he met his match. Wakeham bade Francis to take a seat, lit his customary seven-inch Havana and proceeded to read him the list of the members of Centre Foward, a list that included the bearded Jerry Hayes, who was swiftly to abandon ship. Wakeham also claimed to have seen the content of Pym's 'Oxford Manifesto'. It was proof, yet again, that there are no such things as secrets in the House of Commons and that the Tory whips, save perhaps when led by Martin Redmayne, are past masters of the political black arts. Ted Heath set a new standard at the time of Suez, a standard which Whitelaw, Pym, Wakeham and Richard Ryder were to maintain over the years. Michael Jopling and Tim Renton were less distinguished. If a tribute to Ryder's skills is sought, the reader should buy a copy of Teresa Gorman's book *Bastards*, a slim volume that complains bitterly how 'badly' the Euro-sceptics were treated by the whips in 1992–93. It is pure comedy.

Conservative Centre Forward fizzled out after a week or so of publicity. I had been Pym's *chef du cabinet* in what was, in retrospect at least, the first evidence of incipient revolt within the party against Margaret Thatcher. But in 1985 her position was totally secure. Love her or loath her, and many did, she had won one war and delivered two elections. She had had luck enough to satisfy any of Napoleon's generals. Some of us might have groaned under her yoke but it was not until the Westland affair at the beginning of 1986 that cracks appeared in the marble, cracks wide and deep enough to start the decline in her personal fortunes that was to end with her discharge in November 1990.

When Michael Heseltine, the Secretary of State for Defence, walked out of Mrs Thatcher's cabinet over Westland in January 1986, Heather and I were sailing in *Sea Princess* between Miami and Mexico. James Bishop, the editor of the *Illustrated London News*, had put two free tickets our way so that I could write a piece about cruising in the Caribbean for his magazine. The offer, which came directly from P&O, included free flights to Miami and back together with ten days on board ship. The timing was unfortunate, to say the least. 'Ten days that shook the world' would be something of an exaggeration; but the Westland affair, as it came to be called, certainly shook political London to its foundations. The British public was bewildered and not a little bored as it tried to follow the intricacies of the arguments deployed between rival cabinet ministers: Heseltine seeking a European solution to the problem of Westland helicopters, while Leon Brittan at Trade and Industry, aided and abetted by the Prime Minister, preferred an American buyout. As the *Sea Princess*, loaded to the gunnels with blue-haired American widows, sailed southwards into the sun, I sat in our cabin desperately twisting the knobs of the long-wave radio set in search of the BBC's World Service. It was one thing for Michael to have abandoned ship in so dramatic a manner; quite another for us to do so. There would have been little point in being marooned on the Cayman Islands.

The *Sea Princess* is a majestic ship with a British captain and crew, the officers resplendent in open-necked shirts and El Alamein shorts. It was as if they were being played by John Gregson, Jack Hawkins and the young John Mills. But hell is other people, and it is prudent to discover what sort of people are on board before committing oneself to their company. There were several hundred people in what was a floating Holiday Inn, the great majority of the passengers being elderly American couples spending their insurance money. Even more depressing were the many slot machines that lined the gangways of the ship before which stood, as if transfixed, elderly women desperately pulling levers. Had it not been for the comfortable throb of the engines and the cheerful feeling of being under way, one might have been in the lobby of Caesar's Palace Hotel, Las Vagas, Nevada.

The flight out to Miami was a familiar nightmare. Two hours' delay at Heathrow followed by eight hours in the air, boredom and discomfort culminating in the 'processing' at the airport of several hundred people by US Customs and Immigration. By the time we reached the hotel in downtown Miami we both stood in need of a cruise. The ship sailed the next morning into brilliant sunlight, its decks packed with acres of white flesh browning gently to the scent of Ambre Solaire. The food was American but with some 'English' dishes tucked away on the menu: Lancashire hot-pot, Irish stew. There was a good selection of Californian wines.

It was, however, an unhappy voyage. MPs' wives are supposed to lead, in the words of the song, 'such solitary lives', and after twenty-four years in each other's company our relationship was running on the rims. We had nothing more to say to each other. Heather, although loyal and supportive in Aldershot, was not interested in politics and seemed at her happiest at home with the dogs. Every subject of conversation seemed inevitably to lead to disaster, reverting as it invariably did to my first family. Heather remained silent at lunch and dinner (we had been allocated our own table, which was perhaps a mistake), while during the day I sunbathed, scanning the horizon for the silhouettes of distant islands, or sat in the cabin fiddling with the radio.

Michael, the World Service reported, had changed his tie three times on the day of his departure from the cabinet, so frequent had been his appearances on television. I was intrigued by this piece of information as Michael had taken to wearing his Guards' tie since becoming Secretary of State for Defence. While researching my book on him I mentioned this habit to Major General Bernard Gordon-Lennox, a Grenadier and a constituent. Had he any objection? 'None whatsoever,' was the reply, 'save I do wish the feller would not tie it in a Windsor knot.' I did not admit that it was I who taught Michael to do so, having been shown the fashion by an American who had attached himself to the Hampstead Young Conservatives in the late forties. I thought it rather smart at the time. Stung at second-hand by Bernard's rebuke, I reverted to tying my tie à la George V and not like his son.

The *Sea Princess* anchored off the north coast of Jamaica and we were driven in coaches to a nearby sugar plantation with an old and attractive 'great house' and a splendid outdoor lunch of local delicacies. The drive back to the ship over rutted roads revealed just how poor Jamaican rural life must be: rows of tin-roofed shacks, decrepit shops and many chapels. The people looked sullen, as well they might, but no stones were thrown at the white faces gazing out from their air-conditioned buses. No wonder, nearly every Canadian athlete is of Jamaican origin, and south London an extension of Kingston, Jamaica. It was with some relief that we returned to the mid-American security of our British ship.

I was obliged to cut the cruise short as I had promised to attend the annual dinner of the Aldershot Tories where I was to propose the vote of thanks to a visiting cabinet minister. I left the ship at St Martin, an island half Dutch, half French, leaving a silent Heather to return home via Miami three days or so later.

On my return, after eighteen hours spent in purgatory at Miami airport, the political world was locked in a frenzy of speculation. Had Leon Brittan leaked the contents of the Solicitor-General's letter to Michael Heseltine on his own initiative or had he won the prior approval of the Prime Minister's Private Office as he claimed? Did the Private Office sanction the leak (in order to damage Heseltine and his case) without seeking the approval of the Prime Minister? It seemed unlikely. The very act of leaking Mayhew's private letter (without reference to him) was outrageous and led directly to Leon Brittan's resignation, but not before a particularly unpleasant meeting of the '22 that resembled a pogrom. The hostility shown to Leon personally was an act of political redirection; the bulk of the party transferring its anger over what had been an unsavoury and humiliating affair from Mrs Thatcher to her ministerial colleague. Leon was cast as the scapegoat. We had rooms along the Upper Committee Corridor North; I asked him how long we should wait for the real story to come out. 'Thirty years,' Leon replied grimly. He was then sent to Brussels as a commissioner where he has since avenged himself on Mrs Thatcher by going native.

It would be tiresome to rehearse the saga of Westland. I played no part in it, save that of a spectator, watching with amazement as Neil Kinnock made the worst speech of his career, failing to ask the right questions of the Prime Minister and losing himself in a torrent of Welsh verbiage. Instead, I will offer two quotations which sum up admirably the lasting effect the affair had on Mrs Thatcher's reputation. The first is from Hugo Young's *One of Us*.

We now enter the second stage of Mrs Thatcher's personal Westland crisis. If the first was marked by weakness and lack of control, the next took her into the realm of plain chicanery. It was as if the system, having been thrown out of gear by one minister's impropriety, could recover itself only by descending to a similar or even lower level of dubious conduct. While her own precise involvement in this remained hard to determine for sure, the episode required her to forfeit for ever what the *Belgrano* affair had already compromised; the image of a political leader whose unfailing integrity and flawless honesty and disarming willingness to tell the truth made her different from all the others.

R. W. Johnson in his review in the *London Review of Books* of Lady Thatcher's *The Downing Street Years* is even more scathing. He writes of Westland ' . . . the duplicity of that leak, its role in destroying Leon Brittan and the virtual certainty that Mrs Thatcher lied like a trooper about the responsibility of her own office in the matter were so central to the affair that her account is not very coherent without them . . .'

Had Britain then become a banana republic with its very own supremo? It began to look like it. I can remember running into the Attorney in the Aye Lobby when the affair was at its height. 'Just like Oxford and the start of the Blue Ribbon Club,' said Paddy Mayhew. Michael was, once again, on the loose.

22 Of Books and Boxers

A Labour MP who later became a Social Democrat and lost his seat once said that being an MP 'was better than working'. I know what he meant. The hours may be intolerable, the task frustrating and some of the people dreadful, but the job does not lack interest and excitement. The salary is of middle-management level but the perks (car, secretary, researcher and London home) are more generous. One can also moonlight. There is even a remnant of social prestige still clinging to the 'Member', although, when out of earshot, many people believe MPs to be in the job 'for what they can get out of it'. We rank low in polls of perceived public estimation, although not as low as journalists. Sadly, I have combined both callings. For some reason I cannot understand, doctors top the popularity poll. Could it be their white coats? Their love of euphemism (e.g. 'waterworks')? Or the size of their income?

Among the improvements made to MPs' conditions of work in the last thirty years (a list which includes free stationery and stamps, a free telephone, for calls within the United Kingdom only, an office to oneself if relatively senior), is an annual check-up by a doctor. I took advantage of this service and was sternly told to lose weight. Politics is a sedentary occupation, relieved only by the length of the corridors in the Palace of Westminster and intermittent general elections. We eat and certainly drink too much; alcohol being one of the twin hazards of life at Westminster (the other is adultery). I did not begin to put on weight until the late seventies when I developed irritable bowel syndrome, a condition which continues to baffle the medical profession. Eating relieves the discomfort. The doctor, whose wrist-watch alarm was set for exactly sixty minutes, gossiped cheerfully about his parliamentary patients, many of whom he claimed were unhappily married, overweight or plagued by children who were into drink and drugs. This was a familiar liturgy. He also said that several of 'the colleagues' had complained of severe pains in the kidney region when getting up to speak in the House, caused, so he said, by a surge of adrenaline. That I could believe, for the nervous strain caused by asking questions or making speeches is very great indeed. Which was why I performed infrequently in the House. If I had anything to say I could more easily put pen to paper and sell it to a newspaper. Anyway, nobody read Hansard, and few sat in the Chamber to listen to anyone except themselves.

In 1988 I was invited to become a Steward of the British Board of Boxing Control. It was the Board's practice to appoint a Labour and a Tory MP who would be prepared to defend 'the noble art', as it was once called in a more innocent age, in the Commons, and this I was happy to do. In fact, during the five years I was a director of the Board, the issue was never raised: the Tories willing to leave well alone and Labour not wishing to attack what is at root a working-class sport. The appointment was an unpaid one. There was a meeting once a month in London, the occasional lunch or dinner (at one of which I spoke, along with Frank Bruno and Harry Carpenter) and, best of all, access to the Board of Control's free seats at ringside. They were cramped, but so close to the action that one was in danger of being crushed by a falling British heavyweight.

The Board has a paid staff under the control of its general secretary, the admirable John Morris. Its chairman was Sir David Hopkin, the Chief Metropolitan Magistrate, a bewhiskered, formidable and charming Welshman, and in my early days on the Board the president was Jack Petersen, the old heavyweight champion, active in the thirties, a handsome veteran who nodded gently through the long afternoon agenda. Another prominent figure on the Board, who is today its chairman, was 'Nipper' Read, the policeman who had arrested the Krays. The Board members were a tough lot and they needed to be, for the Board has no statutory powers and floats like a raft on a sport which can be as insalubrious and corrupt as its many enemies claim. There is a mint of money to be made out of professional boxing, and not only by the boxers; the sport attracts characters who can with safety only be called 'Runyonesque'.

Within a day or so of my appointment to the Board I was appointed the steward-in-charge of a promotion in Reading that had, as top of the bill, a fight for the European cruiserweight championship. The post was an honorary one, but it did carry with it the task of climbing into the ring (no easy task for the portly) to fasten the championship belt around the sweaty waist of the victor. As the fight was televised, I was spotted in the Aldershot Conservative Club, my feat impressing mightily the snooker-playing, lager-drinking, former Parachute Regiment non-commissioned officers who might, in the past, have thought of me if not as a library squire, then at least as a snob. So cheered was my constituency agent by the favourable impression I had made that she rang to tell me the good news. 'They couldn't believe it was you,' she cried.

In 1990, the Board summoned the super-middleweight champion Chris

Eubank to appear before it for disciplinary reasons. He had butted his Canadian opponent in the face with the back of his head, knocking him to the floor. This foul had been witnessed by millions on television. Eubank who is black, like the majority of licenced boxers in Britain today, is one of the most successful fighters in the country, undefeated at the time of writing and one of several world champions at the weight. He is articulate, and has cleverly sold himself as the man the crowd loves to hate (he claims to despise boxing). He has possibly made more money than any other British pugilist of his period. He was asked by the Board to explain his conduct.

He was cute enough not to excuse himself, but to apologize at some length, and although flanked by his solicitor, he did all the talking. When he left the room, the Board decided to fine him £10,000, the first punishment I have imposed on anyone since my days as a prefect at Brockhurst. When we moved to the next item on the agenda, I left the meeting to return to the Commons and, unable to hail a cab, stood stoically in line for a bus. As I waited gloomily in the rain, a turbo Bentley drew up at the Board's door, and a uniformed chauffeur opened its door for Chris Eubank to make his entry. He glided smoothly away, leaving me wondering why I had not held out for a higher figure.

The origins of successful fighters are social indicators. Most British fighters today are black, immigration and the decline of heavy industry combining to bring this about. Prosperity has lifted white Americans away from boxing while in Britain the virtual end of coal mining has reduced the number of Welsh fighters (Jimmy Wilde, Jem Driscoll, Tommy Farr, Brian Curvis and many others); the decline of heavy industry like shipbuilding and steel has had a similar effect in Scotland (Jackie Patterson, Benny Lynch, Jim Watt and Walter McGowan). Those white boxers left tend to come from the East End of London, Liverpool and Belfast. But colour makes little difference to the fans. Henry Cooper was a great favourite, but so, too, is 'Big Frank' Bruno. And the best English fighter since the war, Randolph Turpin, was half-caste.

My stewardship gave me patronage. My son Joshua often came with me to the fights. I invited David Lightbown, the twenty-stone Tory whip and former professional ballroom dancer, to Wembley. Lightbown is famous in the popular prints as a 'hard' man, forever shining bright lights into the eyes of sensitive, if rebellious, Tory MPs like Bill Cash, Sir Teddy Taylor and 'Mother Teresa' Gorman. In fact, he has a heart of gold. On another occasion I took Ken Clarke, then the Minister of Health, to the Albert Hall to sit ringside for the Herol Graham vs Mike McCallum world middleweight championship fight. Clarke, who was no stranger to cholesterol, sat cheerfully behind a bank of national press photographers eating a sandwich of sliced bread and fatty, underdone roast beef, at the same time smoking a cigar. 'Your image!' I hissed. 'Sod my image,' was his not untypical response. Happily, the fight was so closely contested that the cameras did not linger on the audience.

I also invited 'Our 'Enery' Cooper to lunch in the Strangers' Dining Room in the Palace of Westminster. Usually the service is unremarkable; motherly and overworked waitresses fighting a losing battle against the clock, but on this occasion two waiters hung attentively at the champ's elbows. Cooper was engagingly modest. 'Surely,' I said, 'the thing to do is to fight the boxers and box the fighters.' 'Easier said than done,' was his crisp response. I noticed beads of sweat trickling down his forehead. Could he have been nervous? A man who had twice fought Muhammad Ali? After lunch I led him through the Central Lobby (the Commons attendants kept stopping him to ask for an autograph) and down to the main entrance in New Palace Yard to see him into a taxi. Two cabbies quarrelled noisily over who would drive him back to Hendon. 'They never want me to pay a fare,' said Cooper, 'but I always do.'

There is a strong case to be made against boxing from a neurological point of view. My father is strongly opposed to the sport, and there is no lack of punch-drunk ex-fighters to use in evidence. Many of the boxers whom I would pay to see perform in the fifties and sixties ended up in my father's consulting rooms at the National Hospital. The fate of Michael Watson is a salutary example of the injuries that can result from the game. Nevertheless, it is better that the sport should continue above ground with properly control and medical supervision, rather than being banned and driven underground with no sanctions save those of the criminal law. In America, the 'fight game' has gone to the dogs, dominated by crooks and spoilt by a multiplicity of so-called governing bodies; such things have not happened here, and will not so for as long as the Board of Control can help it.

It was my Uncle Jack who taught me to box when evacuated to his cottage in Wistanstow, but it was my poor father who took me to my first fight in 1947. My mother was anxious to know what to do with an idle sixteen-year-old while on holiday from school. She persuaded my father to devote an evening to my entertainment. Would I like to go to the ballet? No fear! Did I want to see Ralph Slater, the stage hypnotist? Not much. In the event I forced my fastidious father to take me to the big fight at the Haringey Arena. Bruce Woodcock vs Gus Lesnevich. The arena was patronized by large, slightly battered men in purple pin-striped suits accompanied by girls who looked like the young Barbara Windsor. Beer was drunk out of paper cups, betting was discreet and the humour pithy and Jewish. My father was not enraptured by the scene: in fact, he read his book throughout the bill, even when the patriotic crowd leapt to its feet as Woodcock knocked out the American world light-heavyweight champion in the eighth round. I was not a chip off the old block.

Since the 1992 election there has been published a spate of political biographies. Among the big fish, the most readable were Alan Clark's diaries; the most sententious the memoirs of Nigel Lawson; and the most successful, at least in terms of sales, Margaret Thatcher's *The Downing Street Years*. Clark's personality dominates the events about which he writes so well and so outrageously. I once asked him with which famous figure from the past would he like to have lunch – his answer was Sir Geoffrey Howe.

Lawson did not employ a ghost, although no doubt much of the book was first drafted for him by researchers. It is the best record of the often difficult relationship between Margaret and her principal Chancellor of the Exchequer. Lawson was one of the few cabinet ministers with whom Margaret was wary of crossing swords. Lady Thatcher's 'manifesto' contained almost as many ghosts as a short story by M. R. James (the principal spectre being the journalist John O'Sullivan), and her work benefited hugely from their hauntings. It is worth reading for the account of her fall. Kenneth Baker's apologia was well written, for he is one of the few literate Tories, but the story of his attempt to climb the greasy pole might have benefited from delay. A skilful political operator, his is a talent wasted. We find thus, among the bigger fish, a sturgeon, a puffer fish, a pike and a conger eel. As for the smaller, Norman Fowler's book could perhaps be described as a flounder, and Teresa Gorman's as a tiddler. But we have Geoffrey Howe's book to come; will it be a killer whale?

I have so far mentioned only Tory authors; arguably the best-written of all the recently published political memoirs is Denis Healey's *Hinterland*. That, of course, was not its title (it was called *The Time of My Life*) but Denis did make much of his own hinterland, his name for the cultural and intellectual baggage that prominent politicians carry with them while playing 'the great game' of politics. Denis's hinterland was at least the size of Yorkshire (music, art, photography and literature), Roy Jenkins' the size of Wales (biography in particular), and Quintin Hogg's the size of the Home Counties (religion, polemics and the law). All three men were of prime-ministerial rank, but ill fortune deprived them of the opportunity to gain the highest office. Perhaps I could market a board game called 'Hinterlands, from Balfour to Geoffrey Dickens'; certainly it could be extended to cover many of the middle weights of British politics. Has Margaret a hinterland? It might be Hampstead Garden Suburb.

We Tories have had so many Premiers in recent years that it is not easy to spot those who are, or were, Prime Ministers *manqués*. Maudling and Macleod were professional politicians of great ability, but their hinterlands were not much larger than Rutland. Enoch Powell, on the other hand, was a professional politician of no great ability ('the rivers of blood') but with a hinterland at least the size of Lichfield and the Black Country. Rab Butler was an astute political operator but unwilling to go the last mile. His hinterland, already quite large, was judicially enlarged by marriage. He can have Cambridgeshire.

What then of Labour and Liberal politicians; have they hinterlands? Hattersley could lay claim to the West Riding of Yorkshire, Gerald Kaufman to Wardour Street and Neil Kinnock to Cardiff Arms Park. David Owen's would not extend much beyond Wimpole Street and David Steel's would include the paddock at the back of the manse. But no offence is intended; the bulk of today's politicians is composed of undistinguished professionals whose sole trade appears to be the pursuit of political success as measured either by column inches (John Gummer) or by ministerial office (Michael Portillo). There are no industrialists who are Members of Parliament, no retired generals or admirals, no retired ambassadors. There are two academics: Robert Rhodes James, who retired at the 1992 election, and Robert Jackson. There are no writers of the class of A. P. Herbert or Hilaire Belloc. There are a handful of well-known journalists: George Walden, Austin Mitchell, Hattersley, Kaufman and myself, and a few 'performers' like Gyles Brandreth, Charles Kennedy and David Mellor. The invention of life peers has skimmed the cream from the commons.

Edwina Currie, who published an unreadable but moderately successful celebrity-novel in 1994, tried unsuccessfully to abandon Westminster in favour of the European Parliament. I reviewed her book in the *Telegraph*: in my notice I said she had leapt naked on to a passing bandwagon. It is a book entirely lacking in humour. It also suffers from a common failure, an inability to write erotically. There are, of course, huge dollops of sex, all of which are unspeakably boring. If a back-bench MP is today plucked from obscurity it will be as a result of some peccadillo, the consequence of which will be to act as stand-in for the disc-jockey Jimmy Young.

Peter Riddell's book *Honest Opportunism: The Rise of the Career Politician* did not attract the attention it deserved when published in 1993. Riddell, who is the most reliable of political commentators, takes his starting point from the fact that politicians are today indisputably regarded as a third-rate lot. He asserts that 'In general, British ministers are amateurs in running their departments, and professionals primarily as politicians advancing their own careers.' But as much could be said of Churchill or Lloyd George. The difference lies in the changing social composition of the House of Commons, and the new pressures brought to bear upon MPs as a whole. After the 1992 election 60 per cent of Tory MPs still had been to public schools (not necessarily the Clarendon top five) compared with 75 per cent thirty years ago; more significantly, perhaps, of those who were first elected in 1992, 24 per cent on the Tory side but 38 per cent of the new Labour MPs had previously worked in politics, mainly as researchers, full-time councillors or trade union officials. Riddell stresses something that I had already observed and often written about in the press, namely that nearly all MPs now depend upon their continued membership of the House for their social and economic standing. Johnson once said, 'Politics are now nothing more than rising in the world – a nice but a small gift for self-destruction.'

There have been two other external changes that have borne heavily on the activities, and hence the reputations, of MPs. The Attlee government of 1945–51 saw Labour MPs acting as constituency welfare officers, a tendency that Tory MPs had little choice but to follow. My constituency postbag is full of letters seeking help in areas over which I have no direct control. The phrase 'a good constituency MP' would not have been used or understood before the war; you will not find it in Chips Channon's diaries, Today, it ranks among the highest political praise. MPs have also been obliged to become 'social slaves' (the phrase is Roy Jenkins'), expected to make themselves readily available at countless constituency social functions, often at ward level, which raise money for the party's activities. In Aldershot I was judged by my appetite. I spent the better part of thirty years eating wine and cheese with the same people, hardly a pattern of life conducive to either reflective statesmanship or agreeable self-indulgence. Familiarity can breed a mutual contempt. It is yet another aspect of the fact that the power that Parliament has surrendered to the Executive has in its turn passed, in part at least, to the party organizations.

As for my 'hinterland', I can claim no more than four green fields: an appearance on *Desert Island Discs* (a candid friend said my choice of music lacked 'intellectual content'); the fact that I am always reading more than one book at a time (my favourite novels are *Middlemarch* and di Lampedusa's *The Leopard*); a small taste for music (trad jazz, Elgar and Brahms); and love of poetry (Housman, Larkin, Matthew Arnold and Eliot). 'Hinterland-wise' as Hillary Clinton might put it, I lurk midway between Jack Kennedy and Ronald Reagan.

Can a man be judged by those whom he admires? Harold Macmillan and Iain Macleod were among my political heroes. At the age of ten I modelled myself on Lord John Roxton who accompanied Professors Challenger and Summerlee in search of Conan Doyle's 'Lost World'; much later I admired Fitzroy Maclean who combined a soldier's courage with a writer's flair. Among the great commanders, I preferred Alexander to Montgomery, but admired Bill Slim most of all. Admiral Jellicoe, our greatest sea-captain since Nelson, is the hero of Jutland; 'the only man who could lose the war in an afternoon', having to decide within minutes whether to deploy the Grand Fleet to port or starboard. Arthur Marder wrote the best account of Jutland, devoting a volume of his magisterial series *From the Dreadnought to Scapa Flow* to that most intellectually fascinating of battles. I interviewed Marder for the *Sunday Times.* 'I am the only Jew, born in Brooklyn, who can distinguish between a British general and an admiral,' he told me. It appeared that generals drawl while the speech of admirals is clipped, presumably to prevent their orders from being blown out to sea.

I admired Sir John Verney greatly; sadly he died in 1992. He lived in Farnham, moving later to Clare in Suffolk. John had that most intangible of qualities, 'style'. He wrote like an angel, painted like a man possessed, and had the manners of a more gracious age. Boots' customers will remember him as the begetter of the Dodo Pad: book lovers will remember two of his books in particular; *Going to the Wars*, his account of his experiences in the North Somerset Yeomanry and the SAS during the war, and *A Dinner of Herbs*, his tale of privations as a prisoner of war on the run in Italy. I have several of his paintings: pretty girls with croquet mallets, wearing nothing except a straw hat.

John Verney may have been the last of the Whigs. In 1988 I asked him to paint me a picture of a typical Conservative Summer Fayre. The Young Conservatives were represented by three naked graces; the established church by a purple bishop in hot pursuit. The figure of Mrs Thatcher was to be seen sternly rebuking a nervous candidate. Four Tory ladies of the sort who have sold a thousand raffle tickets, stood in attendance upon Our Great Leader. At one corner was the gross figure of Nigel Lawson opening a magnum of Champagne, seated beneath the words 'To him that hath shall be given'. Lawson's foot is on the head of Verney himself, cast as an OAP striving to climb the ladder of admittance. The picture, painted in the naïve style, hung in my office in the Commons, and I could not resist making it my Christmas card, which was enjoyed by all except for the stuffiest of my local Tories.

Verney was that rarest of birds: a seemingly happy man. He lived to be over eighty, surviving the fleshpots of Eton and the rigours of Christ Church. He captured Syria from the Vichy French and was dropped into Sardinia in order to destroy German aircraft. He spent two months in a cave in the Abruzzi, looked after by a local who walked eight miles twice a week to feed him and his companions. He helped to plan D-day and crossed the Rhine with the Second Regiment of the SAS. He had five daughters, a son and a handsome wife. His *Dinner of Herbs* was arguably the best book to have come out of the Second World War. He painted many a picture and sold not a few. I suppose Conan Doyle would have called him a *beau sabreur*.

23 Margaret's Last Stand (and mine)

The only thing I can remember about the 1987 general election was 'wobbly Thursday'. A week before polling day, Mrs Thatcher, alarmed by what turned out to be a rogue poll, 'did a wobbly' at Conservative Central Office. She was suffering from toothache. She seemed to have tired of Norman Tebbit, her party chairman, rebounding from his sardonic style to the more obliging Lord Young to second-guess him. There were nasty scenes in the building about which both Michael Dobbs and David Young have written, while a nameless but very senior cabinet minister (Geoffrey Howe?) opined at the time that 1987 would be the last election Mrs Thatcher would ever fight. 'The woman is quite hysterical.' The cabinet minister was right. It was to be Margaret's last election. She had been introduced, in the course of the election, to the 'TBW factor' – That Bloody Woman – and she had reacted accordingly. But as for the election itself, victory, in Aldershot and elsewhere, was inevitable. The bubble of the Lawson boom had not yet burst. Neil Kinnock was almost as unsatisfactory a party leader as Michael Foot had been and the Liberals cheerfully split the anti-Conservative vote.

In Aldershot my four weeks' hard labour raised my majority above 17,000, and it is difficult from this distance to remember anything about my penultimate campaign. My days were spent continuously on the move, taking coffee with the rich and retired of Rotherwick and Mattingley or tramping the mean streets near Aldershot station. I was urged to canvass a woman who had 'a mouth on her like the *Aldershot News*'. I did and she had. It was not a rewarding five minutes. I was 'adopted' in a back room of the Aldershot Officers' Club, surrounded by trophies of imperial wars and the stuffed heads of animals, one of which looked ominously like that of my predecessor, Sir Eric Errington. The 1992 election was to be memorable for a variety of reasons but in 1987 I just went through the motions. It seemed a far cry from the frenzied activity of the three elections in Rochester and Chatham all those years ago.

I was beginning to have difficulties within the Aldershot Conservative Association. The president was a Jack Bedser, a former constituency chairman, who had worked until his retirement as a British Rail executive at Waterloo. My chairman was Maureen Cooper. The Aldershot Tories had very largely escaped the quarrels that rive so many local political associations, disputes that are usually centred on rival personalities, not upon ideological differences. But trouble was in the air. My anti-Thatcher stance was bound to make enemies. Bedser seemed lugubrious and limited, decent but unexciting. For some he lacked social prestige in an association that still looked towards the smarter, often military, end of the constituency for its local leadership. Many past presidents had been retired generals, colonels and majors. Mrs Cooper, who lived on a council estate in Farnborough, was a youngish down-to-earth woman of strong personality and undoubted energy with great influence over Jack Bedser and whose relations with the other leading female figures within the constituency (and the Aldershot Tories were dominated by women) were variable to say the least. Although hard-working, Maureen had a reputation for 'shooting from the hip', and it was not long before she fell out with the Association's 'agent' and secretary, the redoubtable Mavis Banham. The ostensible cause of the trouble was undoubtedly me. It was increasingly being said that 'Critchley must go'. But I was to be lucky in my enemies. In the end, it was they who went.

Mavis Banham was a key ally of mine sadly taken by cancer in 1993. She was a large and jolly woman, much loved by the local Tories, who held the fort in the Association's offices above the Aldershot Conservative Club. She was, in effect, the constituency agent, knew everyone, was never off the telephone, and could not bear the sight of Maureen Cooper. In Mavis, Maureen more than met her match. Jack Bedser sat this fight out despite his presidency. He seemed as miserable as sin, and carried no clout with the protagonists.

For a time the rumblings of discontent, as far as I was concerned, were muted. There is, of course, no way (short of bankruptcy or conviction of a criminal offence) that an MP can be forced to relinquish his seat in Parliament. I could sit tight. Bedser and Cooper's objective was to discourage me from putting my name forward for readoption at the next election. I was first made fully aware of this on 9 November 1988 when the two of them invited me to lunch at the Charing Cross Hotel. I thought their insistence upon inviting me, and not the other way around, somewhat ominous. I would have preferred it to be my treat. As I had been tipped off by Mavis that 'something was in the air' I was not altogether surprised when, after a decent lunch, Jack and Maureen asked me to stand down at the next election. I asked what would happen if I didn't and they told me that they would fight me to the bitter end. What was more they would move a motion of no confidence in me there and then at a

Special General Meeting. As the Association's Annual General Meeting was due in March the two functions could be effectively combined, and I might well have found it hard to avoid public humiliation. I thanked them for their lunch and told them to do their damnedest. I can also remember warning them both that their own political careers, such as they were, would also be on the line. 'It is never easy to get rid of a sitting MP,' I reminded them as I left.

Nor was it, but the attempt was not made for nearly two years. I had to wait until December 1990, in the aftermath of Margaret Thatcher's defenestration, for a deselection meeting finally to be held. In the meantime I was saved by my enemies. Apparently unable to persuade the bulk of the executive committee of the wisdom of the course of action they proposed (the no-confidence vote), Jack Bedser and Maureen Cooper promptly resigned, not only from their posts as president and chairman but from the party as a whole. I could not believe my good fortune. How could they have made so foolish a mistake?

It seems that their attack on me proved to be the last straw for them, so unpopular had they both become for a variety of reasons. Indeed, there was talk of a vote of no confidence in the Association's officers being moved on behalf of the executive. Maureen Cooper had offended Mercedes Hudson, the wife of a past president, of whose grand garden in Mattingley Maureen had said, somewhat grudgingly, 'it will do' when kindly offered for the party's annual garden party. 'Feisty' at the best of times, Maureen had left a trail of the offended behind her, and not only in the smarter end of the constituency. She had also fallen foul of Mavis Banham, whose support for me was total and who was universally liked in the Aldershot Conservative Club and party. While Maureen did the talking, Jack Bedser played his second fiddle, the scrapings of which tended to offend the ear of the more sensitive. The sight of a little, bustling Maureen accompanied by a tall, gloomy and balding Bedser might well have depressed any local Tory who wished for little more than a quiet life. They had made not themselves loved, and were the last to know it.

Not only did they both resign (on 29 January 1989), they also issued a statement to the press in which they roundly attacked the local Tories, not for putting up with me but for a series of petty failings that put a swift end to any prospect they might have had of ever re-entering the party. It might be worth quoting from Bedser's statement issued on 31: January 'I never thought I would see the day when this Association would be ruled by an incongruous mixture of sentiment, procrastination, absence of will and self confidence, and insolence. I could say more but it is not my intention to do so now . . .' How not to win friends and influence people. It seemed as if there was scarcely a soul they did not attack. Doctor Monique Simmonds, a scientist who worked at Kew

Gardens, was elected chairman, and an old friend of mine, Esther Chappell (widow of the gallant Mike), was appointed president. Thus I had a slate of officers who were well disposed towards me. Maureen and Jack were left to carry out a campaign of writing peevish letters of complaint to the local newspapers, threatening all and sundry with litigation (which never occurred) and seeking redress from Central Office in London, who did not want to know. Every six months they sought to be readmitted to the party, and every six months the answer was 'no'. In the end they were abandoned by their own ward organization. They were replaced as officers of the Grangefield branch of the Farnborough Tories by Conservatives sympathetic to myself. However, their fortunes were to revive somewhat at the time of my 'deselection' in December 1990.

Nineteen eighty-nine was the year of the stalking horse, the challenge to Margaret's leadership posed by an obscure and dilettante Welsh baronet, Sir Anthony Meyer. It was also the tenth anniversary of Mrs Thatcher's premiership. I wrote a piece for the *New York Times* suggesting that she take the opportunity offered by the anniversary to 'do a Wilson' and bow out of office while the going was good. I paid her many compliments, but the message was plain.

The *Sun* promptly republished the piece and there was the customary fuss, with the tabloid press using words like 'disloyalty' and 'outrageous'. Poor Mavis Banham spent two days in the Aldershot office fielding the telephone calls, the lines blocked by indignant constituents or party workers. When asked for her reaction Mrs Thatcher said she would 'go on and on . . .', a message that had already disheartened her enemies. In the House there was some shaking of grey heads and murmurs about 'rocking boats' but I was amused to see Lord Whitelaw on television in 1993, at the time of the screening of *The Thatcher Years*, tell his audience that 'Margaret should have gone in 1989'. In fact, he had been a prime mover in persuading Peter Carrington to pop over to Chequers one summer Sunday that year (they were neighbours) to give Mrs Thatcher precisely that message. She had not acted upon it. Instead, she embraced the poll tax, and by so doing sealed her fate. Norman Fowler has also since declared that 'Margaret should have gone on her tenth anniversary' but I do not remember him saying so at the time.

I was also writing about restaurants for the *Telegraph* during 1989. I suppose I went to a smart London restaurant once a month, lunched or dined at the readers' expense and wrote a 600-word column for the *Telegraph*'s Saturday edition. Among the many places I patronized were Tante Claire, Le Manoir aux Quat' Saisons, the Castle Hotel, Taunton, and The Riverside Inn at Bray.

Living so high off the hog might not have endeared me to the more respectable of my constituents, and I certainly offended Jack Bedser, then the Association's president, by taking Michael Foot to dinner at The Gay Hussar, a Soho restaurant that served pre-1914 style Hungarian food and had long been a favourite watering hole of the Left. Indeed Michael Foot has his own reserved table directly behind the front door. This act of hospitality was 'the last straw' that led directly to my lunch and grill at the Charing Cross Hotel. Cross-party friendships are frowned upon by the run-of-the-mill party worker who cannot understand how such relationships could ever exist. I like and admire Michael Foot who is a great Parliamentarian, an amusing companion and a kindly man. I would rather have taken him to dinner than three-quarters of the 1922 Committee.

Anthony Meyer, a former diplomat, had long sat uncomfortably on the furthest branch of the Tory tree. Left-wing in Conservative terms and passionately pro-European, he had remained for years on the government backbenches. He had also in the past been threatened with deselection by his North Walian constituents, a challenge that he had defeated in the courts. A tall good-looking man with money, with a loyal and ever-attentive wife, Meyer was a civilized companion with nothing whatsoever in common with Essex Man. He had made little or no impact on Parliament, and to the wider world he was quite unknown. Yet he had more courage than the rest of us.

He declared his intention to stand against Mrs Thatcher in November 1989, taking full advantage of the 'Berkeley Rules' invented more than twenty years previously. He knew that he would become the target for scurrilous journalism (the tabloids duly came up with some lurid story about his sex life) and lots of common or garden abuse ('the stalking donkey'), yet throughout 'the campaign' he behaved with a fluent dignity which his enemies could not fail to respect. He had not a hope in hell of winning, but the sixty votes he garnered (including abstentions) were the writing on the wall. I met Michael Heseltine in the committee room that had been turned into a polling booth. We both had come 'to abstain in person'. I thought Michael looked a little sheepish: had he not spent the last three and a half years on the campaign trail himself? 'See you this time next year,' I told him. 'Could be, could be,' was his murmured response.

In 1989 and 1990, Mrs Thatcher went, as they say in Wales, 'a little funny'. She was full of bombast and bluster. She told Robin Oakley, then of *The Times* that she was 'happy to carry on' by 'popular acclaim'. She staged, with the help of her Environment Secretary, Nicholas Ridley, a cleaning-up operation in St James's Park in which she thrust a pointy stick in the direction of rubbish that had been carefully strewn in her path. It could have been a sketch from Monty

Python. Her eyes, according to Alan Watkins of the *Observer*, took on a manic quality when talking about Europe, while her teeth were such as 'to gobble you up'. More sinister still, she slipped into the habit of using the royal 'we' in public. ('We are a grandmother'). This she explained in the *Express* and on *Panorama*, as follows:

A leader must lead, must lead firmly, have convictions . . . and see that those convictions are reflected in every piece of policy. How can I change Mrs Thatcher? I am what I am . . . I am not an 'I' person, I am not an 'I did this in my goverment, I did that'. I have never been an 'I' person so I talk about 'We' – the government. I cannot do things alone so it has to be 'we'. It is a cabinet 'we' . . . Yes, I do lead from the front. Yes, I do have fundamental convictions . . . but we do have very lively discussions because that is the way I operate. Then we reach collective decisions. That's collective responsibility.

The events of October and November 1990 have been recounted in a score of books, most of which I have reviewed for one newspaper or another. The best is probably Alan Watkins' *A Conservative Coup*. In brief, there was no plot by the cabinet to get rid of Margaret; there was some plotting on her behalf, but in the main events moved inexorably once Geoffrey Howe made his famous resignation speech in the Commons on Tuesday 13 November. Once Geoffrey had spoken she was to all intents and purposes 'dead in the water'.

I watched the proceedings from the upstairs MPs' gallery, looking directly down on to the government benches. The House was packed, the silence broken only by the occasional oohs and aahs from the Labour benches as the enormity of Howe's attack dawned slowly upon them. As for the Tories, they listened silently without facial expression of any kind. It was clear from the moment that Geoffrey began his speech that this was no *tour d'horizon*, no graceful recollection of time well spent in office; it was a carefully crafted, smoothly delivered, destructively pointed attack on the Prime Minister's actions and attitudes. It ended with what amounted to an invitation to Michael Heseltine to mount a direct challenge to her leadership. As a performance it was on a par with Nigel Birch's 'never glad confident morning again' speech of 1963 when he took his revenge upon Harold Macmillan. It was, as Lady Thatcher was later wryly to observe, quite the best speech she had ever heard Geoffrey make. At the time she sat grim-faced, looking neither left nor right. When Geoffrey finished, she left the Chamber. I hurried down into the Members' Lobby where I caught sight of Elspeth Howe running in the direction of Geoffrey's room. Charles Irving, the Tory MP for Cheltenham, claimed that 'it had taken Elspeth ten minutes to write the speech; Geoffrey, ten years to make it'. It was a good crack but inaccurate; Geoffrey had written every word of it. The lobby was crowded with MPs and lobby correspondents in a state of high excitement. 'Now Michael must run' and 'she's dead in the water' were the two views generally expressed. Several days previously I had counselled caution – Michael was doing a trawl of those who were committed to him. Now, unless he wanted his bluff to be called in the most humiliating way, he had no choice. His friends sought him out in the tea-room and the lobbies to tell him so.

A day or so later I was lunching in the Members' Dining Room. Geoffrey came and sat opposite me, with Robin Maxwell-Hyslop on his right hand. Geoffrey and I talked of old times in the Bow Group, of my visit at his invitation to Chevening, the great house in Kent which he was obliged to give up on losing the Foreign and Commonwealth Office. We chatted about everything but his recent speech. Maxwell-Hyslop, who had turned his back on him, shouted some generalized abuse in Geoffrey's direction (Howe took no notice) as he stalked out. It was the only time in thirty years of eating in the Commons that I have witnessed such offensive behaviour; it was a sign of just how high feelings were running.

Poor Geoffrey had just been unlucky in his seating for Robin Maxwell-Hyslop had always been a man to avoid. In the days that followed I spent the bulk of my campaigning either on the box or writing articles in favour of Michael's candidature in the press. No one bothered to canvass me, my colours having been nailed to Heseltine's mast since our Pembroke days. This was, in a sense, a pity, for much of the fun lay in the importunings of 'the colleagues' who, paper and pencil in hand, would sidle up to people with whom they barely passed the time of day in normal circumstances to learn for whom they were thinking of voting. I could have been lunched by Peter Morrison, or dined by Tristan Garel-Jones; but no such luck; in the event I was not required to try to convert anyone (Colonel Mates, the Black Uhlan who was Michael's chief of staff, probably considered such an act likely to be counter-productive) but to sing our candidate's praise on TV and in print. 'No jokes,' warned the massive figure of Sir Peter Tapsell, another of Michael's inner circle. 'Michael has many achievements to his credit.' I promised not to make any jokes.

Michael's election campaign coincided with the Hartley Wintney Christmas Fair which I duly attended. I was soon surrounded by a squad of retired colonels, majors and captains who asked me for whom I would be voting. I suspected their loyalties lay with Margaret, but I spotted at the back of the throng the mackintoshed figure of Field Marshal Sir John Stanier. 'Sir John,' I asked, 'for whom would you vote?' 'Heseltine, of course,' was his reply. The colonels, majors and captains were suitably impressed.

I have looked at my freelance journalism account book for November 1990 and found recorded eighty-four different sources of income ranging from an *Observer* profile of Michael, to *Breakfast with Frost*, to *Newsnight*, *Panorama* and umpteen foreign television stations, the London offices of which were desperate to interview Michael Heseltine's old school-chum. Usually my monthly total of commissions was about twenty. I stressed his stamina, his integrity and his ministerial experience. I claimed that Margaret had outstayed her welcome, and that under her leadership, defeat stared the party in the face. Later, after she withdrew, I claimed that Michael was by far 'the biggest' of the three candidates. I am certain I did not convert any colleague who might have been watching the box; but Michael did remain the public's favourite throughout both elections.

At about half past five on the evening of Tuesday 20 November, I went upstairs to the Committee Corridor to await the result of the first ballot. By six, when the poll closed, the wide corridor had become densely packed with MPs of all parties – I caught sight of Dennis Skinner and of Tony Benn, and a collection of native and foreign journalists, the bulk of whom were strangers to me. The excitement was intense and the heat oppressive. Suddenly there was silence, and someone could be heard in the distance reading out the result: Margaret Thatcher 204; Michael Heseltine 152; abstentions 16. The cry then went up 'second ballot'. Margaret had failed by four votes to win outright. There was chaos in several of the committee rooms which were packed with Tory MPs, enraged that the press had been the first to know. It appeared that Cranley Onslow, the admirable chairman of the '22, had read out the results in the wrong committee room. It was an error that was eventually to cost him the chairmanship of the 1922 Committee. The cry went up 'My God, she's finished'. The crowd then faded away, the hacks to their telephones, the Heselteenies to the Smoking Room to celebrate (Pol Roger '68), the Thatcherites to cabal in a state of gloomy stupefaction.

Mrs Thatcher was clearly finished; 168 Tory MPs had either voted for Michael or abstained. No Prime Minister could survive so large a rejection. A more sinister thought was that if Mrs Thatcher could not heal so wide a breach 'could Michael?' It was this double rejection that sooner or later came to occupy the minds of Tory MPs. We rushed to find a television set to see how Mrs Thatcher would react to the news of her 'defeat'. Foolishly, and for no good reason, she had gone to Paris for a summit. The bearer of the ill-tidings was her newly appointed PPS Sir Peter Morrison. No one watching that evening will forget her dramatic appearance in the courtyard of the embassy, as she elbowed her way past Bernard Ingham to proclaim to the world that she would fight on. '*C'est magnifique*,' murmured Ian Gilmour, '*mais . . .*'

I remember someone saying in the Smoking Room on hearing that she had appointed Peter Morrison as her PPS, 'she's in the bunker now'. Peter was the Thatcherite brother of the 'wet' Charlie Morrison, and son of the John Morrison who had been the chairman of the '22 when I was first elected in 1959. He seemed an unsuitable candidate for a very difficult job. He was both grand and unapproachable. He was to play the role of General Wenck, whose imaginary 12th Army was to relieve beleaguered Berlin in 1945.

Mrs Thatcher's supporters, and especially her 'Court', have found it hard to come to terms with her resignation. In a search for scapegoats they have blamed Tristan Garel-Jones, her cabinet colleagues and occasionally themselves for not working hard enough on her behalf. But they all miss the point. After the first ballot, the more far-sighted believed that Margaret was finished; the fact that the margin of four votes was so narrow was neither here nor there. Even had it been possible to rustle up or to convert another four Tory MPs it would have made no practical difference to her position. She had been holed below the waterline. There is no doubt that a majority of her cabinet colleagues were glad to see the back of her, but they gave their advice freely and frankly. As they saw it, she was unlikely to defeat Michael in a second ballot. And were Michael to win, not only would he recast the cabinet, but he would also find himself faced by a phalanx of irreconcilables who would strive to make his position as Prime Minister untenable. Hence the emergence, almost at the eleventh hour, of the 'unknown' John Major who had offended no one, and about whose political beliefs nobody could be certain.

The Thatcherites listened to their lost leader and voted for 'dear John' in ignorance of the fact that his political hero was Iain Macleod. Whatever John Major's strengths and weaknesses, he did provide the cement without which the Tory party would not have won the 1992 general election. I stuck with Michael to the end. It soon appeared inevitable that he would lose, but it was a brave try. And, writing four years after the event, who is to say that he might not have done better than John Major? He had come a long way from that evening in Long John's restaurant in Oxford in 1952 when he put 'Downing Street' next to the 1990s when he charted his future course.

The repercussions from Michael Heseltine's bid to become leader of the Conservative party, and so Prime Minister, did not end with his defeat by John Major, the candidate hurriedly 'invented' by the party and then put forward as the means of reuniting the Conservatives. Some of his more prominent supporters, Michael Mates, Cyril Townsend and I, among several others, were all threatened with deselection by angry supporters of Mrs Thatcher in the constituencies. According to the Central Office model rules, only fifty signatures are necessary for the calling of a Special General Meeting, at which a motion of deselection could then be moved. The fifty have to be members of the Association, and once a date for the SGM is fixed, no new members are recruited into the party. Despite pleas by the new Prime Minister and the Chief Whip, Richard Ryder, for there to be 'no recriminations', there was a spate of 'deselections' during December 1990 and January 1991.

My own ride in Aldershot had been, over the years, stormy enough, and the opportunity to get rid of me was not one my enemies would easily reject. Even if Jack Bedser and Maureen Cooper were no longer party members (how they must have kicked themselves for having resigned from the party in 1989!), there was no lack of signatures. The officers of the Association did their best to discourage deselection, but were powerless to prevent it. The meeting was thus fixed for Wednesday December 19 to be held in the hall of a school in the village of Hartley Wintney. It was to be a private meeting, closed to television and to the press.

There were immediate complaints, voiced in the two local papers, that the Tories had picked the most inaccessible part of the Aldershot constituency to hold the meeting; eight miles out of Aldershot in what was thought to be 'Critchley territory'. These complaints, which were not unreasonable, were firmly disregarded.

Cheered by the prospects of such excitement the local Tories swiftly took sides and the correspondence columns of the *Aldershot News*, the principal local paper (owned by the *Guardian*), and the *Star*, a free-sheet rag edited by a born-again Christian who was hostile towards me (also owned by the *Guardian*), volleyed and thundered, with Cooper/Bedser adding their well-rehearsed grievances. Critchley 'was never in the constituency' (not true: I was, by necessity, an assiduous attender of fêtes and functions); Critchley 'was a snob who poked fun at the simpler Tories' (some truth in this); Critchley 'had been disloyal to dear Mrs T' (undeniably true); Critchley was not 'a true Conservative' (surely a matter of definition). There were also more sober letters pointing out an MP's right to differ and defending my record in the constituency. I had, after all, twenty years of constituency casework to fall back on. I had an efficient secretary and I was an experienced 'welfare officer'.

On the evening of the meeting Monique Simmonds (the chairman and a supporter of mine, but one who took the chair with admirable impartiality) and the ever-loyal and active Mavis Banham passed themselves off to the media as two 'cleaning ladies' who had come to open up the hall in anticipation of a full house. The school was picketed by television cameras and their crews, to say nothing of various raincoated hacks both national and local. In this way they escaped the attentions of the press. By the time the president, Esther Chappell, and I arrived promptly at eight o'clock the car park and foyer of the school were ablaze with television lights. Maureen Cooper had offered herself in turn to each crew, eager to stir the pot, hopping from one foot to another in antici-pation of my defeat. As she was not a member of the Association she had been barred from entering the hall. She was escorted by a miserable-looking, rainsoaked Jack Bedser.

The hall was packed with 250 people. It was a highly unpleasant occasion and I was not without nerves. It was not as noisy as Michael Mates's meeting, but according to my secretary, Angela Bayfield (a member of the Aldershot and East Hants Tories who had attended both), much more vicious. The motion in favour of my deselection was moved by Ben Franklin, an unemployed Rush-moor councillor well known for having a pleasant wife, innumerable small children and going everywhere on his bicycle. In Association terms he was a lightweight. He complained at some length of my record of hostility towards Mrs Thatcher, going over a lot of old ground in doing so. I marked his speech four out of ten.

Major General Bernard Gordon-Lennox was then called to oppose the motion (at my invitation). I had in the past worked closely with Bernard over the battle of Foxley Wood, which we had won, the developers having failed to build a new town in the heart of Eversley. He was therefore an ally. Bernard had all the authority of a Grenadier, but he did not speak particularly well; he made the case that I had never hidden my support for Michael Heseltine, and was perfectly entitled to vote for whomsoever I wished. What was more I was a good constituency MP who had protected the area from overdevelopment. I was also a friend of the British Army. His speech I also rated a four.

The debate was then thrown open to the floor. Here the passion came from my opponents who largely consisted of right-wingers in general and Young Conservatives in particular. The YCs were very hostile owing perhaps to a piece I had writen in the *Telegraph's* weekly magazine deploring the oafish behaviour of some of the new breed of 'national' YCs who had won for themselves a reputation for political obscurantism fuelled by cans of McEwan's Tartan. Happily for me, the YCs who spoke did so badly, and were personally offensive – which did not go down well with the middle-aged, middle-class audience. Perhaps the most effective was Mark Allnat, a large, balding young man with a taste for right-wingery both within and beyond the Tory party. A Rushmoor councillor mincingly read out a piece of doggerel she had composed especially for the evening, a performance that left no toe uncurled. Monique, in the chair, kept the balance and after a while the more moderate and reasonable speeches came from my supporters. Had not John Major called for an end to recriminations? What was the point in playing into the hands of the party's political opponents locally? Surely the party should reunite so as to win the next election? I saved my ace until last. My case was admirably summed up by Brigadier Bob Thorpe, a remarkable and much-loved local character who, along with the comedian Arthur English, was Aldershot's favourite son. He was robust, dismissive and funny: nine out of ten.

It was then left for me to speak. I was under orders to make no jokes (examples of my humour at Margaret's and others' expense were solemnly read out by the quivering young). I did not speak well; I was somewhat shaken by the intensity of the feelings expressed, but I was brief. The vote was then taken and the motion declared lost by a comfortable margin. I forget the figures, but the vote at all the various deselection meetings was almost exactly the same: one-third in favour of the boot; two-thirds against. As Esther and I left the hall, we caught sight of a disappointed Maureen Cooper still haranguing the cameras. She looked very wet indeed. Of Jack Bedser there was no sign.

Why did I win? I am sure there are still those who believe I did not deserve to. I had been a thorn in Mrs Thatcher's side for ten years and had occasionally written pieces about *la vie politique* to which the more simple could take exception. A speech I had made in the House after the 1987 election, when taking a leaf out of Nye Bevan's book I had warned the newly elected that they were faced 'with hours and hours of exquisite boredom' (Bevan had said as much in October 1959 to the packed and exultant Tory benches), seemed to have given offence to the not so simple, who wondered why if boredom was the end of politics they had bothered to work so hard to get me elected. In politics, jokes are all too easily misunderstood. My opponents in the hall suffered from two handicaps: expressions of personal dislike were counter-productive and accusations of political incorrectness cut no ice with the 'non-political' Conservatives who made up the majority of the audience.

Class, too, played its part. I had the support of the officer class in what was still a military constituency (hence the General and the Brigadier); many of those who spoke against me were either young, unknown, or carried little weight within the local party; and, despite the anger of Mrs Thatcher's supporters, she was never as popular among Tory activists as the popular press made out. Most of mine thought she had long overstayed her welcome. I spoke to Peter Temple-Morris and to Cyril Townsend afterwards; they, too, had noticed a class divide in which the more established voted for the Member, leaving the YCs and the working-class Tories hostile to him or her.

Five months later there was a postscript to my 'deselection'. Anne and Michael Heseltine came as guests to a constituency supper club meeting in Rotherwick. The hall was full to the rafters, and Michael most enthusiastically received. I said I had not seen so large an audience since I was last deselected. By some irony it turned out to be the last meeting in the Aldershot division to which I could walk unaided. Two days later I collapsed and was taken to Frimley Park Hospital.

24 Private Lives

The life of politics does not consist entirely of routs and rallies, flattery and abuse. I enjoyed a private life of sorts. In the seventies, Heather and I took Melissa and Joshua to Alderney for a fortnight's holiday for three successive years. It is a bleak island, tilted the wrong way (to the north), covered with Palmerstonian fortifications, and sinister relics of the German occupation. Provided one could escape the wind, the southern beaches were fine, and the food, 'filling'. But, in the eighties, with the children growing up, and Heather and me growing apart, I would spend August either at my cousin Jane's house in Nether Stowey under the Quantock Hills, or with Rosemary and Alan Laurie whose B&B at Church Bank, Burrington, near Ludlow, I had discovered in the *Observer* small ads.

Alan had been a housemaster at Shrewsbury in the liberal sixties. In Burrington he served at table while his wife cooked excellent four-course dinners for next to nothing. The cottage was comfortable and full of books. Burrington is a pretty village overlooking the Vale of Wigmore, silent except for the twice-daily visits of the Post Office van. The churchyard has iron 'tombstones' marking the graves of Downton ironmasters. August was a month during which I never wore a tie or spoke to a constituent; instead I walked the Somerset and Shropshire hills, lunched or dined *en garçon*, and read all the books the broadsheets told me were worth reading. Peace, perfect peace, with loved ones far away.

In the eighties I finally severed my connection with Rectory Cottage, my maternal home. In 1986 Uncle Jack died – he had lived alone for thirty years (except for his mongrel terrier, Enoch) and I went with his son John to see him aged ninety-six and dying of old age in the cottage hospital at Bishop's Castle. He was gaunt, skeletal. 'Everything is worn out,' he whispered. An even older man filled the small ward with the sound of his laboured breathing. I filled my uncle's glass with malt whisky – the ward sister did not seem to mind – and held his hand. He died a few days later. I once asked him what life had been like in Flanders in the Great War. He struggled to answer, his stammer reasserting itself. 'No one who was not there could begin to understand how terrible it all was.' He then smiled reflectively and told of a raid conducted by soldiers of the Royal Artillery on an abandoned wine shop. 'I was supposed to have been in charge.' Campbell Morris was a lovely man, straight as a die. He never owned a car; only a bike. The only holidays I remember him taking were visits to Harben Road to see the cricket at Lords or the Oval.

In 1972, my Aunt Daisy, mother's elder sister, who had gone with her husband to New Zealand in 1924, paid her first return visit to England. She was in her seventies and had the ruddy complexion of a countrywoman and the stamina of an American tourist. No sooner had we shown her the sights of London than she was off to Shropshire to rediscover lost friends and relations. I persuaded her to talk into an audio cassette. In her tapes she brings the dead to life.

I showed her a sepia photograph of my grandmother which I keep on my desk. She sits at the cottage door, dressed in mourning, surrounded by her six fatherless children. Campbell, the eldest, is twelve, wearing his suit and a black arm band. The youngest child, Beth, is an infant on my grandmother's knee. Aunt Daisy said that as soon as the news of the railway accident reached the Common my grandmother set out to walk the three miles to Craven Arms, carrying the infant. She had not gone three hundred yards before running into her father, a seventy-year-old retired farm labourer called John Davies with whom she shared the cottage. All he said was 'It's no good you'm going, he's jed.' He was a man of few words.

My grandmother received a certain amount of compensation from the LNWR but was kept alive by the Greenes of The Grove. She kennelled Mrs Harriet Greene's dogs, and, having bought a new mangle, washed and ironed the surplices for Wistanstow church. Thus church and squire combined to stand proxy for the social services. A friendly farmer called Hill had long permitted the family to plant two rows of potatoes around one of his fields, a mile or so away at Felhampton.

Such distant memories combine light and shade. Breakfast at the turn of the century was usually 'dukes', pieces of bread dipped in hot milky tea. I had never heard the word before. For other meals eggs were halved but there was always bacon from the cottage pig. Beer was home brewed from mangolds and wine made from elderberries. Treats consisted of giant suet puddings anointed with a crust of butter and sugar.

Summers are remembered by my aunt with affection, but winters must have been vile; freezing children, inadequate school heating and passed-down clothes. But there was a big fire in the cottage and slices of toast and beef dripping. The Great War took the three boys to France; the only work for girls was nursing, teaching or going into service. Aunt Daisy's tapes gave a harrowing account of my grandmother's death from cancer. She took two years to die, being nursed constantly by my aunt who would hold her mother's leg in a comfortable position (the growth was pressing on the sciatic nerve) until she fell asleep. Morphine suppositories soon failed to take effect; she suffered such pain that I can remember being told as a child when living at Leamore Common that her groans could be heard in the lane through the limestone, windowless, rear of the cottage. How much easier her death would have been made today.

My Aunt's legacy – she was the last of her immediate family to die – has been to open windows long shut and, by so doing, to revive ancient memories. Sadly, she too died of her mother's complaint, although swiftly and painlessly, when in her nineties.

In early 1994 I made a sentimental journey to Leamore Common. The cottage and its garden had become a rural slum, its once carefully tended garden a tip, covered with sheds and broken-down cars. The giant pear tree had gone; only the yew that stands by the gate remains. The Morrises who lived in Rectory Cottage for a hundred years were poor, but proud. Dear Auntie May must be turning in her grave.

In the late autumn of 1985 I noticed John Bellak in the Central Lobby. I had known him in my Bow Group days; more importantly from my point of view, he had married Prudence Marshall in 1960. We spoke for a moment, and then, to my delight, Prue herself turned up. Although I had not seen her for twenty years, and then only fleetingly, she seemed barely changed. She was tall, dark slim and graceful with a lovely smile. We reminisced, and parted with the promise of lunch in London. It was to be one of those meetings that mark a turning point in one's life, a chance encounter that led eventually to the abandonment of husband and of wife and setting up house together in Ludlow in April 1992.

I was filled with a strange excitement; my first and lost love for whom I had carried a discreet torch for more than thirty years (not perhaps as discreet as I thought for both my wives had discovered and destroyed photos of her). Could we become lovers again? The thought was tantalizing but surely unrealizable? The affair was slow to develop: an occasional lunch was followed by a monthly visit to one of London's better restaurants (I was then writing about food for the '*Telegraph*', a stately courtship carried on at the readers' expense; Prue was my 'companion' who had pasta as her first course. An afternoon visit to the cinema (as we had so often done in our first incarnation) and a fond farewell outside the elegant doors of the Carlton Club where the Bellaks would put up

225

for the night. Until the summer of 1988 the only variant was a visit by me to Tittensor Chase, a large, cold Staffordshire house where the Bellaks lived – conveniently sited near the City Museum and Art Gallery in Hanley and its world-beating collection of Staffordshire pottery.

Then there were our three August picnics. On the first or second day of the month we would meet outside the Moss Gates, the entrance to Shrewsbury school. I would arrive early and sit on the river bank beneath the school buildings waiting for all the clocks of Shrewsbury to chime midday. Prue would bring the food (stuffed quail, pâté, cheese), I would be responsible for the wine; good white burgundies bought from Tanner's. We drove either to the Long Mynd or as far south as the Wye where we lunched in the river meadow opposite Bredwardine where the diarist Francis Kilvert is buried. We spoke always of the past, of our days in Paris, our tour de France in the Laws-Johnsons' *cochon* and of the end of the affair that happened in some gloomy north Oxford Barbara Pym-like Victorian house early in 1952, leaving me broken-hearted. We wondered at our innocence and our love. The future seemed less certain, and for two or three years we skirted carefully around the implications of our letters and our lunches. Like all those who stand at the brink of love we sent each other books. Prue sent me (among many others) the two Ediths, Wharton and Templeton; I introduced her to Larkin and Robert Graves. For more than five years we bought each other our favourite books, ending up inevitably when we came to live together with two identical sets. Our rendez vous in London were discreet, yet public; I had, at least, 'my love to keep me warm'; we were not yet lovers, but the air was heavy with promise and I was happier than I had been for many years.

Unbeknown to me relations between Prue and her husband came to a head in the summer of 1988 (I was not the cause), and after kissing me goodbye at Euston station in the June our relationship moved up a gear. We had lunched at la Tante Claire. 'Tell me Julian, have you a mistress?' she asked. She was thinner and unhappy. 'Not yet,' I replied and we arranged to meet once again at the Moss Gates on the first of August, more quail; more Puligny Montrachet.

I took her to see Sham Castle, an eighteenth-century folly that I had visited earlier that summer. The 'castle', which can only be approached along cart tracks and through five-barred gates, lies in a bowl of hills open only to the north and The Wrekin. It is a tower built on a mound, beautiful in summer when it is surrounded by cornfields, hideously impractical at any other time of the year. There was a circular drawing-room and much good moulding. It was for rent, having been abandoned by a Shrewsbury solicitor. It was a fairy-tale dwelling. We looked at it, sighed and fell into each others' arms. Later we drove along the side of the Long Mynd overlooking the valley of the River Onny and ate our picnic. 'If only we were ten years younger,' cried Prue. At the ages of fifty-seven and fifty-four we were determined to prove that love, in the words of the old song, 'is lovelier the second time around'. It was, and still is.

The Archdeacon of York would probably have said, had he known of our affair, that we should have had more sense at our age, but thankfully he didn't. He was to save his impertinence for his future sovereign. Many of my constituents and especially the popular press, had they known of our love, would have been predictably censorious, for the English believe morality to be always sexual in kind, and while adultery is a practice indulged in by many, there is always pleasure to be gained from the pillorying of public figures. I wonder, too, whether it is really possible to break up a happy marriage? Surely not in the case of the unpromiscuous. Although I have been twice married and am now 'living in sin', I do not consider myself to be promiscuous, just unlucky, particularly with regard to my first marriage, a mistake for which I am still paying. Even so, Paula gave me two daughters whom I love very much and to whom I have always been close. I was much fonder of Heather. She, too, gave me two children whom I love no less than Julie and Susannah. But our marriage had been on the rocks for years before I met Prue again, and we had reached that dreadful stage of having nothing more to say to each other many years before. Knowing nothing of Prue, Heather told me in 1990 that she had put our house in Farnham on the market (without my knowledge) and that she preferred to live on her own. We were to go our own separate ways. I took advantage of her offer; she may have regretted making it later, I do not know for certain, and it might be hard to escape the charge of having built my happiness on the unhappiness of others. Prue knew full well the nature of my marital circumstances; I doubt if she would have come to me had they been anything other than pretty miserable.

Those two years, 1989 and 1990, were years of intoxication. I had tapped a secret supply of love, and to have done so at my age was beyond belief. Our eight children, who were introduced very slowly indeed into this strange and alarming state of affairs, found it hard to believe. For the young love is a state reserved exclusively for themselves, not for 'wrinklies' of the sort who might well be asked to contribute a piece to the *Oldie*. I could not believe my good fortune.

I was also active politically, involved in the downfall of the tyrant. Aldershot was a round of wine and cheeses, lunches with greedy entrepreneurs and regimental dinners where the band played so loudly indoors as to stop all ratiocination and the wine was wrapped in white napkins for its own protection.

I took David Lightbown, the hard man of the government's whips' office, ringside to see Paul Hodkinson fight at Wembley (he had to be restrained from joining in) and was invited to join 'One Nation' a self-selecting group of like-minded moderate Tories who dined together on Wednesday evenings to put the world to rights. I wrote regularly for the papers, and combed the antique shops for Staffordshire pots and Tinsel pictures.

Prue and I would meet monthly for lunch or dinner, staying the night in 'safe houses' in Lewisham. For some years I had not returned to Farnham during the week as the late-night drive of forty miles had become exhausting; instead, I took a room with my brother Nicholas off the Fulham Road and later lodged in my daughter Susannah's flat in Lewisham. Driving up and down the Old Kent Road morning and evening took me back twenty years to when I lived with Paula in Blackheath Village. Nothing much had changed: the pugs still swopped punches in the first floor rooms of the Thomas à Becket pub, and a faded early nineteenth-century elegance was still visible tucked behind the rows of second-hand cars and garages that sold soft-porn videos. The village had become smarter (Terry Waite country), and Prue and I dined often at a good Thai restaurant opposite the station.

In September 1989 Prue and I flew to Nice to stay for ten days at a friend's villa situated between Callas and Bargemon, a small, modern building, tucked away in the hills at the end of a ferociously dangerous unmetalled drive. 'Provence-wise', it owed more to Dirk Bogarde than to Peter Mayle. The days were hot, the evenings cool. We drove every day to a different village to lunch *en plein air*, spent the afternooons naked in the sun, and in the evenings Prue would cook a dinner of herbs. We were in bed as night fell over the dark blue, mountain-fringed valley. On our first night the thunder rolled incessantly around the house, the rain never breaking as in *Jean de Florette*. Our only human contact was a courtesy visit to the Bonfils, who, living nearby in the village, were the keepers of the keys. When we arrived, Madame was intermi-nably on the telephone to her daughter in Nîmes: we sat smiling at M. Bonfils who seemed reluctant to open the porto, taking it in turns to make stilted conversation in long-forgotten French. At last Madame finished, the corks were drawn with a flourish, and Monsieur, who was an 'unter' (the walls were lined with sporting guns) told us that his hobby was to crouch in the neighbouring undergrowth looking for wild boar. Prue feared he might have been spying on our Eden.

In 1990 Richard Cohen of Hutchinson's suggested that I write two 'celebrity novels' for which he offered £65,000. As it is well known that everyone has one bad novel in them, why not write two? The money was not bad; very good in fact, for me. *Hung Parliament* was published in hardback in June 1991, and *Floating Voter* a year later. At the same time I wrote for John Murray, with the cooperation of Morrison Halcrow, *Some of Us* – a series of profiles of people who had done well out of Mrs Thatcher. It was published in the summer of 1992 and was not a success possibly because it ought to have appeared a year earlier. It did not go into paperback.

The better of the two novels – political farces – was *Hung Parliament* which rose to number 12 in the charts. I was going to call it *Who Killed Edwina Currie?*, and told Edwina so at lunch. She did not seem to mind, 'in fact she beamed with pleasure. I thought it the ideal title for a political thriller of the sort that might be bought by the thousand at Heathrow. Later she wrote to me asking not to use her name in the title and I agreed. They were expensive second thoughts. Hutchinson's took me to the Athenaeum Club for a Saturday morning photo session in which a pretty model's legs were captured hanging decorously over the arm of a well-worn leather armchair. There was not a bishop in sight. Gerald Kaufman panned *Hung Parliament* in the *Sunday Times*, thus keeping its sales out of the top ten; on the other hand, a Cambridge professor of English chose it as his Book of the Year in the *Financial Times*; it had, apparently, cured his asthma. *Hung Parliament* was described by Enoch Powell in the *Telegraph* as 'salacious', a comment which I joyfully transferred to the blurb of the paperback. '*Salacious* . . . J. Enoch Powell.' How our reputations hang in the hands of literary editors. *Hung Parliament* allegedly sold over 4,000 in hardback and 18,000 in paper, but as publishers are such liars when it comes to sales who can tell?

In the late summer of 1990 Prue and I went on a Swan Hellenic cruise in the *Orpheus*, boarding ship at Santander, visiting Santiago de Compostela and sailing majestically into the harbour at Lisbon, where we dined in splendour at the Ritz. From Lisbon, which is my favourite city after Paris, with its magnificent setting, 'Salazar' suspension bridge, (Ponte 25 de Abril since the 1974 revolution) coloured houses, pillar-box castles, Norman cathedral and seven hills, we sailed through the Pillars of Hercules (dense fog), to Algiers, Minorca, Sardinia, Corsica and Nice, disembarking at Genoa. It was my third such trip, for in the late eighties I had persuaded magazines to sponsor two voyages around the eastern Mediterranean on which I took first Melissa and then Susannah. A Swan Hellenic cruise has nothing in common with Miami's *Sea Princess*. The passengers are drawn from the educated classes, the lectures are delivered by clever parsons and garrulous dons, the cabins are Spartan and the food, very Greek. And there are no slot machines. All told, I spent six weeks on board the *Orpheus*, leaving the ship to wander over Delos ankle-deep in the flowers of April, eating splendid lunches at Antayla in Anatolia, and squeezing with difficulty through the Corinth Canal.

Such a cruise is an ideal escape for lovers of a certain age. We were younger than nearly everyone else (although some fond parents brought their clever graduate daughters) and our foxtrot to the ship's three-piece band was half a knot faster than anyone else's. With a combination of courtesy and interest so typical of the graduate classes, we assembled each morning for our lecture: St Augustine of Hippo by Professor Sir Henry Chadwick (a class act if ever there was one); the Franco-Algerian War by Professor Malcolm Todd of Exeter, and 'Whatever happened to the Sards?' by Mr Richard Wallis of Keele. The sea was blue, the sun was high and the company, when we sought it, very good indeed. There was a small library without a single Jeffrey Archer, a travelling doctor with a supply of Dr Collis-Browne's elixir (there should be a statue to that good doctor) – perhaps there is one somewhere and frequent visits ashore where, after a short ride in a charabanc, we would gaze at the ruins of the ancient world. We loved every minute of it.

Prue and I talked over our future and eventually decided to live together. We would delay doing so until after the general election which was likely either in 1991 or 1992. Heather and I had also to sell our house in Farnham so that we could afford to go our separate ways. There was no time to lose as the Lawson boom was beginning to crumble, and house prices with it. That November saw Mrs Thatcher's downfall, and in the New Year the brief and spectacular Gulf War. I survived my 'deselection' in December 1990. What I barely survived was my youngest daughter Melissa's wedding to Robert Schelp on 18 May 1991.

Over the years I had found it more and more difficult to walk any distance. It was partly because of my increasing weight, but more the result of the strain placed on the spinal disc that controlled my withered right leg. There had been two or three warning attacks of hip pain, the first in 1983 while attending the Tory party conference in Blackpool, but they were generally overcome by rest and codeine. My GP seemed largely unconcerned. Perhaps working for the NHS in Farnham put more than enough on his plate? Early in May 1991, my back 'went' again, for the first time I could barely hobble to Rotherwick to attend the Heseltine supper-club. That was a Friday evening; Melissa's wedding was on the next day.

We had hired Sir James Scott's house Rotherfield Park, an early Victorian pile in east Hampshire. Jimmy Scott was the Lord Lieutenant of Hampshire (he died while out shooting in the winter of 1993), and in return for a covenant to repair and restore the roof of Winchester cathedral (a task which I think I am still engaged in) he let his great house be hired for weddings. It was a cold day, the bride was beautiful, her husband handsome, and Rotherfield Park was packed with relations, English and German. Many of the Germans were under the impression that I owned the place. Heather and I did all that was required of us and once it was all over, my speech made and feeling dreadful, I was driven back to Farnham and an early bed. I was utterly exhausted.

The next morning something else 'went' in the small of my back, and I was taken by ambulance to the local 'purpose-built' Frimley Park General Hospital. It had been opened some ten years before by Barbara Castle in a dull ceremony which I attended. I was put in a public ward, but thankfully moved the next morning to a side room which gave me privacy. I had never taken out medical insurance, partly for reasons of cost, partly because I thought Tory MPs ought to pay more than lip-service to the NHS. And I had never worked for a company which would have provided medical insurance as an executive perk. On reflection, it was a grave error. The Health Service is fine in time of emergency; when the problem is chronic, indeed it is not.

I was in Frimley Park for the best part of a fortnight during which my back finally 'went' altogether and I could no longer put weight upon a bent right leg. My room with its view over an unkempt courtyard was dirty, bottles of urine were left on window-sills for more than twelve hours and the younger nurses were noisy and ill-disciplined, especially at night. Whoever got rid of Matron did no patient a service. By eight o'clock at night all I wanted to do was to put myself to sleep, but such was the rigidity of the rules that I either had to toss sleeplessly until the drugs trolley was brought round at ten or was awakened in order to be given a sleeping pill. Unable to walk to the lavatory, I was left ringing bells in increasing desperation. I had a stream of visitors, almost the first being Tony Kennerley, the chairman of the local health authority. He should have stayed longer. There was a half-hearted attempt at physiotherapy; fierce girls in white coats yelling at me to 'look up' while I tried to walk up flights of stairs. In short, the place was a dump: I can only hope it has improved with trust status in the last three years.

I did not appreciate it at the time, but I was on what Health Service doctors call 'the fast track'. I had a room to myself. I was driven to a private hospital in Windsor where I was given an MR scan (unpleasant if you are at all claustrophobic), paid for by the NHS. Back at Frimley I was stuffed full of codeine for its pain-killing properties and laxatives to counter its constipating effects. Somehow a balance was never quite struck, The eventual result was an acute attack of diverticulitis. At home I convalesced for the summer, unable to walk without a stick for more than a few yards or to stand for any length of time and in pain from my leg every evening. As I slowly recovered my strength I adopted a routine of writing in the morning, reading in the afternoon and going to bed at seven with a Zimovane and codeine.

Hung Parliament was published in June 1991. I was not fit enough to promote the book in the way that publishers today think necessary. Speeches at lunchtime, visits to provincial cities, signing sessions à la Margaret Thatcher in Harrods and Hatchard's. Worst of all I was cut off from Prue (we had planned a second visit to Callas in May after the wedding, but it had to be cancelled). We wrote to each other and spoke on the telephone. In July, Joshua drove me to Nether Stowey to my cousin's house for a long weekend where she joined me. It was a blissful reunion. But the polio, from the clutches of which I had narrowly escaped in November 1949, had returned, and returned with a vengeance.

My orthopaedic surgeon in Farnham, Mr Gruebel Lee, arranged for me to have a spinal operation at the National in September. The surgeon there was one of the best in the country. This was, once again, on the NHS. The National Hospital was an order of magnitude better than Frimley Park. The nurses were all graduates, my room was silent, or to be more accurate as silent as it could be given that an extension to the hospital was being built next door, pee was removed promptly and I was paid a visit by the administrator, an admiral no less. In Frimley I was a local MP, but in the National I was my father's son. My only complaint was the food, which was frightful, but I was not hungry and left for home a stone lighter than when I was admitted.

The operation to 'clean up' my disc, and relieve pressure on the nerve, was not a success (I believe it is called a laminectomy). I was promised this, and promised that by the surgeon (walk without a stick; stand without trouble) but after several weeks it slowly dawned on me that I was no better than before. I saw him again two or three times at his Monday afternoon surgeries at Maida Vale; on the last occasion he said 'something may have gone wrong with the operation', but he did not attempt to find out what. It appeared from a letter written to my father that I was 'neurologically deteriorating'. (In January 1994 I had another scan, this time in Stoke. My consultant surgeon, Professor Eisenstein, having looked at the pictures, said there was nothing more he or anyone else could do. I was just unlucky.) In the winter of 1991, I managed to lunch once at Westminster, to make an after-dinner speech at the Savoy, and appear on a Radio Four programme called *Out of Order*, but the strain was immense. My leg was either hypersensitive or painful and I could barely walk any distance whatsoever. Soon I could not sit in comfort. My stamina had gone; and looming before me was the prospect of fighting a general election in Aldershot. For me, 1991 was truly an *annus horribilis*.

Monique Simmonds, the chairman of the Aldershot Tories, was eager to discover my intentions. I said I would ponder my future and let her know. I was still confident that my leg would get stronger and with it my powers of endurance. I had no money to speak of and could not easily abandon a political career which at the very least paid a salary and expenses. And my journalism was, to an unknown degree, dependent on my remaining in the House. I had to pay Paula nearly £1,500 a month in alimony; the same would be true as regards Heather upon our separation. It was clear to me that I had to stand again – if the Aldershot Tories would have me as their candidate. Although I was fitted out with arm crutches in February, I was barely more mobile than I had been before. I told Monique I wanted to stand again, and was confident of making a recovery (which was still the view of my father, and of various doctors). She agreed, and I was formally adopted to fight my seventh general election in Aldershot.

I do not look back on the 1992 election with pleasure. I made one public speech – an evening meeting in a school hall that entailed more walking than was good for me. I spoke for thirty minutes, but at the end of my speech I was 'running on empty'. Fox-hunting seemed to be the flavour of the month, with me as the quarry as I had managed to vote against the abolition of the sport in a Commons debate. I refused to take part in any 'all-party' meetings on which the rival candidates take up moral positions over subjects about which they know little, much to the public annoyance of my rivals. I could not have kept my end up. I spent the mornings being driven to various party committee rooms, lunched publicly in some hotel or public house, and then returned home for the rest of the day, retiring to bed around seven or eight. In short, I was carried by my supporters which was a handsome gesture on their part. On polling day I did a short tour during the day, went to bed early, woke at eleven and was driven to the count in Farnborough by Joshua. Such are the ironies of electioneering that although I had done less than ever before, and had been barely visible, I polled more votes than in any of my previous elections in Aldershot, nearly 37,000. Candidates count for very little. I made the usual speech thanking the Returning Officer, the counters and my hard-working supporters. Adrian Collett, the Liberal candidate, then spoke. He claimed that he had met no one in the campaign who had had a good word to say for me – or, as an afterthought, for any of the Tories. He was heartily booed by Tory and Labour supporters alike. The Liberals are bad losers, and worse winners.

In the early months of 1992 I wrote *Floating Voter*, the second of my two novels. It was published in June and was praised by Julie Birchill. She said I was the Peter Ustinov of the Tory party. The action was set in Brighton at a Tory party conference with a cast of real people and many of the fictional characters from *Hung Parliament*. Both novels had an autobiographical content. Literary critics (usually politicians or political journalists) were divided as to whether Joshua Morris, the hero detective, or Sir Ralph Grunte ('the "e" is sounded, dear boy, as in Brontë') a frightful Tory MP, was the truer self-portrait. 'Felicity', who appears in both novels, is undoubtedly Prue, a fact that did not escape the eagle eye of Lynda Lee-Potter of the *Mail*, who, a month after Prue and I moved to Ludlow, made the connection in the pages of her family newspaper.

The *Sunday Times* said *Floating Voter* was my 'benign revenge on the Tory party'. It got to number 13 in the charts, sold 4,000 in hardback and 13,000 (so far) in paperback. Jeffrey Archer has little to fear from me; or Edwina Currie, whose dreadful *A Parliamentary Affair* went straight to the top of the hardback charts (in the same week incidentally as *Middlemarch* was the best-selling paperback. What does that tell us about the reading public?).

We arrived in Ludlow on 14 April 1992. I had rented a Georgian town house within the conservation area: three brick storeys and a black and white cellar; it had been recently restored by a Reading businessman with an eye to retirement. It has a long, prettily neglected, walled garden ending in a scattering of ancient apple trees. From the front of the house there is an urban landscape (Mill Street is the second most handsome street in Ludlow); from the rear the land drops away to the river only to rise again to Whitcliffe, a hillside on which more Ludlovians have been conceived than would be readily admitted. There are no suburbs. I have long loved Ludlow and it has been my ambition to live in it. And I have loved Prue for almost as long. I still cannot not believe my double good fortune.

I have been happier living with Prue than I have ever been. After two stormy marriages it is marvellous never to have exchanged a cross word. She is loving, she is kind, she is pretty and she is intelligent. And she is also a damned good cook. Through her I have made many new friends. The flip-side to my idyll is the fact that I am a cripple. Since my operation I can no longer sit for any length of time in comfort (I lie along a sofa writing on a portable computer), as well as not being able to walk (I can cross the road and back) or stand for any length of time. I can drive the motor car for a hour or so in the morning (before my leg starts to hurt). I am, in fact, only comfortable on my face in bed.

Hypersensitivity and or pain usually starts in my leg by the afternoon, a fact of life which has meant lunch and not dinner, and bed by seven o'clock. Painkillers blunt the pain but do not get rid of it. A combination of Temgesic and Zimovane sends me quickly to sleep; when I wake in the night the pain has gone. I write in the mornings, watch films in the afternoons and read for a short time in bed. This has been the pattern of my life for the past eighteen months (we travel infrequently to our flat in Olympia), and is likely to remain so. I recount this tale of woe not to seek sympathy, but as an explanation for my political semi-retirement. I still write and broadcast occasionally, but to all intents and purposes I am in dock.

Immediately after the election, I attended a supper club in Hartley Wintney at which John Patten was the guest. He made what I thought was the worst speech by a cabinet minister I have ever heard. He was patronizing, trivial and ill-prepared. In February 1993 I went to the Aldershot annual dinner at which the principal guest was the Secretary of State for Health, Virginia Bottomley. Virginia is an old friend. She spoke well, but I could barely manage the vote of thanks. I went to a garden party later in the year but did not stay very long. I encouraged the Aldershot Tories to pick a candidate who could nurse the constituency in my absence. They chose Gerald Howarth, Margaret's ex-hand-bag carrier who lost his Staffordshire seat at the election. His adoption is as good an example of 'Critchley's Law' as one can find whereby, you will recall, constituency associations tend to pick the direct opposite of the previous Member. Gerald is no Genghis Khan, but he is a shade too Thatcherite for my taste. Nevertheless he is nice bloke and I wish him well. He will inherit my majority; and the Aldershot Tories deserve a quieter life.

As for the House of Commons I have lunched there three times, pushing myself around in a wheelchair (the Palace of Westminster is very badly designed for the disabled: heavy swing doors and numerous flights of steps or stairs), voted for Giles Shaw for Speaker, and have voted in person on only one other occasion. I have been 'nodded through' a dozen or so times, particularly over the votes on the Maastricht Bill and on the vote of confidence on the last Friday of July 1993. Nodding through entails being driven into New Palace Yard where one is checked over by a Tory and a Labour whip. Last July my car was parked alongside Michael Heseltine's ministerial Jaguar. He was recovering from his heart attack. 'It's a pity we've come to this,' was Michael's comment. I am happy to see he seems to have made a splendid recovery.

What I do attend to is my constituency correspondence, which with the help of my admirable friend and secretary Angela Bayfield is handled with dispatch. I talk to constituents on the telephone, put down written parliamentary questions, and harry ministers on my constituents' behalf by letter and by fax. It is something. The irony is that I have become at long last a loyal back-bencher, steadily pro-John Major, who is much to be preferred to his predecessor, and strongly anti-Bill Cash and his tedious group of disappointed nationalists. Were I fit I would by now have become as 'sound' as Sir Tufton Beamish, as decent as Sir Charles Mott-Radclyffe and as loyal as Sir Jackie Smyth. I might even have become a bore.

Richard Ryder, the Chief Whip, could not have been more understanding. He too suffers from a bad back. My area whip is Andrew MacKay, a Berkshire MP of Scottish descent. He is decent but can be a touch dour. When Robert Adley, the Tory MP for Christchurch, died early in 1993 I told Andrew over the telephone how sad I was (Adley was a nice old thing with a weakness for steam engines). 'He has been most unhelpful,' was Andrew's cautious reply. I knew only too well what he meant. Adley's seat was like mine; one which an unexpected by-election could result in a Liberal gain.

I spent much of 1992 writing for the papers, meeting Prue's friends who came over in droves from Staffordshire to 'case the joint', and, for a short time, avoiding the attentions of the tabloid press. A girl from the *Mail* rang our London flat fourteen times in the course of an afternoon. A yob from *Today* hung around Mill Street, banging on the front door at intervals and trying unsuccessfully to persuade our neighbours to permit him to photograph Prue and me from their gardens. With a Salopian's robustness they told him to 'bugger off'. In the end, so as to finish the story once and for all, we invited Lynda Lee-Potter to lunch. She wrote a well-disposed, if cringingly embarrassing piece about us, and since then we have been left in peace. The tabloids have had bigger fish to fry.

In the spring of 1992, my Farnham orthopaedic surgeon kindly arranged for me to be admitted to the rehabilitation unit of the King Edward VII Hospital at Midhurst, once again on the NHS. I was again 'on the fast track' – there are advantages to being an MP. My first stay of a week was an unqualified success: the physiotherapy was as good as Frimley's had been bad, and with exercises and swimming my leg became a little stronger. The hospital was immensely comfortable, the food good, and patients were put in charge of their own medication. No more nonsense of being woken up in order to be put back to sleep. The director, Kit Wynn-Parry was charming. My second visit, however, ended in disaster. Using only one crutch, as I had been encouraged to do, I slipped on the edge of the swimming pool and fell badly on my paralysed leg, cracking a bone in my foot and bruising both knees. There was much consternation and apology (and the introduction of poolside baskets containing cloths on which patients now dry the ends of their crutches). Privately, I considered whether or not to sue. In the end I did not. It was an accident, and doctor's sons do not sue other doctors. I left the King Edward VII swathed in bandages, in a worse state than when I was admitted. Towards the end of the year I paid a third visit to Midhurst for painkilling injections in the spine, but they were not effective. With the best will in the world (which I do not possess), I am 'off' hospitals.

Would I have done better not to have gone into politics? I lack the religious temperament, being incapable of faith without scrutiny. Perhaps I should have read modern history and become a don at an obscure Oxford college, famous for its cellar. Or I could have taught politics at Middlebury, Vermont, in the heart of Alison Lurie country, a tweedy Englishman among the Groves of Academe. I suppose I could have become a full-time political journalist and leader-writer, although I would not have liked to work for Rupert Murdoch. What, however, attracted me to *la vie politique* were its risks and uncertainties. It brought fame but also danger and financial insecurity. My vanity was stroked, but secretly I was slowly filled with self-contempt as the frustrations of being a back-bencher became evident; the humiliations at the hands of the whips, the all too obvious failure to win promotion, the unreal world of party conflict, and the knowledge that people do not really vote for you, whatever your reputation; they 'vote the ticket'. You have been propelled into prominence by the votes of a self-selected body of the unrepresentative; your future depends upon keeping their good will. None the less I will repeat Trollope's dictum: it is no mean thing to have had the letters 'MP' after one's name.

Gore Vidal writes somewhere to the effect that journalism is, after politics, the preferred career for the ambitious but lazy man. He has been a successful writer – his collected essays sit beside my bed – but a failure as a politician. His point about ambition and idleness is, however, well taken. The Commons is full of the disappointed whose horse power never quite matched their ambition, and never more so than today when the 'professional' politician has become the norm. At least the library squire had his books (and his tenants). I have always lacked the staying power and the single-mindedness necessary to take me, if not right to the top then to the cabinet in a poor year. But politics and my pen have given me a living and the privilege of a ringside seat. I have bought Winston Churchill – the real one – a drink (I had no choice), lunched with Ted Heath at Salisbury (he fell asleep in the middle of his own lunch party, something I have always wanted to do; Anna Ford was not amused) and dined with Harold Macmillan at Birch Grove. I have avoided Mrs Thatcher whenever possible. I have written a leader for *The Times* and spoken from the opposition front-bench in the Commons. And this book will be the eleventh I have either edited or written. I have written for newspapers good, bad and indifferent. I have represented two seats in Parliament and fought ten elections of which I have won eight. I have travelled the world at others' expense and I have escaped being made a Knight of either Shire or Suburb. I have been married twice, and have four children. I now live with the woman I have always loved in a charming house in 'the prettiest small town in England'. What have I to complain about? Precious little.

Index